DEFINING A LINGUISTIC AREA

DEFINING
A LINGUISTIC AREA
South Asia

COLIN P. MASICA

THE UNIVERSITY OF CHICAGO PRESS
Chicago and London

Colin P. Masica is assistant professor in the Department of South Asian Languages and Civilizations, University of Chicago.

THE UNIVERSITY OF CHICAGO PRESS, CHICAGO 60637
THE UNIVERSITY OF CHICAGO PRESS, LTD., LONDON

Printed in the United States of America

International Standard Book Number: 0-226-50944-3
Library of Congress Catalog Card Number: 74-16677

Library of Congress Cataloging in Publication Data

Masica, Colin P 1931-
Defining a linguistic area: South Asia.

Based on the author's thesis, University of Chicago, 1971.
Bibliography: p.
Includes index.
1. South Asia–Languages. 2. Areal linguistics.
I. Title
P381.S58M37 491'.1 74-16677
ISBN 0-226-50944-3

To my parents
Peter and Evelyn Masica

CONTENTS

ILLUSTRATIONS

MAPS

TABLES

PREFACE

This book represents an attempt, if only a crude one, to extend some of the methods of dialect geography to problems of areal typology – or, conversely, to make some of the data of areal typology available to cultural geographers (and cultural historians). The specific problem selected for this experiment is that of the territorial delineation of the South Asian, or "Indian," linguistic area, and the establishment of some morphological and syntactic criteria for this purpose.

The Indian area was chosen both because of my personal interest and involvement in it and because its richness in well-attested data of great variety and great time-depth makes it of special general importance for such studies.

At this point, a word of apology is perhaps due Pakistan, Ceylon, Nepal, and Bangladesh for my frequent use of the term "Indian" when referring to the Indo-Pakistan subcontinent and its environs. The convenient term *Indian* – which, of course, is derived from the name of a geographical feature in Pakistan, the Indus River – is so well-established as a general neutral designation for the region as a whole – not least in *linguistic* discussion, past and present – that it is difficult to keep it from slipping in, at least as an adjective. (Emeneau, the father of studies of this linguistic area, simply calls it *Indian,* without further ado.) The new and less convenient term *South Asian,* despite its logic and our best efforts over the past two decades or so, still lacks equivalent clarity for many noninitiates, being too often still confused with South*east* Asia. In other ways, it is perhaps *too* well-defined: there are times when we need an adjective to apply to phenomena that, while centered in and characteristic of the subcontinent, spill over beyond the logical limits of "South Asia" – a readily intelligible yet vaguer term. *Indian* is the obvious candidate. (I do feel the unsuitability of *India* as a noun, since that term now probably most readily indicates a particular country within the "Indian" region.)

Readers interested primarily in the Indian subcontinent, while finding, I hope, much that will interest them, will miss in these pages the kind of detailed *internal* treatment for which an imposing basis of information already exists (or at least could be assembled without too much difficulty). That is because of the nature of the problem addressed, which is the ascertaining of the boundaries of the Indian area as a whole, not the delineation, at this point, of subareas within it. Some indication of such subareas may unavoidably appear, as a by-product of the former quest, but they are not systematically explored and defined here. For the same reason, it may seem that an inordinate amount of space is devoted to extra-Indian matters. This is imposed by the principle of defining things partly by contrast with what they are not, as well as by that of avoiding a priori definitions of the territory involved.

Phonology is not part of this study, though a summary of the phonological evidence is given in an appendix. The whole question of historical development is also deferred.

Even within these limitations I do not pretend to have exhausted the subject. More criteria relevant to the definition of the Indian area could be found, no doubt, beyond those I have chosen to explore here.

It should hardly be necessary to add that this study is not meant to offer new or original research on the various *languages* involved. It sets out simply to *collect, sift,* and *collate* existing descriptive information. On occasion it has been necessary to restate some of this, and I must admit to a little bit of digging when the information I needed was not available but seemed to be obtainable thereby.

Since this is primarily an essay in linguistic *geography,* not linguistic theory or universal grammar, I do not address myself explicitly to those subjects even though the topics dealt with may be relevant to them. As the features with which this study is concerned turn out to be, for the most part, features of surface grammar, what the theoretician will find here will be primarily raw grist for his mill. My aim has been merely to find clear ways of stating the facts for comparison. Occasionally, it is true, that in itself has led to a fairly lengthy discussion, but the aim is the same.

This book is a revised and somewhat expanded version of a doctoral dissertation submitted to the University of Chicago in 1971.* Thanks are due my dissertation committee, especially to A. K. Ramanujan for encouraging me to wrestle with a topic of such immodest scope, more appropriate perhaps to the end of a long scholarly career (and thus to a much greater degree of wisdom as well as of accumulated information), and to Kostas Kazazis for helping me materially over some of the difficulties that not unnaturally followed upon that decision. I am grateful also to the great multitude of persons in and out of academic life, too numerous to mention here, who have given their help on particular points involving particular languages; some, but not all, of these are accredited in the notes to the text.

The roots of an undertaking such as the present one naturally go back further than the circumstances surrounding the final product. I owe a great deal to all my mentors: to those who taught me linguistics at the universities of Pennsylvania, Michigan, and Chicago, particularly Henry M. Hoenigswald who encouraged my exploration of areal typology in the writings of Jakobson and Trubetzkoy; to my friends and mentors in India, especially Bh. Krishnamurti and P. B. Pandit, who, together with colleagues in this country, Canada, and Great Britain, have encouraged me with their interest and inspired me by their example; and, much further back, to those in the Department of Geography at the University of Minnesota, then led by Jan O. M. Broek, who taught me to find meaning and fascination in areal correlations.

Norman H. Zide, James Lindholm, K. Paramasivam, Howard Aronson, Bill Darden, and again A. K. Ramanujan have been especially helpful in advising me during the preparation of this revision.

Thanks are due the *International Journal of Dravidian Linguistics* and its editor V. I. Subramoniam, for permission to use material in chapter 2 which appeared in a preliminary version in *IJDL 3.1* (January 1974), pp. 154-180.

*Its title was *A study of the distribution of certain syntactic and semantic features in relation to the definability of an Indian linguistic area.*

1

INTRODUCTION

Various resemblances between contiguous languages have probably been noted for a long time. It was only when the nineteenth-century comparativists had done their work, however, that the genetic factor in these resemblances could be abstracted and the remainder seen in their true significance. (Where great amounts of comparative work have yet to be done, as for example – despite much recent progress – in the Americas, the picture is still muddled.) That is, a tendency for languages gradually to *converge* in structure and idiom with their immediate neighbors could be recognized as a process complementary to that of their gradual *divergence*[1] from a common ancestor – the other end of it, so to speak. The breaking down of old systems is compensated for by the building up of new ones, and such building up has a direction imparted to it by the structures prevailing in neighboring languages – particularly noticeable when a language finds itself in a new linguistic neighborhood. (This might come about through migration of its speakers, or of its neighbors' speakers, or through important changes in political or cultural configurations.)

The process responsible for these patterns of resemblances is presumed to be borrowing, and the agent the bilingual individual.[2] Borrowing of words and concepts (calques or loan-translations) is familiar enough and generally accepted. A similar process thus seemed the simplest explanation for phonetic, phonemic, morphological, and syntactic resemblances between contiguous languages not related genetically (or not directly related). While this is perhaps now generally conceded for the first of these (the diffusion of the Parisian-French uvular "r" among speakers of a number of West European languages is an example), the others have encountered varying degrees of objection, most often on a priori principles and in the face of strong supportive evidence. Thus some Sanskritists refuse to see the Sanskrit retroflex consonants (/ṭ, ṭh, ḍ, ḍh, ṇ, ṣ/) as anything other than a purely internal development, despite the fact that such sounds are characteristic of the non-Indo-European languages of India and, moreover, can be shown to have gained phonemic status in Sanskrit with the help of borrowed words containing them,[3] a normal way for such changes to occur. In other quarters, particularly those influenced by Sapir, there long ruled the dogma that morphology, in particular, was very unlikely to be borrowed. Perhaps some of this has now been dispersed by the work of Emeneau, but an unfortunate inference from this position, which may remain as a legacy even though the basis for it has been crucially weakened, was that morphological resemblance is an unambiguous indication of *genetic* relationship. (A clear warning against the tenability of such a position, according to Jakobson, should have been those cases where a given structural feature extends from a language over only certain dialects – the nearest ones – of a neighboring language.)

At the opposite extreme were acknowledgments of borrowing and diffusion of all aspects of language so freely and on such a large scale that every language has "multiple roots" and no genetic classification in the old sense is possible. This seems to have been Boas's position (Lackner and Rowe 1955), at least regarding American Indian languages of the Northwest Coast and California, and to some extent is that of the Italian Neolinguistic school.

Such controversies need not detain us here. It may be noted, however, that even by those accepting the validity both of genetic relationships based on sound correspondences and of structural borrowing, the latter is seen as a factor complicating the genetic problem itself. It does so both at the beginning, as in Trubetzkoy's speculation (1939) that the "Indo-Europeans" may never have been one people, but a group of once-unrelated tribes who came to resemble one another – linguistically – through a period of close association, and Andronov's suggestion (1964) that the same thing may be happening in India, and later on, as divergent linguistic "cousins" again come to be neighbors and begin to influence one another's development (e.g., German and French), or as sister languages remain geographically contiguous and continue to influence one another.

INTRODUCTION

Interest in the convergence phenomenon as well as interpretations of it have varied but belong mainly to this century, for reasons noted above. Boas's work on North American Indian languages at the beginning of the century pointed the way, but these promising beginnings were vitiated by his extreme position on the "hybridization of languages," the lack of a comprehensive organized expression of his views either by himself or his followers (Voegelin 1945), and ultimately by the opposite interpretations of Sapir, according to which the similarities in question indicated genetic relationship even when there was no lexical similarity at all[4] – which came to be more influential among American linguists. Both views had the effect of diverting attention from true comparative work (that is, historical reconstruction on the basis of word comparisons and the formulation of sound correspondences) as well as from convergence questions. Conservative views on the historical-genetic question may be taken as perhaps a prerequisite for a clear focus on the convergence problem. Interest in the latter on the part of American linguists (in a narrow sense, as distinguished from emigré linguists resident in the United States) was accordingly minimal until the work of Emeneau, who was well-versed in such matters, on India – where genetic lines were also more clearly established to start with.

Meanwhile, it was left to the linguists of the Prague school – who also were aided in their focus on the problem by prior historical work and clear genetic affiliations of at least some of the languages with which they were concerned – to formulate the basic concepts of linguistic convergence and demonstrate the fact of its occurrence.

This process does not operate evenly. A language generally resembles some of its neighbors more than it does others. For one thing, the world is not one monotonous plain. There are natural barriers of various magnitudes that impede communication and therefore presumably borrowing. To these human beings have added barriers of their own, of culture and of politics. Languages should tend, other things being equal, to converge more when such barriers are less, and where the contact of their speakers is greater.

These factors may lead to the formation of linguistic areas – zones within which the processes of convergence are seen to operate with special strength and urgency, presumably because conditions – cultural, political, or whatever – have been particularly favorable for mutual fertilization among the languages within them. They form, so to speak, an "association." Among them, the convergence processes are also seen to operate in certain definite directions. Emeneau has provided a classic definition of such an area:

> . . . an area which includes languages belonging to more than one family but showing traits in common which are found not to belong to the other members of (at least) one of the families. (Emeneau 1956:16n.28)

The importance of clear genetic affiliations in this definition will be obvious. We might want to qualify the definition slightly by replacing *family* with *genetic stock* or *branch* of a genetic stock to include cases like the Balkan one, where the languages essentially involved – namely Greek, Albanian, Bulgarian, Rumanian, and to a limited extent Serbo-Croat (Hungarian and Turkish being of only peripheral relevance) – all belong to the Indo-European family but to different subbranches thereof.

A number of such areas have been pointed out: the Caucasus, the west coast of North America, the Balkans, southeast Asia, northern Eurasia, Ethiopia, India. Ernst Lewy (1964) has tried to subdivide Europe into such areas. Sometimes the affinity has been phonological only; elsewhere the convergence has been shown to embrace syntax, morphology, and idiom as well (e.g., in the Balkans, Ethiopia, some of Lewy's areas, India).

Such areas, because of the presumed basis of cultural exchange and communication on which they rest, would seem to be of immense importance for cultural geography. Yet we find a dearth of attempts to define their boundaries in terms of a set of criteria and actually to map them.

The neglect of this field by cultural geographers and cartographers is understandable: a fairly sophisticated understanding of linguistic science and linguistic systems is involved. "Linguistic geography" accordingly has tended to remain a mere mapping of languages and their speakers on the one hand, which is perhaps difficult enough, or of word distributions in dialect studies on the other; the latter is, of course, more a branch of linguistics than of geography. Important as this massive undertaking is in its own right, the mapping of abstract phonological and grammatical features, potentially across language boundaries and even genetic boundaries, is something else. (A step in this direction, however, may be seen in the Neolinguistic proposal to map the distribution of individual words and their variations in meaning across language boundaries, or without regard to them [Bottiglioni 1954]. I am uncertain whether this was ever actually carried out.)

Trubetzkoy (1931:345) predicted that structural features, unlike, for example the use of this or that phone in particular words, or of the words themselves, would be neatly mappable as "isoglosses," since a given component of a system, in order to function as such (for example, a phonemic distinction or distinctive feature), "either is or is not present" at any given point on the earth's surface. (This oversimplifies the situation somewhat, to be sure, for as we know there are differences in dialect and even in language coexistent at various points on the earth's surface. Could Trubetzkoy have been assuming convergence of features in such contact situations?) The isogloss would connect like points with respect to a given feature. Each such isogloss would define a "linguistic area" in one sense. Just as dialects within a language are not rigidly demarcated but emerge as identifiable entities from the clustering of various word distributions and the bundling of isoglosses, so also in the larger sense linguistic areas would not be rigidly demarcated but would emerge from the clustering of such structural isoglosses. Their boundaries would not be in the form of sharp lines, but of transitional belts made up of a number of such lines – such belts themselves having presumably some cultural-historical significance. (Sharper, if illusory, lines for certain purposes could be achieved through the use of *isopleths* – lines connecting points sharing a stated *set* of features.)

With a few honorable exceptions,[5] such suggestions have tended to remain programmatic. For their part, linguists have neglected this aspect of the areal problem – that is, precisely defining and mapping the alleged areas by defining and mapping the features involved – for perhaps a number of reasons, aside from a mere disinclination for cartography, although that no doubt played a role. For one thing, it has probably interested them less than questions concerning the historical evolution and internal dynamics of an area, or broader ones concerning the nature of the relations involved. Simply discovering and demonstrating individual instances of convergence has absorbed much of the time and energy of those interested in such phenomena. There is also, no doubt, the fact that some of the proposed areas have appeared to be rather well-defined geographically to begin with – e.g., the Balkan peninsula, the Indian subcontinent, the highland massif of Ethiopia – and thus seem to constitute an "arena" that conveniently can be taken for granted while other work proceeds.

Yet this is not really the case. The areas in question are not really that absolutely defined by natural boundaries – which, in any case, cultural phenomena frequently ignore. We do not really know the area of relevance of a particular feature until we actually explore its distribution; we only know the cases that have happened to come to our collective attention.

Perhaps we also tend to think that the fact that something has been plausibly projected means that it will work: conceiving is equivalent to doing. We do not really know, however, if distributions are such that isoglosses can be drawn until we actually try it. We also do not know if such projected isoglosses will cluster, or if each feature has its own independent distribution unrelated to the others. (The clustering assumption has indeed been disputed by Voegelin[6] and even by Jakobson.[7] Opinions may, of course, differ on what constitutes a significant degree of clustering, even though mathematical procedures would appear to offer a way of deciding.) Hypotheses and projections remain such until actually tested or implemented.

The clearer areal definition of zones of convergence, if it is possible, would have a bearing on some of the historical questions regarding such zones. Distributional information is a valuable kind of documentation. Meanwhile, such purely synchronic study defers for the moment the controversies regarding direction of borrowing and the precise nature of the evolution of various features that have occupied so much attention heretofore.

Perhaps the ideal way to approach this problem would be to plot the worldwide distribution of every linguistic feature, without prejudice, letting the chips fall where they might and any significant areas emerge, if they will, from any bundlings of resulting isoglosses. In that way no questions would be begged and no lurking areas missed. Unfortunately, putting aside my own limitations, neither the state of general linguistic theory nor the state of description of individual languages is at a point where this is even remotely feasible. The problems of premature linguistic macrogeography are illustrated by Fr. Wilhelm Schmidt's pioneering 1926 work, *Die Sprachfamilien und Sprachenkreise der Erde.* The accompanying atlas contains fourteen maps, only six of which (9-14) might be called typological (the rest being maps of languages, language families, etc.). Closer scrutiny of this impressive undertaking quickly reveals some rather questionable generalizations that do not encourage faith in Schmidt's handling of more obscure data. For example, the three-gender system characteristic of older

Indo-European such as Sanskrit or Greek is attributed to *all* Indo-European languages, in India and elsewhere. (The aim here may have been reconstruction of prehistory, as in much of Schmidt's work, but this is not made clear. The result is either anachronism or perhaps error.) We are the fortunate possessors of much more data than Schmidt had in 1926, but that in some ways only complicates our problem. We are aware of greater complexity, without yet having an inventory of all significant features or even of key features.

Nowadays we do have much better data.[8] We are also interested in many more things than interested Schmidt, so the data are still inadequate. And "everything" in the process has become, more than ever before, much too big an order.

One way of delimiting it would be to concentrate on one set of features only – for example, phonology. Trubetzkoy (1931:387) called for precisely that – a phonological geography of the world – in 1931. Plans for a phonemic atlas[9] were developed by phonologists attending the Fourth International Congress of Linguists in Copenhagen in 1936, and were discussed further by a group of linguists at Oslo in 1939-40, but were interrupted by World War II. Jakobson brought up the matter again at the Dobbs Ferry Conference on Language Universals in 1961, adding that linguists at M.I.T. were willing to take up the project, providing help from outside was forthcoming. Apparently it was not. Such a project would be an enormous one in itself, of course, even if everyone could agree, these days, on the criteria. Apparently it has proved too difficult to be implemented.

The mapping of grammatical categories and devices – even a limited set – on such a scale poses far greater problems of theory, of description, and of comparability. Phonological mapping is, at least, within the realm of the possible. To quote Jakobson (1963, 1966:275):

> The number of languages and dialects whose phonemic makeup is already accessible to linguists is fairly high, but – let us admit – at the beginning there will be controversial questions, and some blanks will remain on our maps. Nevertheless, the existence of unexplored areas can never be used as an argument against mapping. The isophones obtained, even if they should be only approximate, will be immensely useful to linguistics and anthropology. Matched with one another, these isoglosses will, no doubt, reveal new implicational rules and present the phonemic typology of languages in its geographical aspect. The phonemic affinities of contiguous languages due to the wide diffusion of phonemic features will be exhaustively displayed. . . .

The existence of blanks on maps, it may be added, reveals the areas where basic descriptive research is needed as nothing else can.

Such mapping of single systems within language, however, is not really suited to the problem I want to focus on here, the delineation and mapping of linguistic areas in the larger sense. The single-trait areas revealed by single system mapping might hint at such areas, but "linguistic areas" in the larger sense by definition are based on the coincidence or near-coincidence of a number of such criteria.

It is for this reason that I propose to take up the problem of a single "area" here, and test against one another the distribution of several criteria proposed to define it. The area chosen for this experiment is the Indian one. It may serve as an illustration of an approach that could be applied to any of the alleged areas.

The Indian area offers especially good material for such an experiment. It is one of the larger areas, involving hundreds of languages from at least four clearly distinct genetic stocks – Indo-European (in two branches, Indo-Aryan and Iranian), Dravidian, Tibeto-Burman, and Munda – plus some others. Partly because of the clarity of these genetic lines, it is also one of the best identified, various scholars having called attention to instances of striking correspondences across these lines since the end of the nineteenth century, correspondences that have been the more striking since they involved transmutations of Indo-European itself. Among these scholars were Sir George Grierson[10] and Jules Bloch[11] in successive eras; the problem is especially associated, however, with the name of M. B. Emeneau, who first applied the linguistic area concept in an organized manner and since the fifties has employed his considerable erudition in historical as well as descriptive aspects of both Indo-Aryan and Dravidian to extend our knowledge of its details (Emeneau 1956, 1969, 1971, 1974). Finally, the availability of data of great historical depth from both Indo-Aryan and Dravidian, the existence of classical languages of respectable antiquity also in Tibeto-Burman (Classical Tibetan) and even for the Austro-Asiatic genetic stock with which Munda is associated (in the form of a distant cousin, Old Khmer), and the considerable progress that historical reconstructions have made or are making in all four stocks all make for a rare opportunity to probe the process of growth of convergence in this area. (I shall not avail myself of it here, however.)

There has been a good deal of work on the Indian area, and even considerable discussion as to how the presumed "Indianization" of

Indo-European in the area may have come about, but, as usual, there has been no attempt to state the boundaries of the area as such in terms of definite linguistic criteria.

The Indian subcontinent, or "South Asia," may seem to be well-defined geographically to begin with, but it is by no means an isolated island. It has land connections to the north, northeast, and northwest, and even the "mountain wall" guarding these approaches has not been a complete bar to either the movement or the intercourse of peoples. The seas may seem to define the other boundaries of the area more neatly. This is an illusion born of superficial cartographic inspection, quickly dispelled when we remind ourselves that in terms of cultural history and cultural geography bodies of water – the Mediterranean, the Caribbean, the seas surrounding insular Southeast Asia, the Baltic – have served to connect as often as to separate. There have been important cultural-historical relations with the lands across both the Bay of Bengal and the Arabian Sea. The question of where India ends typologically is not automatically answerable (and certainly not by reference to the latest in the series of shifting political boundaries). It is worthy of serious attention.

The question of where the Indian area ends is tied up with the question of what defines it; the establishment of boundaries depends on the establishment of criteria. It will be possible to test only a selection of criteria here. Others should certainly be added in the course of time: the more distributions our picture of an area rests on, the more valid it will be; meanwhile, we must make a beginning somewhere.

Because phonology to some extent has been treated elsewhere,[12] I propose to explore some syntactic and morphological criteria here. This will be at the risk of confronting the theoretical difficulties, terminological confusions, and descriptive lacunae that exist with respect to these areas to a much greater extent than in phonology.

My sole aim in the discussions that arise will be to make some sense of the data for typological-comparative purposes. In a better world, all languages would be described not only fully and uniformly, but in awareness of all the typological possibilities at each point. As it is, we have to take such data as exist, in all their theoretical and traditional disguises, and reinterpret in terms of some basic typological framework.

Inadequate data offer obvious problems for comparison. We cannot say positively that Language X lacks Phenomenon N, merely because a scanty description does not mention it; even less can we say that it has it, however much we may suspect it has, without positive evidence. This is in addition to the intractability of certain kinds of data from a comparative point of view. Often it is not a question of yes or no, but of more or less – implying, ideally, statistical measures considered irrelevant to grammatical description by many linguists (and therefore lacking), but potentially very relevant to areal description.

Difficulties also arise from the use by different linguists of different terms (and theoretical frameworks) to describe the same phenomenon and, conversely, of the same term to describe different phenomena. Although old-fashioned accounts are often easier to penetrate, they also present such problems: especially, each area of traditional scholarship – Indology, Sinology, Turcology, Semitics, Finno-Ugric studies, Slavic studies – has existed in its own little world oblivious of the others; in each area a descriptive terminology has been established that owed nothing to the others, even though similar features were sometimes described. Structural linguists, dismayed by this terminological confusion (and by the inconsistencies and lack of rigor that sometimes accompanied it), more often than not ended up by chucking out the window all traditional terminology and inductively constructing a new and ingenious system of their own for the language at hand – which was never used again, and is difficult to relate to descriptions of other languages. This is especially the case since, in accordance with the proposition that every language is a system unto itself and unlike every other language, such relatability was in no way part of their aim and in fact held to be at variance with it.

This study is also a "test" of another sort. Although I have a smattering of a few of the languages involved, I was hardly acquainted with all that came to impinge on it, and a master of none. The test is therefore whether the information relevant to a broad-ranging study such as the present one can be gleaned from the existing descriptions of particular languages by a nonspecialist – in other words, whether linguistic literature is basically intelligible.

As far as this synchronic-geographic study is concerned, my method is simple enough: 1) to ascertain the viability of the feature in question on an all-India basis (although it will have been selected in the first place on that assumption); 2) to trace it outward from India, until the farthest limits of its continuous distribution are reached.

I do not pretend to include all the conceivably relevant sources: that would mean, it turns out, all the linguistic literature – synchronic, at least – pertaining to most of the languages of half the world. My method has been to sift materials until the above questions seem to be answered definitively, checking and rechecking several times if possible. What the materials happened to be is to some extent fortuitous, although I have made an effort to secure good and up-to-date ones.

This survey is hardly linguistically complete: I have not included every tribal language in the vast area that has come within its purview, nor have I descended to the dialect level. I have certainly aimed to hit all the high points and get the basic picture chalked in. It is my hope that this will help make it apparent where such further detailed studies may be most fruitfully and intelligently applied.

Not every instance of convergence that has been observed in the area of the subcontinent is relevant to the question of the boundaries of the "Indian linguistic area" as a whole.

Some – for example, between Marathi and northern Kannada dialects, or between Nepali and certain Tibeto-Burman dialects (Bendix 1974) – involve only two or three contiguous languages. These may be merely instances of what is possibly a universal tendency for contiguous languages anywhere in the world – or at least contiguous dialects of contiguous languages – to resemble each other in one way or another. Even if every Indian language turns out to be linked to its neighbors by special two-by-two relationships, forming a continuous network covering the subcontinent, this in itself would not establish India as a special area, especially if similar arbitrary linkages continue beyond India to the farthest reaches of the Afro-Eurasian continent. A number of the *same* features would have to be shared by all or most of the languages of the subcontinent, and not too many others, to justify talk of an "Indian area."

Another type of convergence that does not help us is one that links a number of Indian languages more closely with languages outside the subcontinent than with other Indian languages. This defines a "linguistic area," at least in the single-feature sense, but it is not the Indian linguistic area. The use of numeral classifiers or "counter words," cited by Emeneau (1956:10-15), in Assamese, Bengali, Telugu, and so on, would seem to fall into this category. It links certain languages mainly on the eastern side of India with the languages of East and Southeast Asia. In this case, the features in the Indian languages concerned are marginal instances of a phenomenon that seems clearly to have its center in Southeast Asia, in the vicinity of Thailand (Jones 1970). We are reminded here of the relevance of quasistatistical measures in evaluating phenomena typologically: these classifier systems show much greater elaboration – in terms, among other things, of the number of terms in them – in the vicinity of their Southeast Asian center than on its peripheries, such as India.

Another example of this is the ergative construction, which links Western Hindi, Panjabi, Marathi, Gujarati, Sindhi, and the Dardic languages with Tibetan, Pashto, and, perhaps, in an interrupted distribution (partially filled in by Tati and possibly other dialects of Caspian Iran), with the languages of the Caucasus. In this case, while the western Indo-Aryan languages cover the wider area, the phenomenon may be described as typologically more "intense" in the lesser languages (Shina, etc.) to the northwest, on the border of the subcontinent and beyond.

A given language, as Jakobson pointed out, may belong to several such single-feature "linguistic areas" at once. Thus Marathi would be, peripherally, part of an "ergative area" and at the same time, according to Emeneau, part of the "counter-word area." The question is, do criteria that hold India together and distinguish it from neighboring areas overshadow – in number or somehow in kind – such criteria as the above, which attach only parts of India to neighboring areas and together form no pattern? In other words, does an "Indian linguistic area" emerge as a significant entity, with the area itself apparently a factor of some importance? To begin with, do such criteria exist at all?

The features I have chosen to investigate for this purpose are: 1) word order, 2) morphologically marked causatives, 3) "conjunctive" participles, 4) explicator ("intensifier") verbal auxiliaries, and 5) "dative-subject" constructions.

2

WORD ORDER

It might be useful, in spite of what was said in the introductory chapter concerning the desirability of independent criteria, if some criteria were to constitute a demarcatable set in themselves. The relative importance of a number of ad hoc criteria vis-à-vis one another and vis-à-vis unexamined criteria may be difficult to judge.

One such readily demarcated set that can be tested is suggested by Greenberg's basic order typology. Looking at Greenberg's article (1963, 1966), one is struck by the extent to which his word-order data (he also deals with a number of other matters) seem to cluster geographically.

Greenberg's purpose was quite different: to ascertain, through examination of a worldwide sample of representative languages, what might be presumed to be true of language universally – either in terms of flat occurrence/nonoccurrence, or, more often, of implication of one grammatical trait in a language given the presence of another. He was particularly interested in working out a theory of "dominance" (based on the co-occurrence possibilities of individual traits) and of "harmonic-disharmonic relations" among traits (based on parallelism – "in similar constructions, the corresponding members tend to be in the same order" – and, apparently, on frequency) leading to general principles on which these implications might rest. For example, a dominant order (which he ascribes to prepositions, subject before verb, verb before object, and noun before adjective) might occur even where other order features are disharmonic with it, whereas a recessive order can occur only where at least one other trait harmonic with it is also present to support it.

Greenberg does not pretend to offer a complete theory, only suggestions for one.[1] There has not been much follow-up of these suggestions, subsequent comment having been largely confined to pointing out exceptions to the empirical generalizations on which the theoretical generalizations are based or correcting the empirical data itself. This is as it should be: the theory has to be based on valid empirical generalizations. Perhaps the time has come to review the data in the light of these additions and emendations and again to make the attempt to derive general principles of the type indicated by Greenberg.

It is not my purpose to do so here. I propose merely to examine individual order-traits from the standpoint of their geographic distributions. These may not be unrelated to the types of correlations Greenberg discusses,[2] but I shall let them speak for themselves.

Fortunately for our purposes, Greenberg is not talking in the overly simplistic terms of, e.g., "left-branching" and "right-branching." In order to come up with his implicational generalizations, he finds it necessary to first treat each order-trait as an independent variable. As noted above, the languages he examines for these traits are drawn at random – or rather, with an eye to the widest possible representativity – from all over the world. Nevertheless, areal configurations are detectable even in this data, when it is looked at from that point of view. They fairly clamor to be filled in and tested against other relevant languages in and around the areas concerned.

The fact that most of Greenberg's implicational generalizations are either one-way (e.g., VSO implies Pr, but Pr does not imply VSO) or not absolute (i.e., having exceptions, or sometimes simply being *tendencies*) not only makes it necessary to investigate and map each trait in question separately – it also makes mapmaking a more meaningful exercise. If a number of traits tend to correlate but do not do so absolutely, by drawing a separate isogloss for each we can expect a bunching of isoglosses at some points and a spreading at others, the steepness of the gradient becoming indicative of the sharpness of the typological boundary. In most kinds of feature mapping, one expects to find such zones of overlap and transition.

Work on word order and deep structure by Ross (1970), Bach (1970), and others makes it necessary for me to make it clear that it is surface structure that we are concerned with. It is surface order that seems to pattern areally, not "deep" order.[3] It appears from the above studies that deep order reflects genetic stock,[4] in other words, at the deep level any convergence patterns dissolve as far as order features are concerned. While it would doubtless be an insight of key importance for the history and process of formation of linguistic areas if intrusive languages conform to prevailing local patterns by means of (structurally) late transformations (and presumably thereby might be identified, even in the absence of other data, *as* intrusive languages), such questions are not expressly addressed here, in conformity with our deferment of historical questions in general. This chapter will confine itself to testing the hypothesis that synchronic surface order features constitute a set of criteria useful in defining linguistic areas in general and an Indian linguistic area in particular.

The features to be examined are largely those taken up by Greenberg, with some additions and modifications. Their selection is not motivated formally by anything in the grammar, except fortuitously. Features produced by transformations and features found in the base component are not distinguished, although there may be some interesting differences between them (depending on the current state of theoretical relegation of a feature to one or the other level). Attributive adjectives are particularly noteworthy here. In general, the features examined are the more salient and readily checkable ones; a brief check has shown that other features confirm the picture revealed.

Theoretical and Practical Difficulties

That is not to say that there are no problems in doing even this much. As Greenberg has noted, "the higher the construction in an immediate constituent hierarchy, the freer the order of the constituent elements." In stratificational terms, this means that sentence elements such as nominal, verbal, and adverbial phrases admit of more alternative arrangements among themselves than do the constituent words of the phrases, and these in turn more than do the generally fixed morpheme-constituents of words.

Unfortunately, the arrangements of the higher constituents such as subject, verb, and object are of particular interest precisely because their greater "flexibility," as it is usually called, seems to make them more susceptible to areal influence. That is, a bilingual under the influence of the norms of a second language may start using a marked (see below) alternative order in his own language with greater frequency than is normal until finally it starts functioning as an unmarked order for him and others like him, whom monolinguals in turn imitate, with the change – a shift in stylistic status – so gradual that it is hardly noticed. Lower-order constituents become progressively less susceptible, barring profound restructuring ("pidginization"?[5]), as we strike closer and closer to the core of the often remarkably persistent genetic heritage. An example is Brahui, which at higher levels of syntax such as those governing the conjunction and embedding of sentences has partly abandoned the "Dravidian" mode of expression (participles) for the "Iranian" (conjunctions), but retains a recognizably Dravidian morphology, including a negative conjugation. The case of Romany is accordingly more extreme, for it has adopted not only the dominant SVO order of eastern Europe but also a system of verbal prefixes analogous to those of Slavic. Although such cases may be more frequent than suspected, it remains a fact that borrowed or shared features are more likely to be found at the higher levels of syntax.

It is here, however, that basic descriptive problems present themselves. Greenberg says that "the vast majority of languages have several [clause-element] orders but a single dominant one." He is evidently using "dominant" here in a different sense than in the dominant-recessive *universal* relation between or among order possibilities proposed for his typological theory. There can be only one "dominant" order in that sense, but any of a number of universal order alternatives might be "dominant," in the nontechnical sense, among alternatives occurring in a particular language. This seems to have been misunderstood by a number of people (for example, even Roman Jakobson, who in commenting on Greenberg's paper at the same conference, remarked, "Greenberg's statements on universals . . . rightly put forward the notion of a 'dominant' order. We are reminded that the idea of dominance is not based on the more frequent occurrence of a given order: actually what is here introduced into the 'order typology' by the notion of dominance is a stylistic criterion. . .".[6] Jakobson then goes on to discuss the variant orders of Russian. "Dominance" as a universal category is not based on more frequent occurrence (i.e., among the languages of the world), to be sure (Greenberg 1963, 1966:97). That is not what is in question here, but "dominance" as a descriptive category within a language. Greenberg in fact offers no clue as to how he isolated this.[7]

Jakobson (1963:268) puts his finger on it when he calls it *stylistically neutral.* The "dominant" order is the "neutral," "basic," or "unmarked" order, from which permitted deviations (to use Jakobson's phraseology) are either "experienced by native speakers and listeners as diverse emphatic shifts," or are conditioned by such factors as interrogation, subordination, and negation, or lexically (e.g., certain French and other Romance adjectives – sometimes, only in certain meanings). In a later article (1966b), Greenberg is much concerned with the relation of the marked/unmarked distinction to universals, but he makes no attempt to apply this to word order norms specifically.

Characterization is one thing, identification is another. All might agree that basic word order in a language is "unmarked," but how do we find it? Even native speakers of languages permitting great freedom of order (which naturally are the ones that pose problems in this regard) are sometimes so conscious of that freedom that they have trouble identifying the (unconscious) underlying basic order.

The neutralization principle of the marked/unmarked theory, cited by Greenberg as a means of identifying other unmarked categories, might conceivably be invoked in the word order problem also. According to this principle, the unmarked member of an opposition may represent the whole category in a marked environment or when a second category is marked in the same place. This helps identify the unmarked member of an opposition (or the most unmarked member of a series of oppositions). That is, we note which member is left representing the rest in a neutralizing environment. In phonology, this is clear: in German and Russian, for example, the voiced/voiceless distinction is neutralized in the marked environment "before pause," the voiceless member representing both and emerging thus as the unmarked or basic member. In the case of grammatical categories, this is not always so clear in that there may be syncretization rather than neutralization in the presence of the second category, which is not the same thing: although the first set of distinctions is suppressed, what represents them is not one of their number, but something different (e.g., English *he, she, it* vs. *they*), which is therefore of no help in deciding which among them is basic. Word order may be more akin to phonology, however, in that what is "left" in a marked environment – for example, a subordinated clause – may well be one of the initial order alternatives, not something new.

In practice, this is difficult to apply – certainly universally – because in a number of languages word order itself is one of the marks of the marked environment. In the extreme case, the result may be in addition something new (e.g., word order of subordinate clauses in German).

Dezső, who has done some of the most significant work on general word order typology after Greenberg, stresses the link between recessive order alternatives and special intonation and stress patterns – the more recessive the more abnormal the sentence intonation and stress required in order to use it.[8] This may be very true, but again it is certainly difficult to apply without a detailed analysis of those patterns – and without a completely native command of every language.

For practical purposes, what do linguists do when they have trouble deciding the order norms of a language and have not worked out all the transformations, all the marked/unmarked relations, and all the prosodic features? We see that they fall back on *frequency,* after all. Two extreme examples of order-indeterminacy are Hungarian and Georgian. The frequency criterion is implied by Dezső (1968: 125-32) – "das häufigste, neutrale Glied", and Hans Vogt (1971: 220-24) explicitly refers to counts he has made.

There is nothing wrong with this, since frequency at the very least is a basic symptom of these other relations, as Greenberg also states. Displacement for emphasis or other stylistic or semantic purposes depends for its effect on a violation of a frequency norm; conversely, it is difficult for an infrequent order to avoid producing some effect by that mere fact. Stylistically affective (emphatic) as well as structurally or lexically conditioned orders are probably always less frequent than their unconditioned counterparts; this corresponds with the more general principle that the unmarked is always more frequent than the marked.

Greenberg seems to have underestimated the scope of this problem for Dravidian, Indo-Aryan, and similar languages. He assigned them to a special subtype of SOV languages having very rigid clause structures: only OSV as an alternative order, and nothing except question particles and a few other particles permitted after V. This is simply not so for Tamil, for Hindi or Bengali, or even for Turkish (as Greenberg later acknowledged in an appended note). All permit displacement for emphasis or stylistic effect, not only to OSV, but also to SVO, VOS, and, perhaps most commonly, OVS. Adverbials can occasionally follow the verb – especially locative or destination adverbials. (A locution rather characteristic of Hindi is the postposed genitive modifier – worked to death by poets and songwriters but also fairly common in conversation, e.g. *ranjiit naam hai uskaa* – "Ranjeet name is, his' = "Ranjeet is his name"; *bahut dinõ ke baad yaad aaii dostõ kaa* – "many days-after memory came friends-of' = "He remembered his friends after a long while"; *saamaan kahãã hai tumhaaraa* – 'baggage where is, your?' = "Where is your baggage?") It would seem that rigidity of word order is a function of the clarity or non-clarity of morphological marking of sentence function, not of order type. Characterization of Indian languages as SOV-types accordingly will have to rest heavily on frequency (and all it implies).[9]

Like Greenberg, I shall shun the burden of proof on the plea that there is too much else to do. In what follows the reader will have to assume that there are good grounds for taking word order to be as stated in a given language, and that in most cases this is the prevailing (at least, pre-deep structure grammar) opinion. When incorporating Greenberg's data, I have rechecked most of it, for it is sometimes subject to dispute or inconsistent.[10] It is inevitable, when attempting to cover so vast a ground, that some missteps will occur. I can only hope that mine will be as clear and susceptible to correction by concerned specialists.

The Indian Syntactic Norm

The problem for investigation presents itself in two parts. The first is to establish that there is substantial agreement in word order among languages of different genetic stocks on the subcontinent and to note in what precisely that agreement consists. The second is to discover the areal extent of these traits, in terms of isoglosses and the configurations they define – if indeed they can be drawn. That of course remains to be seen.

We might approach the first question with the abstract premise that Indian languages are, for example, "left-branching," and measure them and others against that yardstick. However, this would assume in advance that Indianization is equivalent to Dravidianization. I shall adopt the empiric approach of selecting representative languages from each of the three allegedly converging stocks in India – Dravidian, Indo-Aryan, and Munda – and ascertaining which order-traits are common to them.

For this purpose I have chosen Hindi, Bengali, Telugu, Malayalam, and Santali, representing respectively western and eastern Indo-Aryan, central and southern Dravidian, and Munda. Features of surface syntax shared by these five languages include the following:

(S)OV. — The important thing here is the last part, object precedes verb, as contrasted with Greenberg's other two main types, SVO and

VSO, in which verb precedes the object. As noted above, this is a norm, not an absolutely fixed order, in Indian languages.

Examples (1):
(H.) raaman *hindii* boltaa hai - 'Raman speaks *Hindi*'
(H.) *duusraa upaay* socũũgaa - 'I will think up *another way out*'
(B.) she *ẹkṭa gaṛi* kineche - 'He's bought *a car*'
(B.) ami *tãr nam* jani na - 'I don't know *his name*'
(Te.) kamala *puulu* koostunnadi - 'Kamala is plucking *flowers*'
(Te.) *annam* tinaṇḍi - 'Please eat *the food*'
(M.) avasaanam *maanine* kaṇṭupiṭiccu - 'Finally he spied *the deer*'
(M.) *paṇi* veegam tiirkku - 'Complete *the work* quickly'
(S.) *uni hoṛ*-ko toḷkedea - 'They bound *that man*'
(S.) *ac'ren golam*-e kolkedea - 'He sent *his servant*'

Counter examples may be found, generally under special conditions of emphasis (see also above, p. 00):

Examples (2):
(H.) kar cuke *duusraa upaay* - 'You've already exhausted *other ways out*'
(Te.) aydunelalanunci aṇṭunnaaw *padirozulu padirozulani* - 'For five months you've been saying "*ten days, ten days*" '
(H.) tum choṛ do abkii se *khetii* - 'You give up *farming* right now!

A friend who speaks both Hindi and Telugu feels that Hindi lends itself to this sort of thing more than Telugu does. Dravidian languages have other means of conveying emphasis (mainly suffixal). So strong is the force of the norm even in Hindi, however, that it may be used as one criterion for setting up agentive and dative "subjects" as special categories in several Indian languages (see chap. 6).

Examples (3):
(H.) kutte NE *pũũch* hilaaii - 'The dog wagged *his tail*'
(H.) MUJHE *ek ciṭṭhii* likhnii hai - 'I have to write *a letter*'
(M.) ENIKKU *raamane* ariññilla - 'I didn't know *Raman*'
(Te.) aameKU *amerikaa* tsuuḍaalani undi - 'She wants to see *America*'

The examples have so far been confined to noun objects, but pronoun objects behave no differently. Santali might appear to constitute an exception because of object-incorporation in the verb.

Examples (4):

iń ạgu*ko*a - 'I shall-bring-*them*'
bako sap'led*e*a - 'They did-not-catch-*him*'
gidrạko benaoked*iń*a - 'They treated-*me* as a child'

This might appear to constitute a pronoun object structure *Vo*. (The "adhesion" is no bar: there are many other examples of suffixed pronoun objects, e.g., in Spanish, Italian, Persian, and Amharic.) However, this same structure occurs when nominal or separate-pronominal objects also occur.

Examples (5):

mẹrọm-e gọc'kede*tiń*a - 'He killed *my goat* (*Goat*-he killed-*it*-my)'
ẹṇḍẹkhan *iń* hō̤ cet'*a*ńme - 'Then teach *me* too (*me* too teach-*me*-you)'

These "infixes" are in all cases except the third person singular recognizably the same morphemes as the separable pronouns. A notion that personal endings have to be different from the pronouns, however, is an Indo-European prejudice, and this phenomenon accordingly may be called mere object-indication in the verb inflection. As the separate pronoun subject is ordinarily not used except for emphasis in languages where it is already sufficiently indicated by the personal inflection of the verb, so also in Santali the separate pronoun object is ordinarily not used, being already sufficiently shown by the verb, as in Examples (4).

For Indian languages, and many others as well, the term *object* might as well be broadened to *verbal complement*, for goals of motion, predicate nouns and adjectives, so-called adverbial complements, infinitival complements of catenatives, and certain other items tend to occupy the same position as the direct object, whether in SOV or SVO languages. Compare the English translations of the examples below.

Examples (6):

(H.) sab log *apne apne ghar* jaao - 'Everybody go *home*'
(B.) ami *shomdeber baṛite* jacchi - 'I'm going to Somdev's house'
(Te.) *inṭiki* weḷdaam - 'Let's go *home*'
(M.) kaakka *maaninṯeyaṭutta* parannu cennu - 'The crow flew *to the deer*'
(S.) onko *oṛak'te*-ko sẹn akana - 'They've all gone *home*'
(H.) ham sab *muurakh* hãĩ - 'We're all *fools*'
(B.) tini *ẹkjon ḍakṭar* chilen - 'He was *a doctor*'
(Te.) ciire *nallagaa* undi - 'The sari is *black*'

(M.) caaya *tayyaaraayi* - 'Tea is *ready*'
(M.) *rakṣappeṭaan* nookukayaayirunnu - 'He was trying *to escape*'
(S.) noa katha dọ *sari* kangea - 'This story is true'
(S.) ar ạḍi ọkọc'ak'ko *cet'a*ko-e portonket'a - 'And he began *to teach* them many things'

The order is the same, only more rigid, in subordinate clauses, and it is the same in interrogative and declarative sentences, except in Malayalam, where there is a tendency to put the question-word first.

Examples (7):
(M.) *aar*-aaṇ-avaḷ? - "*Who* is she?'
(M.) *ent*-aa nii nirutti-kkaḷaññatå? - '*Why* did you stop?'

This is merely a stylistic tendency, dependent moreover on a peculiar use of the quasicopular element /aa(ṇ)/ and pronominalization of the verb, if there is one. The pan-Indian order, putting the question-word in place of the word used to answer it in a declarative sentence, is also possible:

Examples (8):
(M.) nii-y *-eṅṅine* iviṭe vannu? - '*How* did you come here?'
(M.) niṅṅaḷ-*aar*-aaṇå? - 'Who are you?'

V + Aux. —— The definition of *auxiliary* needs some attention here. Let it be clear that here I do not mean by *aux* what it has meant in transformational descriptions of English. Greenberg's definition, on the other hand ("a closed class of verbs inflected for both person and number . . . in construction with an open class of verbs not inflected for person and number"), makes strange demands that are unsuited to Indian languages (and many others), where the main (open class) verb may be inflected for number (Hindi), where no verbs may be inflected for number (Bengali), where auxiliaries in certain tenses may not be inflected for person (Hindi), or where no verbs may be inflected for either person or number (Malayalam). Our purposes would not be served by adopting such a definition.

Although a simple open *vs.* closed criterion would serve well enough for Indian languages, it would (by admitting modals, etc.) lead to too many complications – interesting complications, but best deferred. For the purposes of this book, let us define *aux* as a *tense*-carrying word or quasiword in complex verb forms. In the sample Indian languages, tense-carrying auxiliaries invariably follow the main verb and close the construction.

Examples (9):

(H.) aa rahaa *hai* - 'He *is* coming'
(H.) aa rahaa *thaa* - 'He was coming'
(H.) aayaa *hai* - 'He *has* come'
(H.) aae*gaa* - 'He *will* come'
(B.) phire eshe*che* - 'He has returned'
(B.) ja*cchi* - 'I *am* going'
(B.) ja*bo* - I *shall* go'
(Te.) tsadawa*leedu* - 'I/he/you/we/etc. *did not* read'
(Te.-lit.) tsadiwi *unṭini* - 'I *had* read'
(M.) pa*ranni**rikunnu* - '. . . *has* flown'
(M.) pa*ranni**runnu* - '. . . *had* flown'
(M.) varunnuṇṭaay*irunnu* - '. . . was coming'
(S.) calak'*kana* - 'is/are going'
(S.) gọc'*akadea* - '. . . have killed'

"Standard colloquial" Telugu (i.e., of the northern coastal districts) presents certain problems for this working definition in that the common auxiliary *unnaanu, unnaaw,* etc., has submerged the distinction between present and past: tsaduwut*unnaanu* = 'I *am/was* reading'.

Po. – Our Indian languages are postpositional rather than prepositional. Moreover, they generally possess two kinds of postpositions, a small set of short particles resembling suffixes (or as older descriptions would have it, "case endings") and more numerous, longer forms derived from nouns (or less commonly, verbs) added to genitive or dative case forms of the noun or pronoun.

Examples (10):

(H.) ghar *mẽ* – '*in* the house, *at* home'
(H.) ghar *ke piiche* - '*behind* the house'
(B.) baṛ*ite* - 'at home'
(B.) bon*er mọddhe* - '*in the middle of* the forest'
(Te.) gumpu*lo* - '*in* the crowd'
(Te.) ḍabbu *koosam* - '*for* money'
(M.) muriy*il* - '*in* the room'
(M.) aa mara*ttinte kiizhe* - 'beneath that tree'
(S.) oṛak'*re* - '*in* the house, *at* home'
(S.) bir *sẹnre* - '*toward* the forest'

Adj + N, Gen + N, Dem + N, Num + N. – In the Indian sample languages, adjectivals,[11] genitive expressions (defined either specifically in terms of a relationship of "possession" or merely in terms of the subordination of the one NP to another by the same means used to indicate possession, or by other means), demonstratives, and numerals all precede the nouns they modify (for certain exceptions in the case of Malayalam see below).

Examples (11):
(H.) *andherii* raat - '*dark* night'
(B.) *shundor* chele - '*beautiful* child'
(Te.) *pedda* samasya - '*big* problem'
(M.) *nalla* hooṭṭal - '*good* hotel'
(S.) mit '*ṭhutkut*' sahan - 'a *small* piece of firewood'
(H.) *raam kaa* bhaaii - '*Ram's* brother'
(H.) *pattiyõ kaa* ek ḍher - 'a pile *of leaves*'
(B.) *shomdeber* baṛi - 'Somdev's house'
(B.) *boner* raja - 'the king *of the forest*'
(Te.) *kaantaaraaw* koopam - '*Kantarao's* anger'
(Te.) *aandhradeesa* caritra - the history *of Andhra*'
(M.) *kaakkayuṭe* muṭṭa - '*the crow's* egg'
(M.) *enṯe muṟiyuṭe* taakkool - 'the key *of my room*'
(S.) *johan babaptisic'reak'* bọhọk' - '*John the Baptist's* head'
(S.) *bir reak'* dare - 'a tree *of the jungle*'
(H.) *vah* aadmii - '*that* man'
(B.) *ei* lokṭi - '*this* man'
(Te.) *ii* niiḷḷu - '*this* water'
(M.) *ii* aama - '*this* turtle'
(S.) *nui* họṛ - '*this* man'
(H.) *do* ghaṇṭe - '*two* hours'
(B.) *pãcṭa* kukur - 'five dogs'
(Te.) *muuḍu* nelalu - 'three months'
(M.) *naalpatu* kuzhi - 'forty holes'
(S.) *bar* poesa - 'two pice'

It will be noted that Telugu marks the genitive relationship, in the case of nouns, by *position only.*

Qualif + Adj. – Qualifiers of adjectivals precede them. This includes not only intensifiers (words for "very," "somewhat," etc.) but also *qualifiers by comparison* – the equivalents of "than X," which also may be viewed as qualifying an adjectival: *How big? Very big. Bigger than an albatross.* The criterion (following Greenberg) is the position of the marker (M) of comparison (= "than") and the standard (S) of comparison relative to the adjectival (A); equivalents, if any, of – *er, more,* etc., are ignored. Indian languages have the comparison structure SMA, the modifying elements SM preceding the modified A, rather than following as in English (A-MS: big(ger) – *than/an albatross*).

Examples (12):
(H.) *bahut* acchaa - '*very* good'
(H.) *us-se* acchaa - 'better *than that*'
(B.) *gọtokaler cee* besi gọrom - 'hotter *than yesterday*'
(Te.) *tsaalaa* ettugaa undi - 'it is *very* high'
(Te.) *kamala kanṭe* andangaa unṭundi - 'she's *more beautiful than* K.'
(M.) kiṭṭu *valiya* dhavaanaayi - 'Kittu became *very* rich'
(M.) haliimaa *ninte mumtaasine kkaal* etrayoo uyarnnavaḷaaṇǎ - 'Haleema is much greater *than your Mumtaz*'
(S.) *ạdi* marań sadọm - 'a *very* big horse'
(S.) *ińren khọne* marańa - '(it is) bigger *than mine*'

Santali, significantly, also permits the order Adj + Qualif: maran *ọkọc'* hati – a *very* large (large-very) elephant (S.)

All the features so far described have indeed been instances of *left-branching* – the modifier *precedes* the modified. However, it would be incorrect to say that Indian languages as such are left-branching. Only Dravidian languages – and not all of them – are consistently and exclusively left-branching. The crux of the matter is the complex sentence. Although conditional, temporal, and adverbial clauses normally precede the main clauses to which they are subordinated in all the languages, only Dravidian (that is, in our sample, Telugu and Malayalam) forces nominal object clauses to precede their verb and adjectival ("relative") clauses to precede the noun they qualify; in Hindi, Bengali, and Santali they normally follow. The typical Indo-Aryan device of relative *marker* preceding the noun, with the main body of the clause (including the verb – Greenberg's criterion) following the noun but preceding a *correlative* in the main clause, may be considered a compromise as far as relative clauses are concerned. The noun and the correlative pronoun, as it were, trade places, so that the clause does precede the noun's proxy, the correlative.

Examples (13):

'the very stone which the builders rejected' =

(H.) jis patthar ko / raajmistriiyõ ne / nikamma ṭhaharaayaa / *vahii*
which stone-*acc.* the builders-*ag.* rejected *it*-only

(Te.) –– / illu kaṭṭuvaaru / niraakarincina / *raay*
(the) (by) the builders rejected stone

(M.) –– / viiṭu paṇiyunnavar / aakaa ennu taḷḷiya / *kallu tannee*
(the) (by) the builders rejected stone-itself

The Hindi verb is not adjectival here. Moreover, a form without a correlative, with the marker *following* the noun as in English, seems to be equally common: 'the fig tree/which you cursed' = yah anjiir kaa peṛ/*jise* tuu ne sraap diyaa thaa.[12]

Despite the awkwardness of the Aryan construction when compared with the Dravidian one, it is often imitated – if that is not begging the question – by the Dravidian languages themselves.

Examples (14):

(Te.) *eemi* dzarigindoo *adi* dzarigipooyindi - 'What has happened, has happened' Cf. (H.) *jo* huaa *so* huaa.

(Te.) ii ḍabbu *ekkaḍanunci* vaccindoo, *akkaḍikee* pampu - 'Send this money back where it came from' Cf. (H.) ye paise *jahãã se* aaee, *vahĩĩ* bhej do; (B.) ei ṭaka *jar kach theke* esheche *take* dao.

Participial constructions subordinating a VP to an NP are possible in Hindi more readily than in English, but the point is, they are not compulsory – and even then need not always precede the noun.

Examples (15):

(H.) *giraa huaa* bairii - 'a *fallen* enemy'
(H.) *rotaa huaa* baccaa - 'the *crying* child', 'the child who is *crying*'
(H.) *peṛ par caṛhaa huaa* aadmii - 'the man *who climbed up the tree*'
(H.) *zamiin par leṭaa huaa* aadmii - 'the man *who lay on the ground*'
(H.) *bace hue* log - 'the people *who had been saved*'
(H.) *rakkhaa huaa* khaanaa - 'the food *which was kept*'

Statistical measurements of the frequency of such constructions *vs.* equivalent relative constructions in texts of various languages under consideration here (including English, German, and Russian) would no doubt be of great interest, but let us adopt as a crude taxonomic principle the behavior of the VP's *with complements* when subordinated to a noun. On that basis, the five-language sample exhibits no common pattern (participial constructions are particularly uncommon in Bengali), only tendencies.

That is not to say that the five headings above exhaust the points of agreement in syntax among our sample languages. They would seem also to include, for example, *adverbials* – both their position in the sentence and vis-à-vis one another. This is merely too time-consuming to be gone into here, for the information gained.

The Areal Configuration

We now come to the second and most important stage of the investigation – determining whether the syntactic points of agreement among our sample languages are indeed characteristically "Indian" and useful in establishing, in terms of isoglosses, an "Indian linguistic area."

We shall do this by attempting to trace outward in all directions each order-trait established above until resistance is met in the form of an *opposing* trait; at that point an isogloss is to be drawn.

This is putting it too simply, to be sure. Our "isoglosses" will have to be basically highly generalized and representative of whole languages in their standard form, rather than of dialectological or reporting-station information. This will serve our purpose, however, which at this point is a basic blocking out of the pattern. Further refinements become meaningful once that is established. The problem posed by mixed or conflicting traits in a language will be dealt with cartographically by adopting the convention of drawing the isogloss in question through the *middle* of the speech-territory concerned (rather than around it), without implying that there is a boundary at precisely that point on the ground.

But let us go back a step. Are the traits in question so distributed as to permit the drawing of isoglosses at all? A mere irregular concentration is conceivable. However, this does not seem to be the case: languages that are exceptions to an areal pattern, although always posing intriguing historical questions, are rare enough to be recorded merely as exceptions. The patterns stand.

This will only become clear as we proceed to trace the distribution of the traits:

OV (or, except where noted, Complement + Verb). – This basic pattern includes not only the remaining Dravidian and Indo-Aryan

MAP 1. Word Order Feature Distributions

Key:

———— Object precedes Verb

(Note: this also implies Postpositions except where marked as follows:

Prepositions, inside OV

Postpositions, outside OV

Ambipositions, both Prepositions and Postpositions and other transitional phenomena, either inside or outside OV

------- Adj+N order dominant

- - - - Celto-Romance area of mixed N+Adj/Adj+N order, former dominant

—·—·— Genitive precedes Head Noun

··········· Standard+Marker ("than")+ Adjective order in comparisons

Exceptions: 1 Kashmiri, 2 Khasi,
3 Basque 4 Kanuri.

Note: certain cases of mixed phenomena, such as Burmese adjectivals, Greek genitives and English genitives, are indicated by running the isogloss through the middle of the speech-area concerned. Other, minor types of equivocation, such as position of pronoun objects, verb position in German subordinate clauses, etc., are not indicated at all on this map. The highly equivocal word order of Hungarian is indicated by the special symbol ┬┬┬┬┬┬┬.

Anti- features:

oooooo Numeral follows Noun

++++++ Demonstrative follows Noun

×××××× Qualifier follows Adjective

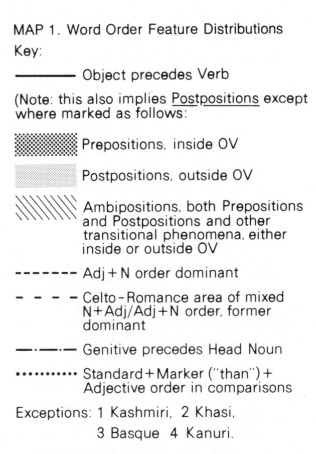

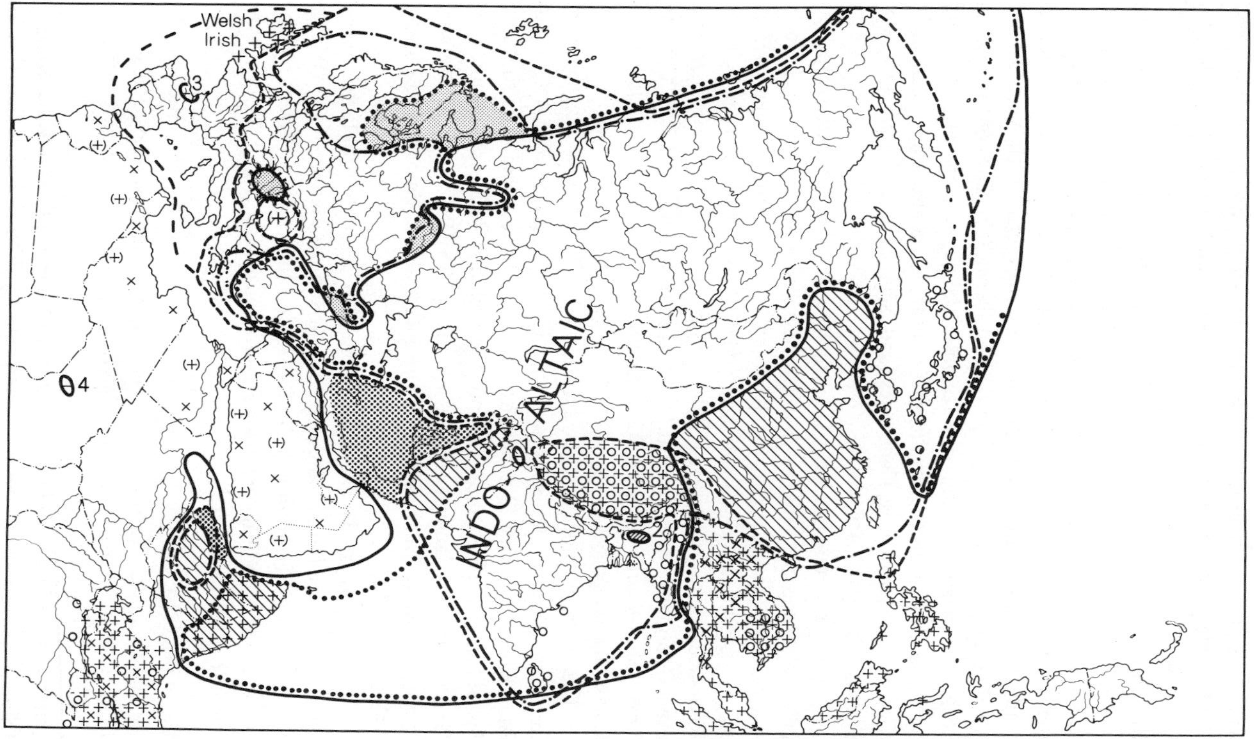
Welsh
Irish
INDO
ALTAIC

languages of the subcontinent, but also the Tibeto-Burman, Iranian, and Dardic languages of its borderlands (including specifically Tibetan, Burmese, Pashto, and Persian) – with the important exception of Kashmiri. It also includes Burushaski and the Tai-affiliated Khamti language of Assam, and extends to Armenian, Kurdish, and Ossetic on the west, and the Turkic and other Altaic languages, Korean, Japanese, the Paleoasiatic languages, and Eskimo on the north. Thence it continues even farther, some distance into northern North America, but we shall not pursue it there. On the southwest, it reaches out to take in both the Hamitic and the Semitic languages of Ethiopia and Somaliland, and on the southeast it appears to include the Andamanese (but not the Nicobarese) languages (and, according to Greenberg's data, most of aboriginal Australia).

Beyond this massive bloc, OV languages stand as isolated exceptions in equally massive blocs of VO languages: Basque in Europe, Lolo in southern China, Hottentot and a few other scattered languages in Africa. A western VO bloc includes Arabic and Berber, Greek, Romance, Celtic, Germanic, Balto-Slavic, most African languages, and even Georgian[13] and Finnish.[14] An eastern VO bloc takes in Chinese, Thai, Mon-Khmer languages, Vietnamese, and Indonesian languages (including Malagasy).

The eastern bloc reaches in, through the Palaung languages of northern Burma, to subtract the Khasi language of Assam (of Mon-Khmer affinity like Palaung) from the Indian area. The southern Munda language Sora must also only be included with reservations. Free lexemes in this language order themselves (S)OV, but in compound forms, which are very numerous, the ancestral (see Pinnow 1960) order VO is preserved.

The Indo-Aryan language Sinhalese also presents problems. As we have seen, most Indian languages permit some violation of the OV rule for purposes of emphasis. In Sinhalese, this is formalized by the presence of a special "emphatic" verb form (*-nne*), and VO patterns become quite frequent.[15]

Examples (16):

(Sinh.) mahattea *suruṭṭu* bonạwa - 'The gentleman smokes cigars'

(Sinh.) mahattea paawicci karaNNE *mee suruṭṭu* - 'The gentleman uses these cigars'

(Sinh.) mee basekạ *kalutạrạtạ* yanạwa - 'This bus goes to Kalutara'

(Sinh.) mee basekạ yaNNE *kalutạrạtạ* - 'It is to Kalutara that this bus goes'

Other kinds of attrition are to be seen on the west. In Ethiopia and in Iran and its borderlands *pronominal* objects may be suffixed to the verb, thus presenting a structure *Vo*:

Examples (17):
(Pers.) didam-*esh* - I-saw-*him*'
(Balochi) man aagiraan-*ish*-'I will-seize-*them*'
(Brahui) xalkuṭ-*ta*-'I-struck-*him*'
(Amharic) gaddalhu-*aachaw*-'I-killed-*them*'

Although separable pronoun forms also occur in the normal position (SoV), generally with emphatic value in speech, these enclitic forms appear to demolish Greenberg's Universal No. 25 as presently stated: "If the pronominal object follows the verb, so does the nominal object." Bach, in the paper on Amharic cited earlier, notes that such exceptions to Greenberg's universals occur where the deep structure order differs from the surface order, which in turn occurs where the typical order of the genetic stock to which a language belongs differs from that of the area in which it now finds itself. An additional qualification may now be added: such exceptions also occur near the margins of major syntactic zones geographically.

Across the OV/VO boundary it is interesting that the reverse of this pronoun phenomenon occurs, namely the proclitic pronoun object structure *oV* – the pronoun *precedes* the verb – in the VO languages Greek, Rumanian, Bulgarian, Italian, Spanish, French, Swahili, etc. (The enclitic *Vo* structure also occurs in some of these languages, to be sure, in restricted environments, such as imperatives and gerunds, e.g., Gk. *afísteME* - 'let me go', Sp. *dejadLO* - 'let him/it go', *abriéndoLO* - '[on] opening it', but these may be regarded as exceptions. In Spanish, the exceptions may be carried quite far [Stevenson 1970: 108]. Spanish is also farthest from the boundary region among the languages mentioned.)

The broader category *Complement + Verb* also breaks down in the western borderlands. In colloquial Persian, Kurdish, and Turkish, the order *norm* for goals of motion verbs is *VG*, even though direct objects are *OV*.

Examples (18):
(Pers.) boro *manzel!* - 'Go home!'
(Kurd.) bá bchin *bó bazar* - 'Let's go to the market'
(Kurd.) haatim-*aa shaarii* - 'I came to town'
(Turk.) gel *buraya* - 'Come here!'

The distribution of *V + Aux* broadly coincides with that of OV. Again Kashmiri is an exception in India, with *Aux + V.* A shadow of this even falls on Panjabi, in that the *past* auxiliary precedes V when construed in the negative: (Panj.) *ó andar aundii SII* - 'she used to come in', but *ó andar nā̃ĩ SII aundii* - 'she didn't used to come in'. Again there is vacillation in Iranian: the Persian perfect auxiliaries follow, but that of the future (not used in spoken Tajik) precedes (*rafte AST* - 'has gone', *rafte BUD* - 'had gone', but *XAAHAD raft* - 'will go'). In Pashto, tense-forming "particles" (added to *finite* verbs) precede, but true auxiliaries (added to participles) follow.

Examples (19):
(Pashto) za *bạ* xat likạm - 'I *will be* writing a letter'
(Pashto) maa xat likạlay *vu* - 'I had written a letter'

According to Penzl's analysis, the particles are essentially modal in function. However, he cites the same order transformation with the negative that was noted above for Panjabi, bringing the auxiliary itself (and no longer just the past auxiliary) before the verb:

Examples (20):
(Pashto) staa axbaar raagạlay DAY - 'Your newspaper has come'
(Pashto) staa axbaar NEDAY raagạlay - 'Your newspaper hasn't come'

Again there are analogous reverse phenomena across the VO boundary. In Bulgarian, Serbo-Croat, Slovak, Czech, Polish, and Ukrainian, certain auxiliaries (generally those of Perfects and Conditionals) *normally* follow but precede under special conditions, while others (typically Futures – the pattern varies slightly from language to language) normally precede but may follow under special conditions (as may certain Rumanian auxiliaries). This brings us finally to the German feature of inversion of auxiliary and main verb in subordinate clauses.

The distribution of *Po* follows that of *OV,* but with certain noteworthy discrepancies, again in the border regions. Persian and Tajik have exclusively prepositions (or possibly one postposition, if the accusative particle = RAA is so classified).[16] Closer in, Balochi has appropriately a mixture of the two. Pashto has also, plus a development that points to an inadequacy in the Po/Pr dichotomy – namely, both simultaneously, that is, discontinuously, "framing" the N; they might, following Greenberg's *"ambifixes,"* be called *ambipositions.*

Examples (21):
(Pashto) *da* kor *tsaxaa* - '*from* the house'

(Pashto) *pa* kor *ki* - '*in* the house'
(Pashto) *ta* mez *laándi* - '*under* the table'

Hindi itself has one ambiposition, sometimes preposition, the item *binaa . . . (ke)* 'without'. Kashmiri is postpositional. Several languages of the Pamirs (Wakhi, Ishkashimi), however, follow Pashto in being ambipositional.

A similar situation is found on the southwest frontier: Tigré has prepositions, Amharic, Tigrinya, Gafat, and Gurage have ambipositions and prepositions, while Harari, Agau, Galla, Beja, and Afar have postpositions. (According to Ferguson, Amharic should be classified as postpositional and Tigrinya as ambipositional.) Somali exhibits another new category: the equivalent relational elements are attached to the verb rather than to the noun to which they refer, which may occur anywhere in the sentence (generally, however, somewhere before the verb).

Examples (22):
(Amharic) *wada* wanz - 'toward the river'
(Amharic) *ba* aalgaa *taach* - 'under the bed'
(Somali) 'ali la'agta *ka*-qaad - 'Ali the-money from-take (= 'Take the money from Ali')

A somewhat similar phenomenon occurs in Kurdish. Here the "prepositional" element is suffixed rather than prefixed to the verb:

(Kurd.) *haatim-AA shaarii* - 'I came-to town'

The reverse effect on the other side of the VO/OV border is this time exemplified by Georgian, which, though VO, is exclusively postpositional, and perhaps Swahili, which has a locative suffix *-ni.* Finnish and Estonian have developed a few prepositions, however, while in the same vicinity Latvian, Lithuanian, and even German have a few postpositions (*entlang, entgegen, gegenüber, halben, halber, wegen*).

Are there comparable shadow effects across the eastern frontier? Chinese is of some interest here. It presents certain classificatory, because first of all descriptive, problems – such as Thai, Cambodian, Malay, and other Southeast Asian languages do not. Relations such as those expressed in other languages by prepositions or postpositions are expressed in Chinese partly by noun-like words that *follow* the noun (wūdz*li* 'in the room', chwáng*sya* 'under the bed', chyáng*shang* 'on the wall'), partly by verb-like words that *precede* it (*dzài* jyā 'at home', *yán* lù 'along the road', *gēn* wǒ 'with me'). Just as the former may plausibly be rendered "room-inside," "bed-bottom," "wall-surface," so the latter may be seen, especially in context, as retaining their verbal meanings ("located-home," "edging-road," "following-me": e.g., *gēn wǒ lái* = "follow-me-come" = 'come with me'; *dzwò fēijī chyù* = "sit-plane-go" = 'go by plane'). Complicating the matter further, there are members of the verb-like class that seem to have no ordinary verbal function, such as TSÚNG 'from', as well as one undoubted postposition in the "genitive" particle DE (is English 'S a postposition?). Finally, members of the two classes frequently occur together (*dzài* fángdz*de hòubyar* - 'behind the house' = "located-house's behind"), analogous to the situation in Pashto and Amharic. Perhaps the fairest thing would be to call Chinese ambivalent, *Po/Pr.* If the verb-like forms are taken to be prepositions (or something other than verbs), the effect is often to leave another verb alone at the end of the sentence, thus pushing Chinese away from the VO-Pr norm in any case.

The Lolo language appears to be postpositional, while Khamti and Shan as well as Khasi and Palaung are prepositional. The line in this respect, therefore, unlike the OV line, neatly follows the genetic one of Tibeto-Burman *vs.* Tai and Mon-Khmer.

The various modifiers of the noun that patterned alike in our Indian language sample turn out to be separate variables when we trace them further.

The feature *Adj + N* defines an isogloss considerably at variance with OV, though still circumscribing the same general area. The main differences are a wide flaring out in the north, to include in addition to the OV languages the Slavonic and Germanic groups, Chinese, Finnish and Hungarian, Georgian, and, less securely, Greek, and a marked narrowing at the waist, to exclude Persian, Kurdish, and Tajik on the one hand (though not Ossetic, Pashto, or Balochi) and Tibetan, Garo, the Naga dialects, Khamti, and Shan (and of course Khasi and Mon) on the other. Somali, Eskimo, and Aleut are also excluded.

Burmese, Manipuri, Lushai, perhaps Kachin and other Tibeto-Burman languages waver. That is, to take the Burmese case, modifiers of nominal origin precede (*sa* dai' - '*letter* building' = postoffice), while those of verbal origin follow (nwa *pyau'* - '*lost* bullock') *unless* they have to do with "use or cause" (*thau'* ye - '*drinking* water') *or* use the particle *thau;* phrasal modifiers also precede, *except for* a special list, which follows. This confused situation arises partly from the transformational nature of attributive adjectivals and partly from the fact that this is a border situation. Two of the early insights of generative grammar, namely, that attributive adjectives are derived transformationally from predictive ones and that languages differ more in their transformational structure than in their basic phrase structure, seem to be borne out when the Adj + N isogloss is compared with the OV and similar isoglosses.

Greek, with normative Adj + N but permitting adjectives in postnominal position under special conditions, may be regarded as transitional to Romance with allegedly normative N + Adj but permitting (rather frequently) prenominal adjectives under special conditions, and the latter as transitional in turn to the more rigid N + Adj order of Arabic and Berber.

The *Gen + N* isogloss follows OV more closely, including Chinese, Georgian, and Finnish, but stopping short of Slavonic, unless we take note of the special "possessive" adjectives derived from proper names and a few other nouns (names of animals). Persian, Tajik, Kurdish, and Somali are excluded, but Tibeto-Burman remains unambiguously inside this time with Indo-Aryan and Dravidian. A slight shadow falls on otherwise excluded Greek, in the case of noun phrases containing other modifiers, or genitive phrases themselves containing modifiers (pame *stis adelfis MU* to spiti - 'Let's go *to MY sister's* house').

Dem + N excludes Somali and Tibetan (as well as the already excluded Thai, Indonesian, Swahili, Tagalog, Cambodian, and related languages). At two points along this southern boundary, namely Tigré-Tigrinya and with Malagasy, the typically border phenomenon of *ambifixation* occurs *(dem + N + dem)*.

Num + N cuts out all Tibeto-Burman languages, Andamanese, Korean, and, most significantly, Sinhalese. A numeral *may* follow the noun under certain (quasi-appositional) conditions also in Tamil, Kannada, and Malayalam as well as in Japanese.

Ordinary adjectival qualifiers follow the adjective only in extreme right-branching languages: Arabic, Swahili, Thai, Cambodian, Javanese.

The qualifier of comparison, however, yields an isogloss useful in distinguishing languages of the Indian type from mixed-type as well as right-branching languages. The *SMA* trait characterizes all Indo-Aryan and Dravidian languages (including Sinhalese, Kashmiri, and Brahui), Munda, Tibeto-Burman and Altaic languages, Korean, Japanese, Finnish, and Somali. Then follows a transitional type MSA, in Amharic, Balochi, Pashto, Tajik, Chinese, Khasi, and partly in Persian. (Colloquial Tajik has also developed an SMA form.) Beyond these are the AMS types of Europe (such as English), as well as of Arabic (and competing in Persian) and of further Southeast Asia, and unrelated constructions (typically using a verb "is greater") in Africa.

Conclusions

It can be seen that the successive isoglosses of surface order features common to a sample of Indian languages do define a definite area of the Old World and ultimately set off within it a smaller region very closely coincident with what might be taken a priori to be the "Indian linguistic area." This area, moreover, is not an area of transition (formed by the *intersection* of isoglosses) but a *trait-core* area, surrounded by *concentric* isoglosses.

First, the basic OV isogloss defines a massive middle segment of the world, a largely left-branching syntactic zone in which India is the main southern anchor. In keeping with its basically north-south trend, we might name this macrozone *Indo-Altaic*. It is flanked by two equally well-defined opposing VO zones (well, perhaps not *equally* well-defined, as Europe is rather mixed), the Euro-African and the Sino-Indonesian, within which Greenberg's category VSO appears in more or less isolated fragments as an extremist subvariety. (Such fragments in the west include Maasai, Arabic, and Celtic – and interestingly enough, strong tendencies in Spanish[17] – and in the east, Polynesian and Philippine languages, and Nicobarese.)

Subsequent isoglosses, especially those involving the noun phrase, cut the OV zone almost in two at its waist and set the subcontinent apart as a separate subzone.

The subsequent isoglosses at the same time set up three transitional subzones where the basic OV syntax begins to give way to right-branching phenomena: the *Iranian,* the *Tibeto-Burman,* and the *Abyssinian.* Of these, the latter two show the closer typological affinity to India, despite the genetic affinity of the first. This is especially apparent with regard to relative clauses, not used as a criterion here. To these three a fourth perhaps should be added where left-branching traits begin to assert themselves strongly across the VO line – *China.*

A thick bundle of isoglosses separates India from Southeast Asia beyond Burma (see Table 1) from Arabic (see Table 2) and from Africa beyond Ethiopia (see Table 3). There is more affinity with Europe (see Table 4) and with China (see Table 5) than with these areas. A number of significant order isoglosses also separate Indian languages from Persian (see Table 6).

TABLE 1
Word Order: India and Further India

Hindi, Telugu, Burmese	Thai, Cambodian, Javanese
OV	VO
Po	Pr
gen + N	N + gen
dem + N	N + dem
V + aux	aux + V
standard + marker + Adj	Adj + marker + standard
qualif + Adj	Adj + qualif

TABLE 2
Word Order: India and Arabic

Hindi, Malayalam	Arabic
OV	VO
Po	Pr
Adj + N	N + Adj
gen + N	N + gen
standard + marker + Adj	Adj + marker + standard

TABLE 3
Word Order: India and Africa

Malayalam	Amharic	Swahili
OV		Vo
Po	Ambi/Pr	Pr
Adj + N		N + Adj
gen + N		N + gen
rel + N		N + rel
num + N		N + num
standard + marker + Adj	marker + standard + Adj	(verbal)
V + aux		(tense prefix) + V
qualif + Adj		Adj + qualif
dem + N		N + dem

TABLE 4
WORD ORDER: INDIA AND EUROPE

Telugu	OV	Po	Adj + N	gen + N	dem + N	num + N	qualif + Adj
Hindi	OV	Po	Adj + N	gen + N	dem + N	num + N	qualif + Adj
Swedish	VO	Pr	Adj + N	gen + N	dem + N	num + N	qualif + Adj
Russian	VO	Pr	Adj + N	N + gen	dem + N	num + N	qualif + Adj
German	VO(OV)	Pr(Po)	Adj + N	N + gen	dem + N	num + N	qualif + Adj
French	VO(oV)	Pr	N + Adj (Adj + N)	N + gen	dem + N	num + N	qualif + Adj

TABLE 5
WORD ORDER: INDIA AND CHINA

Bengali	OV	Po	Adj + N	gen + N	dem + N	num + N	qualif + Adj	N + rel
Telugu	OV	Po	Adj + N	gen + N	dem + N	num + N	qualif + Adj	rel + N
Chinese	VO	Po/Pr	Adj + N	gen + N	dem + N	num + N	qualif + Adj	rel + N

TABLE 6
WORD ORDER: INDIA AND PERSIA

Hindi	Persian
OV	OV/Vo
Po	Pr
Adj + N	N + Adj
gen + N	N + gen
V + aux	V + aux/aux + V
SMAdj	MSAdj/AdjMS

Of the two anomalies within the subcontinent, Khasi and Kashmiri, the former is only slightly intruded from the territory of its typological allies on the east, but the latter, although near the point where the Iranian and Tibeto-Burman transitional zones approach each other most closely (these are anyway defined in particular by N + Adj, a peculiarity it does not share), is far from any VO language. If retention of genetic heritage is the explanation in both cases, it can be noted that the Khasi Hills and the Kashmir Valley share a notable degree of geographic and historic isolation.

On the northwestern border, Pashto and Balochi constitute a further subtransition between India and Iran proper – they may be called partially assimilated Iranian.

3

CAUSATIVE VERBS

PROBLEMS FOR THE COMPARATIVIST

In proposing to discuss causatives we immediately find ourselves in an area of immense descriptive confusion. A statement such as "Indian languages typically have causative verbs" might be made by anyone familiar with these languages in a first, naïve attempt to express what seems to be one of their common and characteristic grammatical features. An attempt to illustrate this, however, and to proceed to comparisons in a universal framework, soon reveals that (1) there is considerable disagreement on the application of the term *causative* (or "causal") even among traditional grammarians, and (2) the notion is the focus of considerable current discussion among theoretical linguists, one effect of which is to extend the common range of the term even further.

Traditional grammarians have generally used the term to refer to an overtly marked verbal category, whereas the modern usage refers to the inferrable presence of a causative component in the deep structure of the verb, whether or not it has any immediate surface manifestation. For example, English *drop, kill,* and *break* are deemed causative verbs, since they involve causing something to fall, die, or break (be broken) respectively, even though their overt relationship to these latter verbs is only suppletive or even homonymous (distinguished only syntactically). In this sense, *all* languages "have" causative verbs. In the other sense, not all languages have (overtly marked) causative verbs, and it is still a usable typological category.

Of course, causality may be overtly marked either analytically (*make it go*) or morphologically, and it must be further specified that it is the latter that is in question here. Our statement then becomes something like "Indian languages typically have *morphologically marked* causative *verb stems.*"

Even this is not quite satisfactory, however. There are a number of different semantic relations that exist between morphologically related verb stems in Indian and other languages. Which of these (if not all) are to be labeled "causative" is a matter on which reputable grammarians of even the same language disagree. Among these relations are that of an intransitive verb and a corresponding transitive and that of a transitive verb and a corresponding factitive. The former might be called direct or "contactive" causation. If only the former is present morphologically in a language, the derived transitives in question are usually labeled "causatives" in the literature. If both are present, as is the case in many languages of India, either both derivatives may be called "causatives," perhaps distingushed as "first" and "second," or only the latter may be accorded the title.

It is also possible to have indirect causation of intransitive concepts, and some languages (traditionally Tamil) are said to distinguish this from mere transitive formation: *ooṭu* 'run', *ooṭuvi* - 'have s.o. run', *vs. ooṭṭu* 'drive; chase'. Finally, some languages have intransitives that might be considered secondary rather than primary, derived from transitives with suppression of any causative agent (hence a kind of passive). This further complicates the question of where to apply the term "second" causative – to derivatives of semantically causative concepts, or to derivatives of morphologically causative forms? And which are which?

Even if our basic concern is with linguistic *forms* (that is, with the surface structure where typological differences primarily manifest themselves), it is obvious that there must be first a clarification of the conceptual framework to which they are to be related. The use of English as a metalanguage has caused and continues to cause problems here, for in some ways English is rather aberrant in its own causative system.

Many English intransitive verbs can be used transitively (="causatively"): *run the motor, walk the dog.* Many transitive verbs, on the other hand, can be used intransitively (= "passively"): *this book reads easily, the tickets sold briskly.* These phenomena may lead to statements that English verbs are "unmarked" or infinitely flexible, i.e., basically neither transitive nor intransitive but acquiring one or the other meaning only in context. This is hardly the case. One or the other meaning is clearly the basic one and the other clearly secondary and derivative. The derivative meaning in both cases seems to be confined to much more limited contexts than that of the parent verb (in the transitive-to-intransitive case, to the environment of a small set of adverbs). This could be called a characteristically English type of derivation with zero-affix, which is quite productive, but still by no means has extended itself to all verbs. All this is relevant to the metalanguage problem, in that writers are sometimes uncertain as to which is the basic meaning of a verb, such as, e.g., *break,* and carry this confusion over to their description of another language.

English also has a small vestigial class of intransitive/transitive pairs distinguished by internal vowel change: *rise/raise, fall/fell, sit/set, lie/lay.* Here, again, as a rule the second member cannot be used as the causative of the first in all its contexts. It is more limited, sometimes drastically so (*fell*). It is noteworthy also that there is a strong tendency to lose or confound these distinctions in substandard English speech. They are already undermined by the overlap of *fell* and *lay* with the preterites of *fall* and *lie. Fell* is saved only by its extreme lexical specialization.

For the remaining contexts of the intransitives in the preceding paragraphs, and for all other verbs in the language including all transitives, English has to express causativity periphrastically or by lexical suppletion: *He causes the sun to rise and the rain to fall* (not **He raises the sun and fells the rain*). However, there are several auxiliaries commonly employed for this purpose, each with its own peculiarities. The "causative verb" par excellence (according to dictionaries), *make*, has the additional connotation of *compulsion* when used with transitives (*Make him eat it*), but less consistently with intransitives (*What made it fall?*) or as a denominative-causative (*Make it red*). *Get* brings in an element of *persuasion* in one construction (*Get them to do it*) but not in another (*Get it done by them*). The most neutral auxiliary is the ubiquitous *have.* Taking the construction *Have the house built by them,* noting the passive participle *built* and the agentive phrase *by them,* one might be led to insist that the causative of transitives is really the causative of the *passive* of the transitive rather than of the transitive itself. But the construction *Have them build the house* also exists, with a double accusative and an active verb. *Make,* of course, takes only the latter construction.

The verb *cause* itself is a rather artificial item, found more in discourses on philosophy, law, theology, and linguistics than in real life. Seemingly "scientific" and precise, this word can play some strange tricks. The fact that we can paraphrase, e.g., *cut* as *cause something to be cut*, does not mean that *cut* is a derived transitive-causative verb.

Allow, let, and *help* also express meanings conveyed by causative forms in some languages.

The generalization may be hazarded that, while the causative of intransitives may be sufficiently conveyed by context alone (the presence of an object), the causative of transitives always requires an additional overt element of expression, be it a morpheme or an auxiliary word. The fact that we often say in English *He built a house,* meaning *He had a house built,* must be put down to the special case of *semantic ellipsis* (see below, p. 74): the sentence is accordingly ambiguous.

Clearly, a naïve competence in English does not constitute a very good basis for a universal typology of causatives; that can only emerge from a comparison of many languages. Introspective analysis, through English, of the "logical" possibilities must be strongly tempered by objective awareness of what the actual possibilities are in other real languages. Languages differ in what can be causativized as well as how it is to be causativized. English can also be an ambiguous and awkward medium in which to describe (and especially to paraphrase) the causative mechanisms of another language, or causative systems in general. We can get all tangled up simply on the basis of which English auxiliary we employ and which construction we happen to employ it in. Although translation equivalents constitute one of the bases of comparison, we must beware of hasty generalizations on the basis of mere accident of paraphrase.

Let us take the facts of Hindi as a more concrete illustration of the descriptive (hence also of the typological) problem.

The morphological facts of Hindi may be stated fairly succinctly:

1. Many Hindi verb stems occur in sets of three, *base* (usually equivalent to *root,* except for a few forms with vestigial prefixes) /base + suffix –AA/base + suffix -WAA, as follows:

   gir-/giraa-/girwaa-
   likh-/likhaa-/likhwaa–
   ban-/banaa-/banwaa-

paṛh-/paṛhaa-/paṛhwaa-
cal-/calaa-/calwaa-
etc.

a. bases ending in a long vowel add /l/ and shorten the vowel to /i/ or /u/ or /a/ before adding the suffixes:[1]

pii-/pilaa-/pilwaa-
dee-/dilaa-/dilwaa-
soo-/sulaa-/sulwaa-
khaa-/khilaa-/khilwaa-
etc.[2]

b. bases with a long *internal* vowel (not, however, the diphthong /au/, and inconsistently the diphthong /ai/) also shorten the vowel before the suffixes:

siikh-/sikhaa-/sikhwaa-
jaag-/jagaa-/jagwaa-
etc.

c. as a purely phonetic matter, bases of the pattern CVCaC slur over the /a/ of the second syllable before the suffix -AA, restoring it, however, before the suffix -WAA:

samajh-/sam'jhaa-/samajhwaa-
pakaṛ-/pak'ṛaa-/pakaṛwaa-
laṭak-/laṭ'kaa-/laṭakwaa-
pighal-/pigh'laa-/pighalwaa-
also *nahaa-/nah'laa-/nahalwaa-*

2. Many other Hindi verb stems exhibit in addition to the above both long and short vowel bases, making sets of *four*:

khul-/khool-/khulaa-/khulwaa-
mar-/maar-/maraa-/marwaa-
kaṭ-/kaaṭ-/kaṭaa-/kaṭwaa-
dikh-/deekh-/dikhaa-/dikhwaa-
lad-/laad-/ladaa-/ladwaa-
cf. also *dhul-/dhoo-/dhulaa-/dhulwaa-*
etc.

It will be noted that the suffixes are again added to the *short*-vowel base.

a. sometimes the -AA term in this set is rare or missing (although it is hard to be sure about this as it often occurs dialectally or colloquially somewhere):

nikal-/nikaal-/______/nikalwaa-
phaṭ-/phaaṛ-/______/phaṛwaa-
bik-/beec-/______/bikwaa-

b. there are a few irregularities and morphophonemic changes involving consonants (see examples in previous paragraph) that need not concern us here.

3. Not all verbs have three or four stems:
   a. some have only two, a few for obviously phonological reasons (*gaa-/gawaa-*), others for less obvious reasons (*bac-/bacaa-, bhaag-/bhagaa-*).
   b. some have only one. These include:
      1) onomatopoeic and other denominatives or apparent denominatives in -AA: *kaṭkaṭaa-, hinhinaa-, khujlaa-, sataa-*. There are a large number of the former.
      2) an arbitrary list of verbs, most of which have important grammatical functions as auxiliaries, either exclusively (*sak-* 'be able') or in addition to their main verb function (*jaa-, aa-, paṛ-*, etc.). Not all verbs used as auxiliaries are defective in this way, however (nor are the same verbs necessarily defective in other Indic languages).

The *semantic* (and syntactic) facts, which do not correspond in any simple way to the above, are basically as follows:

1. The -WAA forms are always unambiguously *indirect* causatives (involving use of an intermediate agent):

calwaa- 'have someone drive'
likhwaa- 'have someone write'
khilwaa- 'have someone feed'
banwaa- 'have someone build' etc.

a. this intermediate agent is expressed by an NP + SEE 'by'.

b. Bahl (1967:17-23) points out, however, that certain -WAA forms (as well as certain -AA forms when these have the same meaning) may also take an agent with -KOO (="dative") instead of -SEE, in which case the causation is somewhat more direct, though falling short of "contactive"–i.e., translatable as *help to, allow to*, etc., rather than *have* or *get to*.

2. The *base* in the three-term sets (p. 43, above), whatever its phonological shape (short vowel closed, long vowel closed, long vowel open, disyllabic), may be either intransitive (*cal-* 'go', *jaag-* 'wake up', *soo-* 'sleep', *laṭak-* 'hang') or intransitive (*likh-* 'write', *siikh-* 'learn', *khaa-* 'eat', *pakaṛ-* 'grab').
   a. if the base is intransitive, the second or -AA term will be what is usually called the "corresponding transitive":

      uṭh- 'rise, get up' *uṭhaa-* 'raise, pick up'
      phail- 'spread (intr.)' *phailaa-* 'spread (tr.)'
      jal- 'burn (intr.)' *jalaa-* 'burn (tr.)'
      gir- 'fall' *giraa-* 'drop'

      1) Bahl (1967:17) alone points out that these terms may have another value also—that of indirect causative of the intransitive, e.g., *uṭhaa-* = not only 'pick up' but also 'cause someone to get up'.
   b. if the base is transitive, the -AA term may have exactly the same meaning as the -WAA term (namely, indirect causation):

      kar- 'do' *karaa-/karwaa-* 'have someone do'
      dee- 'give' *dilaa-/dilwaa-* 'have someone give'

      2) for a small set of verbs, however, having in common a semantic feature of *taking something into* the body or mind (literally or figuratively), the -AA form is distinct from the -WAA form. It is rather a *double transitive* (taking an direct and an indirect object rather than a direct object and an instrumental of agent), signifying helping or causing *someone else* to do this ingesting. (They are thus to be distinguished from primary double transitives such as "give," "write," and "send," which have an inherent, not a derived, double object.) The -WAA forms are the indirect causatives of these double transitives.

khaa- 'eat' *khilaa-* 'feed' *khilwaa-* 'have s.o. fed'
pii- 'drink' *pilaa-* 'give drink to' *pilwaa-* 'have (etc.)'
sun- 'hear' *sunaa-* 'relate' *sunwaa-* 'have related'
samajh 'understand' *samjhaa-* 'explain' *samajhwaa-* 'have something explained'
siikh- 'learn' *sikhaa-* 'teach' *sikhwaa-* 'have taught'
paṛh- 'read' *paṛhaa-* 'teach' *paṛhwaa-* 'have taught'
cf. also *deekh-* 'see' *dikhaa-* 'show' *dikhwaa-* 'have shown'

It is not without significance that English and other languages usually have distinct lexical items for the -AA terms above (although one is missing in English for *pilaa-*), but not for other -AA terms derived from transitive bases.

The two bases in the (potentially) four-term sets (p. 44, item 2, above) have sharply contrasting meanings depending upon their phonological shape. The form with the long vowel is always *transitive.* The corresponding short vowel base is *intransitive*; only in some cases, however, is it what might be called an "active" intransitive: *nikal-* 'emerge', *utar-* 'descend', *ubal-* 'boil', *ruk-* 'stop', *mar-* 'die'. In the majority of cases it is semantically a passive (or "mediopassive") of a verb that presupposes an active agent acting upon an object, which in this construction becomes the subject (with the erstwhile agent deleted or, better stated, simply not brought into the picture): *kaṭ-* 'be cut', *bik-* 'be sold', *phaṭ-* 'be torn', *ukhaṛ-* 'be uprooted', *khud-* 'be dug', *bãṭ-* 'be divided', *khul-* 'be opened', *juṛ-* 'be raised; brought up', *jut-* 'be plowed', *lad-* 'be loaded', *ṭal-* 'be fended off', *sudhar-* 'be put right', *chid-* 'be pierced', *dhul-* 'be washed', *bãdh* 'be tied', *mãj-* 'be scoured', *bhun-* 'be fried', etc.

Although these all involve actions that subjects cannot do for themselves, which – logically – they can only *undergo* at the hands of some agent, the special forms in question serve to focus attention only on the change of state of the object, without reference to any agent, which occasionally may be desirable: *kapṛee dhul gaee hãĩ* - 'the clothes have been washed', *fasal kaṭ gaii hai-* 'the crop has been cut'. For similar purposes Western languages press into service their passive (English) or their reflexive forms (German, French, Spanish), and in certain contexts English uses its zero-affix derived intransitive forms – (p. 41, above) *sells, cuts, reads,* etc. (e.g., *easily*).

For the group of verbs first mentioned above, the "active" intransitives, it would seem that, semantically, the "corresponding transitive" forms are derivative (although this judgment may merely betray a lack of imagination):

nikaal- 'take out (= cause to emerge)'
utaar- 'lower (= cause to descend)'
ubaal- 'boil (= cause to boil)' cf. *faire bouillir*
rook- 'stop (= cause to stop)'
maar- 'kill (= cause to die)

But for very many verbs in Hindi it would seem that the "corresponding transitive" is semantically primary and it is the "passive-intransitive" that is the derivative: cf. the meanings of the long-vowel (transitive) bases – *kaaṭ-, beec-, phaaṛ-, ukhaaṛ-, khood-, bããṭ-, khool-, jooṛ-, paal-, joot-, laad-, ṭaal-, sudhaar-, cheed-, bããdh-, mããj-, bhuun-* = 'cut, sell, tear, uproot, dig, divide, open, join, rear, plow, load, fend off, set right, pierce, wash, tie, scour, fry'.

For most two-base verbs of both types, the -AA form, if it exists, is equivalent to the -WAA form: *bãdhaa-, bãdhwaa-* = 'have someone tie'.

For a few verbs whose semantics permit it, however, there is a shadow of a difference. If the verb denotes an action that one can get done either to or for oneself *or* for others, then both the -AA and the –WAA forms may be used for the former (although the -AA form may be regarded as more specialized for the function), but only the -WAA form may be used for the latter; e.g., *kaṭaa- (kaṭwaa-)* 'to have (one's) hair cut', *silaa- (silwaa-)* 'to have clothes stitched (for oneself) by a tailor', *dhulaa (dhulwaa-)* 'have (one's) clothes washed', *maraa- (marwaa-)* 'sens. obscen.'. These correlate with the use of the 'reflexive adjective' *apnaa* 'one's own' and the 'reflexive verb' *lenaa* (see chapter 4).

Some verb-sets may be missing certain terms for phonological reasons, or because the resulting form would be the same as another existing form in the language. For example, the transitive verbs *likh-* 'write' and *paṛh-* 'read' lack short-vowel passive-intransitive correlates because, among other reasons, *they cannot have them because their vowels are already short.* The verb *khaa-* 'eat' and *pii* 'drink' have the alternate stems found in *khilaa-* 'feed' and *pilaa-* 'give drink to', analogous to *dhoo-* 'wash', *dhulaa-* 'have washed', but whereas *dhul-* 'be washed' is found, *khil-* and *pil-* by themselves happen to be stems of different verbs meaning 'blossom' and 'attack', respectively.

In addition, it may be true that there is less occasion to refer to something being written, read, eaten, or drunk with no implication of agent than there is to something being washed, cut, fried, and so on. The "ingestive" verbs as a group might be regarded as occupying a halfway station between intransitives and transitives, since the object in question can frequently be dispensed with in favor of concentration on the activity as such: one can speak of eating, drinking, seeing, hearing, etc., just as one does of walking, flying, swimming – as an *activity,* without reference to a particular object in the former case or a particular goal in the latter case. Hence, these verbs would be too close to intransitives to permit an intransitive correlate. This would also explain why their -AA derivatives are (double) transitives and not indirect causatives as is the case with normally transitive bases.

However, we must not push this too far. 'Eat' and 'drink', in particular, cannot in fact dispense with an object as easily as their English counterparts: they normally require what seems to an English speaker a redundant object – *kyaa aap-nee khaanaa khaayaa hai* = 'Have you eaten?' (lit. 'Have you eaten *food*?'). Moreover, it happens that the primary double-transitive verbs (*dee-* 'give', *bheej-* 'send', *likh-* 'write', etc.), as well as the double-transitive *derivative*-forming "ingestive" verbs, do not have passive-intransitive correlates in Hindi. It is harder to find a semantic reason for this.

Hindi verb stems are not in *every* case clearly marked as to transitivity. Among the defective verbs, *jaa-* 'go', *aa-* 'come', and *paṛ-* 'fall' are intransitive only, *sataa-* 'torment' is transitive only, but *badal-* 'change' and *khujlaa-* 'itch/scratch' may be either, and certain of the numerous one-stem basically intransitive onomatopoeic verbs in -AA may be used transitively (= causatively) in the sense of 'make the noise in question by using Obj'.

How is all this dealt with in various descriptions of Hindi? To be sure, these differ in quality as well as in intended audience and scope. It therefore says something about the importance of the causative formations in the language that any account of Hindi grammar, popular or pedagogical as well as scientific-academic, finds it necessary to discuss this subject, which some might consider "derivational" (i.e., pertaining to the lexicon) rather than part of the grammar narrowly defined. Good or bad, lengthy or brief, these accounts may be classified according to their handling of certain descriptive problems.

The first of these problems is manifested by the question of what to call the *second* term (with suffix -AA) in three-term sets starting with an *intransitive* base. On this hangs an author's whole philosophy of causatives, as it were.

A popular treatment, i.e., found in Phillott (1918), Harley (1944), Saighal (1958), but also in more serious descriptions such as Forbes (1855), Katenina (1957), Pořízka (1963), Elizarenkova (1962), Dimshits (1966), Pray (1970), is to call it simply *transitive,* giving the threefold scheme intransitive-transitive-causative in which the term *causative* is reserved for the third, or -WAA member – in other words, for indirect causation. For some, it just happens to turn out that way; others, however (e.g., Dimshits, some of the other Russian writers) explicitly intend to restrict the notion "causative" to "action through an intermediary agent."

The other alternative, perhaps more in line with the terms of the current discussion of the subject in linguistic theory (but restricting itself to *formally signaled* relations) would call any *derived* transitive a "causative." Therefore, the -AA term is called the *First* causative, and the -WAA term *Second* causative (or causal). This is the scheme followed by Kellogg (1875, 1938), Greaves (1933), Bailey (1938), Kamtaprasad Guru (1952), Scholberg (1940, 1955), S. V. Sharma (1956), A. Sharma (1958), Fairbanks-Misra (1966), Kachru (1966), Bender (1967).

The first position above might better seem to reflect the traditional Indian threefold scheme of *akarmak-sakarmak-preraṇārthak,* but the leading Indian authority, Kamtaprasad Guru, adopts, as we have noted, the second position. Beames (1872-79, in his *Comparative Grammar of the Modern Aryan Languages of India*) adopts essentially the second position, but both positions continue to crop up in accounts of other Indian languages beside Hindi. Some hedge, and Bailey (1933a:33) perhaps points to the essence of the problem when he says: ". . . in *practice* it is most useful to call the causal of an intransitive verb its 'transitive.' "

There is an additional point of confusion. Writers of the first group above often use the terms *First* and *Second* causal/causative for the -AA and -WAA derivatives, respectively, of *transitive* bases – that is, where the former are noticed at all. (A number of writers in both groups find it convenient not to notice them, perhaps because of their apparent redundancy, or because they upset the symmetry of their schemes.) Some writers of the second group (e.g., K. Guru, A. Sharma, Fairbanks-Misra), resting exclusively on form, call all -AA derivatives first causals regardless of whether they are derived from intransitives and hence semantically distinct from -WAA forms, or from transitives and hence in most cases semantically identical with -WAA forms. Bahl, on the other hand, would call -WAA forms themselves first degree causals when they are used with a -KOO agent (meaning "help NP+koo to V") as derivatives of "noncausal" transitives – derived or primary. (He distinguishes between causal and merely transitive -AA derivatives of the *same* V^{in}.) Kachru (1966:62ff.) talks about "one level of causativization" (in transitive verbs of the "*kərna* type") with "two phonological shapes."

The widely used Scholberg grammar (3d ed., 1940) affects to see a distinction between *karaa-* and *karwaa-*: *yah kaam karaao* is allegedly 'have this work done (by somebody)' and *yah kaam karwaao* is 'Cause (someone) to have this work done (by somebody)'. The -WAA form is supposed to mean to cause someone to cause a *third party* to do an act. Much nonsense of this sort involving nonexistent "third parties" and the like has been written as people get carried away by the spirit of the thing and start interpolating various presumed extensions of the system according to the requirements of the model of it they have worked out, which is usually based on too simple a relationship between form and function. They are insensitive to what Elizarenkova calls the "asymmetries" of the system, namely, that:

1) one form may be connected with different meanings (e.g., V + -AA may be a) merely "transitive" -direct causative, such as *uṭhaa-* 'lift'; b) "doubly transitive," such as *paṛhaa-* 'teach'; c) indirect causative, such as *karaa-* 'have someone do'; and even d) intransitive onomatopoeic, such as *hinhinaa-* 'whinny' – depending on the meaning of the underlying base).

2) Two different forms may have the same meaning sometimes (but not at other times, e.g., the synonymy of -AA and -WAA derivative stems for certain verbs).

The special status of *khilaa-, pilaa-,* etc., is noticed by only a few writers. Several indeed cite them as paragons of the causative formation. One would think that the different syntactic relations of this set of verbs would have merited more attention, but most writers have been exclusively preoccupied with the intricacies of the morphology. Those who treat them as causals sometimes refer to the next degree of derivatives (*khilwaa-, pilwaa-*) as "double causals." Kachru calls the first degree "double object" verbs and notes that these verbs are unlike other transitives in undergoing "two levels of causativization." Dimshits, true to his definition of "causative" as "done via an intermediary," says verbs such as *khilaa-* 'feed', *paṛhaa-* 'teach', etc., cannot be causatives since the feeding or teaching is done directly by the subject himself. Greaves (1919:314), anticipating case grammar, is concerned to show that sentences such as *laṛkee koo rooṭii khilaaoo* 'feed the boy bread' involve not two accusatives but an accusative and a dative. (The accusative and dative are not distinguished in Hindi: the particle *koo* may signal either, although indefinite inanimate nouns, such as 'bread' in this sentence, are generally unmarked in the accusative.) "The bread is Accusative, whether I eat it or cause another to eat it." Bailey (1933b:29), on the other hand, insists on the *passive* meaning of causatives of transitives, including these transitives. According to him, *khilaa-* would essentially mean '*cause to be eaten*', just as *karaa-* would mean '*cause to be done*' – in both cases, "by" someone, which may be signaled either by *-see* ("strong causation") or by *-koo* ("weak causation"). Meanings such as 'cause to see, hear, eat', as well as 'cause to do', are "not permissible."

The common *semantic* element (+reflexive +"ingestive"?) in the set of verbs underlying these formations has been noticed by none of the writers mentioned.

Suppose derived transitives are treated as ("first") causals. This leads to a further question – and a further split among our writers: which transitives are derived? In addition to the -AA derivatives, there are also the long *vs.* short vowel stems. Which are derived from which? Whether or not an author has been struck by the essentially "passive" meaning of many of the intransitive short vowel stems, the almost universal practice has been to regard them as primaries and derive the transitives from them by vowel lengthening or *guṇa* (+ certain other changes). Apparently the feeling is that a "longer" form *must* derive from a shorter form, just because it is longer. Yet semantically the transitive form often seems the primary one, and the intransitive the derived. This seems to have occurred only to Greaves, Bailey, and Pray. The semantic and formal *directions* of derivation need not coincide, but here there would seem to be nothing against even the formal derivation of the short forms from the long by "reverse *guṇa*" (or some such variation on the theme, as proposed by Pray). This view has the added advantage of explaining by one rule both the "intransitive" and the causative, which generally *share a common derivative stem.* (The prevailing, clumsy practice is to derive the transitive from the intransitive by lengthening the vowel, and then to derive the causative from the transitive by shortening it again before adding the suffix.)

This is also the historical truth in a sense: it is known that many such derivations have indeed occurred and are still occurring – for the process is a productive one. What has apparently happened is that an old Indo-European process of apophony, which *did* produce transitives from intransitives (Eng. *rise/raise*) has been extended analogically in reverse. The whole system has reorganized itself on a new principle. A minor problem is the persistence of pairs inherited from the old rule, e.g., *mar-* 'die'/*maar-* 'kill; beat'. (We must not be too hasty, however, in assuming which is which. It would seem that, e.g., *nikal-* 'emerge' is a normal nonpassive intransitive verb, from which *nikaal-* 'take out; cause to emerge' is derived: historically, it is *nikal-* that is the derivative, by back-formation.)[3] Are we to reinterpret these in accordance with the predominant new direction of derivation in the language (i.e., *mar-* as 'to be killed')? Or may we tolerate again (as with the suffix -AA) an imperfect correlation of form and function in the language?

A more serious problem, from a comparativist's point of view, is that these passive derivatives are less numerous in other New Indo-Aryan languages, particularly those to the east – including eastern dialects of "Hindi." This is, moreover, a gradual phenomenon. At what point do they become un-numerous enough to force another interpretation upon us? And how is the Hindi phenomenon to be compared with formally similar but relationally different phenomena in related languages?

1. If the long-vowel bases are treated as *primary* transitive bases, there is no question of their being "causatives."
2. If they are regarded, as has usually been the case, as *derived,* writers who regard middle-term -AA forms as merely transitive naturally regarded these also as merely transitive. Writers of the group that regard middle-term -AA forms as first causatives, however, differ among themselves as to how to regard the long-vowel transitives. Some (Kellogg, S. V. Sharma, Fairbanks) regard them as first causatives of a different formation. Quite a few, however (including Kamtaprasad Guru), look upon them as merely derived transitives, distinct from causatives. Those that regard them as causatives are then confronted with the problem of what to do about the remaining -AA and -WAA derivatives. If, e.g., *khool-* 'open' is a first causative, does that make *khulaa-* a "second" and *khulwaa-* a "third" causative? Usually this issue is sidestepped by ignoring *khulaa-,* or by a sudden switch to "meaning" as the arbiter of degrees of causation. Greaves (1919:314) is adamant in his rejection of this whole process. To call a verb like *khool-* 'open' a causative, he says, just because it can be thought of as 'cause to be opened', is "a misuse of language . . . the true causal verb indicates the causing of something to be done by another instead of doing it oneself, not . . . merely the causing of something to *take place.*"

Thus it may be seen that the terms "causative" or "causal," as well as the terms "first" and "second" causative, have by no means a clear and agreed-upon meaning in the literature dealing with these phenomena in Hindi. And there are other complications as well. The foregoing gives an inadequate idea of the multiformity of descriptions. What then about other languages, which have to be compared with regard to such features? This writer knows them even less well, and their causative systems as a rule have been less subjected to investigation than that of Hindi. The available description may be incomplete or inaccurate and misleading. This is in addition to the various points of view that may be adopted by an author, as described above. It should be abundantly clear by now that for all of these reasons a comparison cannot be made by simply juxtaposing the accounts left by various writers on the several languages concerned. This increased awareness of what to look for and in what ways a description can be inadequate or misleading is very important. There is something else that is desperately needed, however, if the descriptive confusion is to be cut through with any degree of success. That is a general typology of causatives.

A Framework for Comparison: A Typology of Causatives

Greenberg made the work of chapter 2 easier by providing the basic outlines of a general typology of word order. After struggling with various ad hoc formulations of the causative problem – always dangerous when one's focus of attention is a particular area rather than universal typology – it was therefore with great joy that this writer discovered a similar guru-pioneer in Kholodovich. I refer to A. A. Kholodovich (ed.), *Tipologii͡a kauzativnykh konstruktsiĭ: morfologicheskiĭ kauzativ* (Leningrad: Academy of Sciences of the USSR, Institute of Linguistics, 1969). This 310-page monograph is the collective work of a group of Soviet linguists and specialists in various individual languages who collaborated on the causative problem in a four-year project. It consists of two theoretical chapters (and an appendix) and fifteen chapters exploring specific languages in terms, more or less, of the agreed-upon descriptive framework. The languages that have special chapters devoted to them (many more are discussed in the general chapters) are Old Chinese, Abkhaz, literary Arabic, Batsbi (Caucasus), Hungarian, Georgian, Indonesian, Kamchadal, Gilyak, Swahili, Tajik, Finnish, Chuvash, Chukchi, and Japanese. (No Indian languages are represented, nor are, for that matter, Western languages or Russian.) Although the individual chapters have different authors, or groups of authors, despite natural differences of emphasis the whole thing hangs together remarkably well for a committee product.

The theoretical spadework of the Kholodovich group is quite thorough. There is no need to recapitulate their full scheme and the arguments behind it in all their elaborateness here, as I intend to extract from it a rather simpler working model for our purposes. The essence of the Kholodovichian position and conclusions deriving therefrom is as follows:

1. "Causative" is an essential universal category demanding expression in languages, among other places in verb phrases. Hence all languages "have" causative verbs semantically. The question is how they are expressed – purely syntactically, or by suppletion, auxiliary words, formal derivational relations involving the verbal stem and/or paradigm, or a combination of these.
2. A causative verb denotes an action that calls forth a particular action *or condition* in another person or object. This causation may be principally of two kinds, "distant" and "contactive." In the latter the agent does something to the object, bringing about its new condition by direct contact; in the former he makes use of an intermediary agent and serves only as the "instigator" of the act. Contactive situations are very common and quite basic to any dealing of a speaker with his environment; indirectly causative situations are less basic and therefore less common, but also exist in all languages. (Their frequency and pervasiveness probably depends less on universal norms than on the degree of social differentiation and functional specialization developed in a given society. This is a statement that seems to apply happily to the Indian society but needs to be tested against, or have its terms carefully defined in terms of, "primitive" societies: unfortunately, this interesting question cannot be explored here.)
3. "The *morphological* causative exists in those languages where there are parallel sets of verbs, causative and noncausative, and the causatives are connected with the corresponding noncausatives by derivational relations" (Kholodovich 1969:206).
4. Of the various expressional devices noted above, the one characteristic of English, namely, purely syntactic relations (the verb otherwise remaining the same) is, surprisingly, one of the rarest. Morphologically marked causative stems, on the other hand, seem to be *found in most of the world's languages* at least vestigially.
5. As it becomes confusing as well as cumbersome to talk about these matters in ordinary language (especially English, but also Russian), a set of symbols is developed:

   V_i = noncausal verbal base (transitive or intransitive)

   V_j = a derivative of V_i; "1st degree causative"

   V_e = a derivative of V_j: "2d degree causative"

Superscripts may be added to V_i to indicate the transitive or intransitive character of the base: V_i^{in}, V_i^{tr}. V_j and V_e derivatives are of course all transitive.

6. In terms of a scheme of verbal "valences" (the number of agent or patient entities implied by a verb) each derivational step adds one: if V_i is 1 or 2, V_j is 2 or 3, and V_e is 3 or 4.

   Semantically, therefore, causative derivatives are always more complex than the verbs they are derived from.

7. They need not be *formally* more complex, however. That is, the formal derivation may go in the *opposite direction* from the semantic derivation. This is the case, for example, in Russian and a number of other European languages where an "intransitive" use of a verb is marked by a reflexive or similar form:

varit'sa ← *varit'*
'boil, cook (intr.)' → 'boil, cook (tr.)'

otkryvat'sa ← *otkryvat'*
'open (intr.)' → 'open (tr.)'

Although the forms in the right-hand column are semantically more complex (+O+Ag--vs. +O for the left-hand column) it is the forms in the left-hand column that are morphologically more complex. This marking to *reduce* the verbal valence by 1 is given the name *anticausative* and the symbolization *ak* (*vs.* *k* for

---

MAP 2. Morphological Causatives

Key:

——— domain of morphological causatives ($V_i > V_j$)

—•—•—•— domain of second causatives ($V_i > V_j^{k'} > V_e^{k''}$)

xxxxxx causative marked by prefixes, infixes, or confixes (otherwise, by suffixes

---

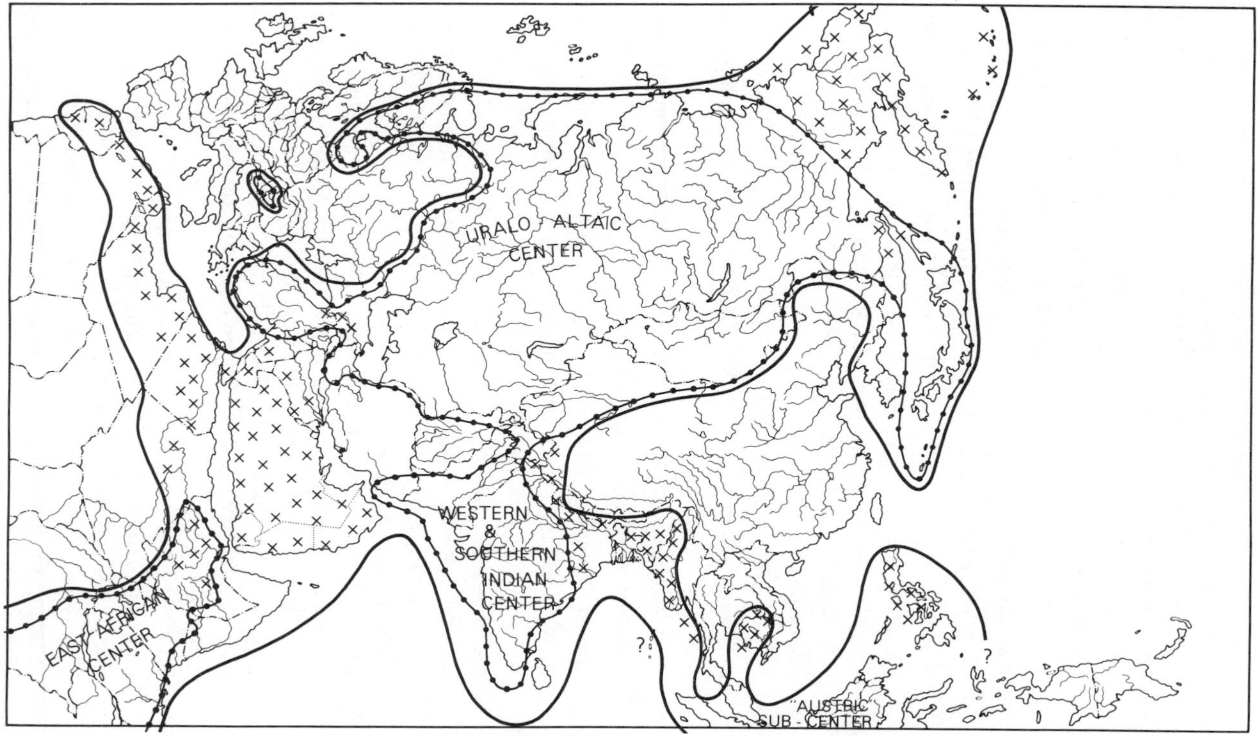
URALO ALTAIC
CENTER
WESTERN
&
SOUTHERN
INDIAN
CENTER
EAST AFRICAN
CENTER
"AUSTRIC"
SUB - CENTER

causative). This "negative marking" of the causative relation is less common than the positive marking.

8. The kind of derivation that is most widespread, hence "found in most of the world's languages at least vestigially" (English *'sit'* → *'set'*, etc.) is that of transitive verb from intransitive , $V_i^{in} \rightarrow V_j^k$ (Hindi *cal-* → *calaa-*). Derivation from a transitive primary, $V_i^{tr} \rightarrow V_j^k$ (Hindi *kaaṭ* → *kaṭaa-*, *kaṭwaa-*), is less common. Derivation may be exclusively from V^{in} in a language, whereas derivation from V^{tr} only occurs if there is also derivation from V^{in}.
9. Often $V_i^{tr} \rightarrow V_j^k$ form a small class in a language. If only a few transitive verbs form causatives, they are generally of the "ingestive" or semitransitive subtype described above (pp. 46-47) and include such pairs as *'see'* → *'show'*, *'eat'* → *'feed'*, *'understand'* → *'explain'*.
10. $V_i^{in} \rightarrow V_j$ derivation is of greater variety in a language morphologically than $V_i^{tr} \rightarrow V_j^k$. $V_i^{tr} \rightarrow V_j^k$ affixes are sometimes complex in structure.
11. $V_j \rightarrow V_e$ (causatives from causatives) are even less common (Hindi *uṭhaa-* → *uṭhwaa-*). Sometimes they are restricted to a particular type of V_j, e.g., those of less "regular" formation, or to those derived from V_j^{in}. Second degree causatives from originally *transitive* bases – especially, "fully" transitive bases (as against the "ingestive" subset) – are quite rare, but do exist in languages.
12. Beyond points at which its system is blocked, a language resorts to circumlocutions to express the needed causative relations, when the need to do so arises.
13. Kholodovich then attempts to restrict the term "morphological" causative, previously defined above, to those whose formation is "*regular and productive*." Others, including apparently the Slavic type described by Gołąb 1968 (which is *fairly* regular and was *once* productive, but is so no longer), he labels "*lexical*" causatives.
14. To avoid being trapped by atypical exceptions, Kholodovich and his collaborators work with the concepts "all or most" and "few or no" rather than a pure yes/no.

This provides a good basis for constructing a matrix of questions through which to determine and map the causative typology of India and its environs. Although it can be divined ahead of time that what will be typical of India is causatives from V^t and 2° causatives (which is what has prompted one group of writers to accord the title *causative* to these alone), if the more universal format, as clarified by the Kholodovich team, is adopted, these will be seen in their proper context, both typologically and areally.

Their definition of "morphological" *vs.* "lexical" causative is the only thing that causes some discomfort. For one thing, it gives to the term *morphological* itself a rather narrow meaning, one perhaps acceptable in certain European circles but apt to be confusing to those in the habit of opposing *morphological* primarily to *syntactic*. More important, it lumps together in the category "lexical" both purely suppletive causatives (Eng. *die/kill*) and nonproductive derivational patterns sharing a common root (Russ. *umeret'* 'die' → *morit'* 'exterminate', *sidet'* 'sit' → *posadit'* 'seat', *tech'* 'flow' → *tochit'* 'secrete', *gustet'* 'become thick' → *sgustit'* 'make thick', *mrachnet'* 'grow dark' → *omrachit'* 'make dark', etc.). It might help somewhat if a further distinction were made among "lexical" causatives between suppletive and vestigial-morphological forms. Perhaps this distinction is less important, however, than the one between productive and nonproductive patterns. It is, after all, the productive patterns that interest us here more than the nonproductive ones, which become mere footnotes to the problem.

Even though existing descriptions are often not so comprehensive or explicit, the questions to which we would *like* to have the answers, then, would be the following:

1. Does the language morphologically derive transitives (= causatives) from intransitives in any regular and productive manner ($V_i^{in} > V_j^k$)?
2. Does it derive intransitives (= anticausatives) from transitives in such a manner ($V_i^{tr} > V_j^{ak}$)?
3. Or is there a morphological passive?
4. Does it have causative derivatives from *transitive* bases ($V_i^{tr} > V_j^k$)?
5. Are different subgroups of verbs treated differently (e.g., semi-transitive "ingestives")?
6. Are there causatives of the second degree (= causatives of causatives – $V_i > V_j^{k'} > V_e^{k''}$)? From V_i^{tr} or just V_i^{in}?
7. What is the manner of the marking? Is the same or a different marker used with V_i^{in} and V_i^{tr}? For $V_j^{k'}$ and $V_e^{k''}$?

8. Is the causative marker, or one of the causative markers, also used to form denominatives in the language (that is, as a verbalizer)?
9. If the answer to all the above is No, how *is* causativity expressed in the language (i.e., by suppletion, analytically, purely syntactically, by other means)?

There remain some problems in applying this yardstick. There is the difficulty of ascertaining how "productive" something is on the basis of a superficial acquaintance with a language, whether gained from a brief descriptive account that does not go into this or otherwise. There is also the problem of judging whether something is indeed morphological or not – that is, of distinguishing between (bound-) morpheme and independent particle or auxiliary word status. This problem arises especially with some of the so-called isolating languages to the east of India, but by no means only with them. Then, do Indian languages have anticausatives? An anticausative is defined as something that is formally more complex but semantically less complex (specifically, involving fewer obligatory case relations). Can somethings which are "shorter" be made to fit the definition of *formally more complex*? When is an inflectional "passive" really an anticausative? "Anticausative" is not the same as "passive," to be sure, being more akin to "middle," but certain forms in some languages partake of the nature of both, and there is an area of overlap and uncertainty.

I dwell at length on the inadequacy and unreliability of descriptive data for many languages. The Kholodovich conclusions suggest that the following working assumptions may be made in utilizing such data:

1. Second degree causatives are absent in a language unless specifically cited or mentioned.
2. Causatives from transitive bases are absent in a language unless specifically cited or mentioned.
3. Causatives from transitive bases are confined to the "semitransitive" ("ingestive") subclass unless other examples are specifically cited.
4. Remarks as to syntactic construction, etc., should also be checked for evidence of pertinence to special subclasses only.
5. Similarly, in reverse (cf. Greenberg's universals), if a language has causatives from transitives, it also has them from intransitives; if it has them from "full" transitives, it also has them from semi-transitives.

Before passing on to a look at the languages of the area in this Kholodovich framework it might be worthwhile to examine an alternative typology such as the one proposed (although not fully developed) by Emeneau (1971:38-42). This essentially is an application of the structuralist principle according to which any term is defined and meaningful only in the context of the system of contrasts operative in a specific language. The same terms may be used for different – generally closely related – languages if exactly the same system of contrasts obtains, but "to show the difference of the [Dravidian] system from that of NIA, a difference of terminology is called for: the NIA [New Indo-Aryan] system contains simplex, causative, and causative of causative, and the Dravidian system contains simplex, mediative of simplex, causative, and mediative of causative; the terms 'intransitive' and 'transitive' are too burdened with connotations and too inexact, considering the membership of the basic sets, to be usable" (Emeneau 1971:39).

Such a typology of whole systems, if it could be fully worked out, might be especially useful in bringing out basic systemic differences among languages. There are problems in applying it, however. For one thing, a very thorough understanding of not only the mechanisms but also the semantics (e.g. regarding such matters as mediative *vs.* causative of intransitives) of each and every language so compared is necessary before its "basic system" can be identified. The overlooking or misunderstanding of even one component could place it in a completely different system-category. Such a complete descriptive understanding is available for very few (if any) of the world's languages – partly, of course, because it has not been sought in these terms. This is true of even the best studies (e.g., Subrahmanyam 1971).

There are a number of more theoretical objections that could be made to the proposed typology as it stands in embryo.

For one thing, I would take strong exception to the proposed exclusion of the terms "intransitive" and "transitive" from the formulation. The intransitive or transitive character of the "simplex" is demonstrably relevant to whether or not, for instance, secondary derivative forms occur (second causatives, in Kholodovich terms), and even to whether or not primary derivatives occur. That is, as noted earlier and as will be amply illustrated in the remainder of this chapter, secondary derivatives from intransitive bases are found in a good number of systems, whereas secondary derivatives from transitive bases are very rare. Similarly, the causative system of a language may be confined to making transitives out of intransitives. The next step usually lies in making double transitives out of semitransitives ("ingestives") – making identification of this latter class relevant as well.

It is also undesirable to use the same terms in different senses in describing different systems, or to describe some but not all of the same relations by different terms. It is precisely such confusing usage that the earlier portion of this chapter has been concerned to find a way out of. If the terminology employed to describe different systems is not to have reference to universals, let it then be totally arbitrary and discrete: let there be no partial overlap. Emeneau uses *causative* generally in the sense of "derived contactive-transitive" (except in the case of Munda languages, p. 42). His term *mediative* is a felicitous innovation for *indirect* (*vs. contactive*) causative, which it might be wise to generalize and retain. He himself applies it only to his postulated Dravidian system, where it is necessary to distinguish between "contactive" and "indirect" *first* causatives. *Second* causatives are of necessity very largely "mediative" (using the term in a descriptive rather than an arbitrary sense). This is as true of Indo-Aryan as it is of Dravidian. So why not call the same phenomenon by the same descriptively expressive term? ("The same," that is, in a syntagmatic, not a paradigmatic, sense.) Likewise the "causative" construction of Munda?

One way around both of these problems, to a quick typology that would be at once systemic and universal, might be to speak in terms of two-term, three-term, or four-term (or greater) systems, based on the possibilities for a typical *intransitive* stem. What I am proposing, in other words, is a typology based on maximal distinctions. Much else, though not everything, could be inferred from that, with the aid of implicational universals. For example, a language with secondary derivatives from intransitives (three-term) would be likely to have at least primary derivatives from transitives. We would not know, however, whether there were secondary derivatives from transitives (unlikely in any case, but important if it occurs) or, more importantly, in a two-term system whether derivation was confined to intransitives or to intransitives and semitransitives, or also extended to full transitives. (If desired, refinements could be added to show this: *2+* for intransitives + semitransitives; *2++* for intransitives + semitransitives + full transitives. Conceivably further investigation may show, however, that the last does not occur unless intransitives show a three-term system.) Such a typology does not distinguish between "mediative" and "contactive" – although conceivably a universal might be discovered according to which a three-term system necessarily includes one mediative, a four-term system two mediatives, and a two-term system none, which would make such a distinction unnecessary. In roughly the same way, Greenberg's basic order typology VSO-SVO-SOV does not tell us everything we might want to know about word order, even of sentence elements; it merely selects one aspect of it, namely the position of *nominal* subjects and direct objects relative to *transitive* verbs in *declarative* sentences, as the basis of a classification and, as it happens, much else follows. Indeed, our proper concern in establishing the basis of a typology should be not to try to include in it every fact, but to select those facts that are the keys to others.

A typology of whole systems necessarily highlights differences at the expense of obscuring similarities. There is a point, prior to the establishment of the implicational universals on which the refinements to Emeneau's typology proposed above rest, where a clear view of partial similarities and partial differences, and fragments of systems in general, is not only of interest but necessary. To handle both this and the problem of incomplete data, the Kholodovich framework (or one similar to it) is a necessary first step. (For a discussion of Emeneau's postulated system for Dravidian languages, see p. 72, below.)

A Look at the Languages of the Area in the Kholodovich Framework

Hindi-Urdu, as we have seen, has numerous causative derivatives from both transitive and intransitive bases, as well as causatives of causatives. It also conceivably has anticausatives from many transitive bases. There is, apart from this, no morphological passive. (By another analysis, there would be two types of first causatives, quite different in formation from one another and correlating with two large semantic subclasses of intransitives, namely those with "passive-intransitive" meanings and those expressing something the subject actually *does* – *laugh, cry, speak, sleep,* and all kinds of motion.)

However, semantically distinct second causatives from transitives are confined for practical purposes to the ingestive subclass – *eat, drink, see, hear, understand, learn, read* – (although many other transitives also yield two causatives formally that in the main are not semantically distinct). This same subclass of transitives, along with primary double object verbs (*give, send, write*) does not yield anticausative derivatives. (The analytic passive is used instead.)

The mode of causative marking is by suffixes + vowel reduction, that of anticausative marking, vowel reduction only (plus certain consonant changes). There is a strong tendency toward specialization of the two causative suffixes, -AA and -WAA, the former always indicating first, and the latter second, causative where these are semantically distinct.

The first causative suffix -AA is also a verbalizer: it forms denominatives from nouns, adjectives, and imitative polysyllables. Except for the onomatopoeics, however, these are not very numerous or productive at this stage of the language. For a different analysis see Pray (1970:92-114).

A similar situation prevails in Panjabi, Nepali, and the several Hindi "dialects" (Braj, Awadhi, Bhojpuri, Magahi, Maithili), except that the causative suffixes are respectively -AAW and -WAAW[4] – the forms Pray postulates as underlying Hindi-Urdu also.

Vowel reduction (and consequently also anticausative formation) is somewhat less in evidence in Panjabi as many bases already have short vowels. This aspect of the system also becomes progressively less operational as we move eastward through the (Hindi) dialects, for different reasons.

Nepali has a passive in -I (according to Kellogg 1938:292-93, there are traces of the same in Braj, and according to Tiwari 1954:258, in Panjabi – but he may be referring to Western Panjabi: see Lahnda, below): *gar-* 'do'/*garaau-* 'have done by someone'/*gari-* 'be done'.

The same labial element is present in the Kashmiri suffix, -AAV, which however is simply repeated (with a transitional element -/ɨn/-) to form the second causative (in -AAVƗNAAV, therefore): *con* 'to drink'/ *caavun* 'to give drink to'/*caavɨnaavun* 'have someone give drink to'. According to Kachru (whose examples these are), a number of verbs cannot be causativized in Kashmiri that do yield causatives in most other Indian languages: *see, wear, come out, get up,* etc. There appears to be no development of anticausatives, and no organic passive. No examples of second causatives are cited which are not of the ingestive subclass.

In Gujarati, the element -AAW/(AW) has to share honors with an element -AAḌ/(EḌ), with vowel-reduction in the case of /aa/ but not other vowels: *jaaṇ-* 'know'/*janaaw-* 'inform', but *dekh-* 'see'/ *dekhaaḍ* 'show' (cf. Hindi *dikhaa-*): this is no doubt because there is no more "short" /i/ and /u/ in Gujarati. There appears to be no (subclassificatory) semantic basis for the use of the several suffixes, and there are a number of further variations and irregularities.

Gujarati does clearly have two layers of causatives: the second almost always contains the sequence /ḌAAW/, either added as such to the stem with the first causative suffix in -AAW/(AW) or produced by adding /aaw/ to first causatives in -AAḌ/(EḌ): the second degree stems thus end in -AAWḌAAW, -AWḌAAW, -AAḌAAW, or EḌAAW, but there is a strong tendency to generalize -AAWḌAAW regardless of the form of the first causative (see Cardona [1965] for further details).

Gujarati has a few transitive and intransitive stems related by vowel change, principally AA/A (*mar-* 'die'/*maar-* 'kill, beat'; *ughaḍ-* 'come open'/*ughaaḍ-* 'open [tr]'). Whether this should be regarded as another type of "causative" formation (the traditional view), an "anticausative" as in Hindi, or merely a vestigial anomaly, as in English, is hard to say. If the first, their "second" causative is anomalous in not containing the element /Ḍ/ – in fact, in looking like a "first" causative: *maar-* 'kill'/*maraaw-* 'cause to kill'.

The place of the Hindi anticausative is otherwise taken by an organic "passive" in -AA (plus vowel reduction). It will be noted that this is identical with the Hindi first *causative* – a reminder that passives and causatives are phenomena in the same semantic field and should be considered together. The Gujarati passive differs from the Hindi anticausative (or passive-intransitive), however, in being formed equally freely from "ingestive" and double object verbs (*wancaa-* 'be read', *khawaa-* 'be eaten', *dewaa-* 'be given', etc.). It may even be formed from causatives (*calaawaa-* 'be driven'). It is thus equivalent to the Hindi anticausative + the Hindi analytic passive. Like the latter, it also may express potential and similar meanings. A similarly formed inflectional passive occurs in Bhojpuri and Maithili according to Kellogg (1938:336).

The Marathi suffixes (-AW, -WAW) sort themselves out, insofar as they do so, on a phonological rather than a functional basis (-WAW after vowel stems). There are no vowel reduction rules. The language has two layers of causals, with the second formed by repeating the causative morpheme: *bas-* 'sit'/*basaw-* 'seat'/*basawaw-* 'cause to seat' (Katenina 1963:58-61).

There is a series of verbs related by internal vowel changes, but again this has not developed into anything analogous to the Hindi system. On the contrary, the system of ablaut is so weakened as to produce a group of verbs in which the transitive/intransitive distinction has disappeared: *ughaaḍ-* 'open (tr, intr)' (cf. Gujarati *ughaaḍ-/ughaḍ-), moḍ-* 'break (tr, intr)', *samadz-* 'understand/be understandable'. According to Beames (1872:75), these are distinguished conjugationally. The latter writer, however, was also moved to say that "Marathi stands alone in respect of its causal, and as in so many other points, exhibits a hesitation and confusion which confirm the impression of its being a backward language which has not so thoroughly emancipated itself from the Prakrit stage as the others."

Sindhi also exhibits two layers of causals. The suffixes are -AA (-WAA after vowels) and -RAA, the latter tending to specialize as the marker of the second causal, added to the first: *virch-* 'be weary'/*virchaa-* 'weary'/*virchaaraa-* 'cause to weary someone'. There are two additional features of Sindhi, besides the distinctive element -RAA, that merit our attention:

One is the inflectional passive in -(I)J, which also occurs in certain Rajasthani dialects (e.g., Marwari).

The other is a series of intransitive/transitive correlates after the Hindi manner, except that the intransitive (anticausative) member is formed not by vowel reduction but by *consonantal change.* This change is, moreover, from whatever the original final consonant is to /JJ/ or /JH/ – which reminds us immediately of the passive suffix -(I)J: *bhun̄-* 'fry'/*bhujj-* 'be fried', *chin-* 'pluck'/*chijj-* 'be plucked', *bbandh-* 'tie'/*bbajh-* 'be tied', *khaa-* 'eat'/*khaajj-* 'be eaten'. (In trying to

---

MAP 3. Anticausatives

Key:

——— main as area of <u>reliance</u> on anticausatives for marking of valence distinctions

------- other anticausatives (generally in conjunction with causatives)

‾_‾_‾_‾ post-inflectional suffixes

× × × × semi-analytic formation (movable reflexive particles)

① ⋮ Scandinavian area of weakly marked valence distinction

② ⋮ Balkan area of weakly marked valence distinction

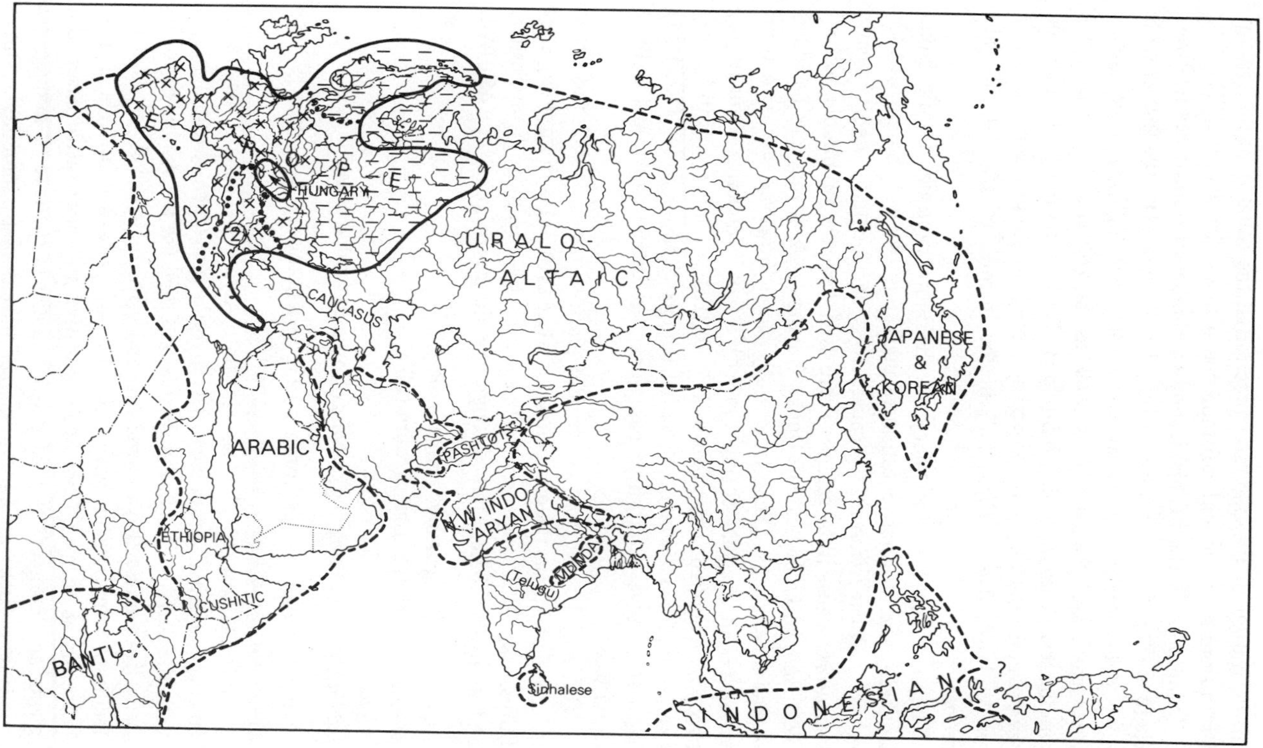

EUROPE
HUNGARY
URALO-ALTAIC
CAUCASUS
JAPANESE & KOREAN
ARABIC
PASHTO
N.W. INDO ARYAN
MUNDA
(Telugu)
ETHIOPIA
CUSHITIC
BANTU
Sinhalese
INDONESIAN

run derivation in the opposite direction in the usual tradition, Sindhi descriptions come up with a formidable array of "irregularities"!)

Lahnda, or Western Panjabi, shows a number of transitional features. There are "passives" in both -II (cf. Nepali) and -(J)J (the former with vowel reduction and the latter without it: *maar-* 'kill'/*marii-* 'be killed', *khaa-* 'eat'/*khaaj-* 'be eaten') as well as in /p/ and /bh/ (*sii-* 'sew'/ *siip-* 'be sewn', *ḍooh-* 'milk'/*ḍubh-* 'be milked' – reminiscent rather of *causative* formation) and by vowel reduction alone (*vaar-* 'put into'/ *var-* 'go into', *paa-* 'put'/*pa-* 'lie') in the manner of Hindi or Panjabi proper.

Beyond the Kashmir valley in the more typically Dardic Shina language, the distinctive causative marker is -AR (cf. Sindhi -RAA): *sidoiki* 'beat'/*sidaroiki* 'cause to be beaten', *khoiki* 'eat'/ *khayaroiki* 'cause to be eaten'. There is a "passive or middle suffix" -IZH: *ṣidizhoiki* 'be beaten'. Unlike Gujarati -AA, it may not be added to causative stems. (The element ZH alone, however, seems to form transitives in irregular correlation with a few intransitive stems in /c/: *pacoiki* 'be cooked, ripen'/*pazhoiki* 'cook [tr.]'.) There seems to be only one layer of causals here. All verbal triplets cited by Bailey (1924:51) seem to involve a transitive base form, an anticausative, and a (first) causative.

This may be the most convenient place to take a look at the exotic neighbor of Shina, the completely unrelated (to Shina or anything else) Burushaski. This language also forms causatives from both intransitive and transitive bases, but through the device of *prefixes* (AS-, A-):

gutsaras 'walk'/*agutsaras* 'make walk'
γulaas 'burn (intr)'/*asgulas* 'burn (tr)'
minaas 'drink'/*aminas* 'give drink to'
baaltas 'wash (something)'/*abaltas* 'cause to wash (something)'.[5]

There is no mention (in Lorimer 1935 or Klimov and Edel'man 1970) of either anticausatives or second causatives.

Shifting now to the east in Indo-Aryan, in Bengali and allied languages (Oriya, Assamese) there is *only one layer* of causatives, all with the suffix -AA. (In this discussion I shall use the symbol *aa* for the Bengali-Assamese-Oriya vowel /a/, and *a* for their vowel /ɔ/, to better facilitate comparison with the rest of Indo-Aryan.) These may, however, be formed from both transitive and intransitive bases, thus giving an "indirect" (= mediative) meaning in the case of noningestive transitives such as *kar-* 'do'/*karaa-* 'have done by someone'. This is accompanied by vowel reduction in Assamese and Oriya (*aan-* 'bring'/*anaa-* 'have brought') but not in Bengali (*aanaa-* 'have brought'). Indeed, in the latter language there is even the opposite shift to /aa/: *cal-* 'move'/*caalaa-* 'drive', *jal-* 'burn (intr)'/*jaalaa-* 'light, kindle'. This is reminiscent of the vowel-lengthening that accompanies the Sanskrit causative in *-aya.* There is no second causative, no morphological passive, and no anticausative. The internal flexion so productive in Hindi has been lost, except for a few vestigial forms such as the ever-present *mar-* 'die'/*maar-* 'kill'. More causative relations are expressed suppletively than in other Indo-Aryan languages: *uṭh-* 'rise'/*tul-* 'raise' (H. *uṭhaa-*). The element -AA is also much in evidence as a verbalizer (in contrast to Hindi): e.g., *haat* 'hand'/*haataa-* 'acquire', *ghum* 'dream'/*ghumaa-* 'sleep', etc. It should be noted that vowel shifts in the Eastern languages, especially Bengali, are preempted by another function, namely vowel harmony, and so are not available to mark verbal valence.

The faraway and aberrant Sinhalese language has, like Bengali, only one layer of causatives, of which the distinctive sign (in the Present – it is different in the Past, a state of affairs more reminiscent of Eskimo than Indo-Aryan) is -WA-: *hadanawaa* 'make'/*hadawanawaa* 'have made', *yanawaa* 'go'/*yanawanawaa* 'send (have go)'. However, consonant-strengthening is also employed: *kapanawaa* 'cut'/*kappanawaa* 'have cut', *padinawaa* 'pedal'/*paddanawaa* 'cause to pedal' – a "Dravidian" device (see below).

These are formed from transitive as well as intransitive and semitransitive ("eat") primaries – hence in the first case yield "indirect" causatives (= getting something done by somebody else). No further derivatives (V_e) are possible from an already derived (= secondary) transitive ($V_i^{in} \rightarrow V_j^k$), however, and when one wishes to express an indirect causative of these, the same derived transitive (V_j^k) is pressed into service in an appropriate sentence context with the added agent phrase (i.e., rather than employing a periphrastic verbal expression).

There is an elaborate development in Sinhalese of anticausatives – called in the literature "passives," "involitives," and by various other names. Their characteristic sign is -E + stem vowel modification (not shortening but fronting): *kapanawaa* 'cut'/*kæpenawaa* 'be cut', *hadanawaa* 'make'/*hædenawaa* 'be made', *ugulanawaa* 'uproot'/*igilenawaa* 'be uprooted'. In view of *maranawaa* 'kill' > *mærenawaa* 'die', we should perhaps be less hesitant about assimilating, e.g., Hindi *maar-*/*mar-* 'kill/die' to the generally Hindi anticausative system, instead of insisting on the semantic priority of 'die' to 'kill'. But a number of other correlations depart from the usual Indo-Aryan pattern in the direction of their derivation as well: *tooranawaa* 'explain' < *teerenawaa* 'understand', *danawaa* 'set fire to' < *dæwenawaa* 'burn'.

Before moving on to Dravidian, let us go back and take a brief look at some of the Austroasiatic languages in India.

The basic Munda causative sign (still extremely productive in Sora) would seem to be the prefix-infix AB- (= Sora; Kharia = OB-, -B-). The /b/ of this affix usually assimilates to a consonant of the verbal root. The prefixal *vs.* infixal position of the affix is explained with reference to phonological conditioning (monosyllabic *vs.* polysyllabic roots, etc.) but it is just possible, judging from the very limited evidence available in the grammars, that a case could be made for $V_i^{in} > V_j^k$ = infix, *vs.* $V_i^{tr} > V_j^k$ (as well as $N_i > V_j$) = prefix. Cf. Sora *kəjed/kajjed* (*kəeabjed) 'die/kill', *gəlo:/gallo:* (*gəablo:) 'fall/throw', *bəton/batton* (*bəabtoŋ) 'fear/frighten'; Kharia *bhore/bhobre* 'be full/fill' *vs.* Sora *jum/ajjumjum* (*ab-j-) 'eat/feed', *omda:/adomda:* 'leave/cause to leave', *sukka/absukka* 'happy/make happy'; Kharia *ñog/obñog* 'eat/feed'. The Kharia prefix can be generally applied also, however (i.e., in the place of the infix).

This element exists vestigially in the Kherwarian languages also (Mundari *jom/ajom* 'eat/feed'), but these languages have replaced it for productive purposes with a "suffixal" element (Santali OCO, Mundari ICI or RIKAA). I put "suffixal" in quotes because these elements (which are usually written separately, for what that is worth) are perhaps more properly auxiliary words, analogous to our English *make, have, let,* etc., in similar contexts. In other words, we have here the first instance of the what-is-a-word problem that will plague us in Southeast Asia. Santali *duṛup'ena/duṛup ocokedea* '(He) sat down/(They) made him sit down', *hẹc'ena/hẹc' ocokedeako* 'He came/They caused him to come'.

It is also typical of these languages that the root is not clearly "transitive" or "intransitive" (or, for that matter, even "verbal"); Santali *gọc'* can mean 'die' or 'kill', *cet'* can mean 'learn' or 'teach', *beret'* can mean 'rise' or 'raise', etc., according to context. Transitivity *vs.* intransitivity is marked, however, at certain points in the conjugational paradigm, e.g., "simple past" is indicated by -EN(A) for intransitives and by KET'(. .A) for transitives. (Thus *gọc'ena* = '[he] died', and *gọc'kedea* = '[They] killed him'.) The element

OCO seems to be used to indicate *indirect* causation only, not mere transitivity (direct or contactive causation).

On the other hand, the *intransitive* use of many roots, and many intransitive roots as such, are often (though not consistently) marked by a genuine suffixal element, the so-called passive -OK': *jorok'* 'to warm oneself', *pạc/pạcok'* 'abandon/withdraw oneself', *pẹrẹc'/pẹrẹjok'* 'fill/be filled', *(ju)jut/jutok'* 'to correct/be correct', *hoyok'* 'become, happen'. Thus Santali could be described as having a predilection for anticausative rather than causative morphology. Kharia has a "passive" in -ḌOM: *yoḍom* 'be seen'. The Sora "reflexive augment" in -N- (Ramamurti 1931:26) would seem also to be a kind of anticausative sign. A. Zide (1972), however, develops a more complex interpretation ("+ affectedness of subject") of a similar element (*-nuH*) in the closely allied Gorum or Pareng language (of Koraput District, Orissa), which may conceivably also apply to the (dissimilar) elements just noted in the other Munda languages. Moreover, in Gorum, at least, this element is not incompatible (i.e. not mutually exclusive) with the causativizing prefix *ab-*, or even with certain kinds of "objects".

In Khasi, there is a causative prefix PN-: *hiar/pnhiar* 'descend/lower', *tip/pntip* 'know/inform', *iap/pniap* 'die/kill'.

Dravidian systems bear more analogy to Indo-Aryan ones than the Austroasiatic systems do. Rather than prefixes, or the auxiliary-like particles of Santali, it is a question of genuine stem-building by means of suffixes – complicated by the fact that in these languages there are several layers of it. There seem to be ancient suffixes that have become fused with the root, vestigial suffixes whose meaning may still be discerned, suffixes of limited productivity, and fully regular and productive suffixes. (There are, in addition, sometimes causative auxiliary verbs bearing a striking phonetic resemblance to the causative suffixes.) In analyzing the system, one of the problems is where to stop in peeling off these layers of accumulated derivation. There is a considerable amount of formal and semantic overlap among the elements involved, which adds to the difficulties.

When this section was first written, I had observed that all this had, unfortunately, not been the object of extended investigation and attempted systematization even to the extent that the Indo-Aryan (especially the Hindi) systems had. The most notable efforts had been those of Lisker (1951) for Tamil and of Krishnamurti (1961) for Telugu, both largely concerned with morphology. Since then, however, at least three important contributions have appeared that should be taken into account here: Emeneau (1971), already referred to earlier in this chapter, Subrahmanyam (1971), and Krishnamurti (1971).

Both the suggestions of Emeneau and the rich assemblage of data in Subrahmanyam are animated by a concern for the historical aspects of the problem – the reconstruction or hypothesization of basic forms and categories for Dravidian as a whole or for its various branches and languages, and the history of various morphemes. That, of course, is not our concern here, and it is important for our purposes that we try to separate this from the synchronic descriptive facts.

Emeneau, as we have seen earlier, has postulated a Dravidian causative system with the categories *simplex/mediative of simplex/ causative/mediative of causative.* He bases this on his "fieldwork on Toda, Kota, and Kodagu, and . . . observation of Malayalam" (Emeneau 1971:39). He also says there are traces of this in Kolami (a Central Dravidian language). For other languages he infers that the system either may not apply (Kui, Parji) or merely has not been adequately described (Tamil). What he is describing, then, is a protosystem of some kind, either Proto-South-Dravidian or, possibly, Proto-Dravidian. (The same is true, by the way, of his characterizations of the NIA system and the Munda system. The former would appear to apply only to Hindi-Punjabi-Gujarati-Sindhi, and explicitly excludes Bengali and Oriya, as well as – apparently unjustly – Marathi.) It is not meant to describe the systems actually found in all the modern languages – although it suggests a dimension one should look for in surveying them.

What dimension? If we rearrange the order of Emeneau's categories slightly, so that we have *simplex/ causative of simplex/ mediative of simplex/ mediative of causative,* we see that this corresponds in Kholodovich terms to *base/ first causative*^{a} ("lexical" and contactive)/ *first causative*^{b} ("morphological" and indirect)/ *second causative.* What we are looking for therefore is verbs with two first causatives, which contrast semantically and, presumably, also morphologically. Since (Emeneau notwithstanding) these are only likely to be found with intransitive or semitransitive bases, we may further amplify the first derivative category as (lexicalized derived) contactive-transitives (or double transitives, in the case of semitransitives). Second causatives (like causatives of full transitives) are likely to be necessarily indirect, as we have noted earlier.[6] The feature "mediative" may thus potentially occur in two environments: 1) in direct combination with a simplex base (intransitive, semitransitive, or transitive) and 2) in combination with a *derived* transitive. In the case of occurrence with intransitive bases, in contrast with a feature yielding "direct transitive," it would be in the interest of linguistic logic and economy if it were to be expressed by the same morpheme that expresses "mediative" with derived-transitives (which is presumably different in such systems from the morpheme expressing "direct-transitive").

Practically speaking, then, what we are looking for is mediatives from intransitive verbs (presumably using the same morpheme as the second causative uses in the language), since that would seem to be the most distinctive category. It is also likely to go unreported, or to be inaccurately reported. Subrahmanyam, despite his extensive coverage, is only of limited help, because he was not specifically looking for this category – nor, most of the time, would the level of semantic information provided by his sources have allowed him to do so. Dictionaries also generally confine their reporting to direct-transitive derivatives (which Kholodovich has appropriately termed "lexical" causatives) and only rarely or sporadically include even second causatives, presumably as a more regular formation; the same consideration may apply to mediative (morphological) first causatives. The formation may well be, statistically, relatively rare: combing of texts is not likely to be very productive. What is really needed is work with informants. In the absence of precise syntactosemantic information, we can only fall back on the hints given by the overt morphology. We look, in other words, for different morphemes occurring with the simplex – although this is still complicated by the fact that we may not know that one of them (the mediative) *can* occur. Meanwhile, even stray occurrences are of some value.

This is complicated in Dravidian by complex conditioned allomorphy as well as by subsequent lexicalization in the direct-transitive marker, which may give the impression of separate morphemes unless the conditioning can be shown. The situation is also complicated by the great phonological economy of Dravidian in derivational and inflectional processes, with consequent overlap in phonic material involved in verbal and nominal derivatives as well as inflections.[7]

Subrahmanyam notes that causatives of causatives, to use his terminology (= second causatives, in Kholodovich's, and mediatives of causatives, in Emeneau's) – that is to say, the fourth member of the Emeneau equation – are confined to Tamil, Malayalam, Telugu, Malto, and Brahui, and "absent in all other Dravidian languages" (Subrahmanyam 1971:93). We shall examine the evidence below. The presence of mediatives of the second causative type does not, of course, guarantee or even indicate the presence of mediatives of the first causative type (= the third member of the equation, as I have rearranged it). Nevertheless, it is probably a safe hypothesis that the latter do not occur unless the former, more widespread category is also present. Meanwhile the distribution of the languages cited by Subrahmanyam should be noted. The list includes languages of the southern, central, and northern branches of Dravidian – reason enough to suspect the existence of at least the second causative category in other languages of the Dravidian group as well, perhaps as yet merely insufficiently reported. As will be seen, there is evidence warranting the addition of Kannada to the group. Emeneau indeed bases his hypothesis heavily on Toda and Kota, which are not on Subrahmanyam's list either and would be difficult to put there on the basis of published analyses alone. Now to specific languages:

The Tamil system would seem to illustrate, or to have illustrated, Emeneau's thesis nicely. There is a contrast between the "direct-transitive" morpheme, -TTU, which enters into the formation of lexical first causatives, and a "mediative" morpheme -VI(~PI~PPI), used to form both first and second causatives. (The latter are formed only from first causatives of the direct-transitive type; in other words, morphologically, the morpheme -VI may not follow itself; semantically, there are no mediatives of mediatives.)

The problem is that the morpheme -VI belongs to the classical language (and to grammar books), and is dead in modern Tamil. The mediative categories remain, however, and are expressed in modern Tamil by the collocation *infinitive* + *vai* 'put', e.g., not *ooṭuVI, ooṭṭuVI* 'cause to run; cause to be driven' (from *ooṭu* 'run' and *ooṭṭu* 'drive, chase'), but *ooṭa VAI, ooṭṭa VAI* – which, however, sound suspiciously similar. (Perhaps it is not quite accurate to say that the categories remain. I am told that it is common in Tamil – in contrast with, for example, Hindi – to use the first causative in place of the second – morphological or syntactic – when the context is otherwise clear or the distinction is unimportant.)

The pressing into service of auxiliaries analogous in sound may perhaps be one of the ways Dravidian (and perhaps other stocks?) replaces wornout morphemic material. (Dravidianists are not too happy with this suggestion, but it has been made before, in various ways. For example, Ramaswami Aiyar 1928 saw *vai* behind the old *-vi* in the first place. Subrahmanyam finds it necessary to say in refutation that there is "no indication in any of the languages to prove that these causative constructions *were originally* periphrastic" [p. 95. Italics mine]).

The direct-transitive (= lexical first causative) morpheme -TTU exhibits a complex allomorphism. Some of its allomorphs are phonologically conditioned, triggering simultaneous changes in the final consonant of the stem. Thus "regular" *para-/paraTTU-* 'spread(intr/tr)' but *tuyil-/tuyi(R̲)R̲u-* 'sleep/put to sleep', *kaaṇ-/kaa(Ṭ)ṬU-* 'see/show'. However, there are also *covert* allomorphs, triggering in one case changes in the final consonant of the stem (single consonant or homorganic nasal + single consonant become geminated consonant) and in the other case changes in the *initial* consonant of the *tense suffixes* (again, in the direction of gemination and "hardening"):

eer̲u-/eeR̲R̲u- 'rise/raise', *ir̲aṅku-/ɨr̲aKKu-* 'descend/lower';
uṭai-/uṭai(X)- 'break(intr/tr)' (= 'past'*uṭaiNT-/uṭaiTT-;*
'pres.' *uṭaiKIR-/uṭaiKKIR-;* 'fut.' *uṭaiV-/uṭaiPP-.)*

The latter had traditionally been called "transitivity by change of conjugation." Each of these classes has a fair number of representatives.

There is a second overt "allomorph," -PPU (sometimes -VU), apparently not phonologically conditioned and indeed sometimes occurring as an alternate to -TTU with the same verbs: *kiṭa-/kiṭaTTU kiṭaPPU* – both glossed as 'put down, lay' (from *kiṭa-* 'lie'). Whether this is a matter of genuine free variation or of vestigial or actual contrast of some sort (transitive/mediative?) is a question, at least for this writer.

The covert allomorphs of the direct transitive in Tamil have counterparts or echoes in some of the other languages. Going by Subrahmanyam's data, the "change of conjugation" allomorph (Lisker's *X*) is found in Malayalam, Kota, and Kodagu, while the "hardening (depending on geminating or devoicing, with dropping of nasal) of stem-final consonant" allomorph (Lisker's *) is found in those languages and in Toda and Kui, and, vestigially, in Kuvi, Konda, Pengo, and Kannada. Both allomorphs seem to be absent in North and much of Central Dravidian. The mysterious -P- allomorph, however, seems to be found in most of Dravidian except Toda and Kota, Kurukh, and Malto.

The Malayalam system seems to be considerably more intact than the Tamil. That is, its mediatives are still fully operative. Indeed, it may have elaborated them further: as Emeneau notes, mediatives of mediatives seem to be possible in Malayalam. The direct-transitive morpheme -TT has allomorphs analogous to those of Tamil. The mediative morpheme, corresponding to (Old) Tamil -VI, is properly just -I, but since (like Tamil -VI) this implies a "strong" conjugation, we may take it to be -I(KK) for certain morphophonemic purposes.

At this point, however, our would-be system seems to break down, in that morphological first causatives in -I(KK), if they exist, end up looking exactly like lexical first causatives from bases ending in -I derived through the change of conjugation allomorph of -TTU: e.g.,

ett- 'arrive' + *i(kk)* = *etti(kk)-* 'cause to arrive' *vs.* *oṭi-* 'break(intr)' + *X* = *oṭi(kk)-* 'break(tr)'.[8]

The distinction remains for some verbs, those that have lexical first causatives based on some other allomorph of -TTU (e.g.,

kaaṇ-/kaaṭṭ-/kaaṇi(kk)- 'see/show/demonstrate')

or are "strong" in conjugation to begin with (e.g., *naṭa(kk)-* 'walk-'). The semantics of this distinction is not very clear, however; there seems to be a strong tendency toward lexical specialization, perhaps only originally relating to a contrast "direct/mediative."

The function of -I(KK) as a marker of a category "mediative" is weakened still further by the fact that it is also the morpheme used to form denominative verbs (very numerous in Malayalam) – some of which are *intransitive*: e.g., *oḷi* 'concealment', *oḷi(kk)-* -hide(intr)'. Some are semitransitive; e.g., *paaṭham* 'lesson', *paṭhi(kk)-* 'learn, study'.

Where a verb has only one first causative derivative, and that is ambiguously in -I(KK), the direct-transitive category would seem to have first priority. However, there seem to be verbs with only one derivative, which is clearly the morphological, not the allomorphic-lexical, variety: e.g., *etti(kk)-*, referred to above. In such cases the derivative seems to fulfill both functions, not just the mediative.

We are thus reminded that the lexical and morphological categories may simply be different means of forming the general first causative and do not imply different semantics, at least of a generalizable sort. Even the occurrence of both with the same verb is not quite sufficient to establish an operative distinction, since such verbs show a tendency to lexical specialization on the one hand and interchangeability on the other.

The morphophonemic rule referred to above changes (KK) – whether from the causative morpheme -I(KK), the denominative -I(KK), the lexical change of conjugation allomorph, or original strong conjugational (KK) – to PP before -I(KK) is added again, thus producing a sequence -(I)PPI(KK)-, which closes the construction. That is, this operation may be performed once, but not more than that. The rule does not apply to the sequence /kk/ produced by the "hardening" allomorph ("*") of -TTU from underlying /k/ or /ṅṅ/.

The category reached by the closing sequence -(I)PPI(KK)- depends on that of the immediately underlying construction. Intransitives or semitransitives with denominative or conjugational (KK) close as first causative transitives or double transitives: *oḷi(kk)-/oḷiPPI(KK)-* 'hide(intr/tr)', *paṭhī(kk)-/paṭhIPPI(KK)-* 'learn/teach', tool(kk)-/toolPI(KK)- 'lose/win, defeat'. Transitive verbs of these types close as first causatives with a mediative function: *sneehi(kk)-/sneehIPPI(KK)-* 'love/cause to love'. Verbs with a first causative only in -I(KK), whether conjugational or suffixal in origin, close with a second causative, of mediative value:

oṭi-/oṭi(kk)-/oṭiPPI(KK)- 'break(intr)/break(tr)/ cause to break',
tiriy-/tiriyi(kk)-/tiriyIPPI(KK)- 'turn back(intr)/enforce the customary distance between castes/cause to " " '.

(The latter verb also goes *tiri/tiri(kk)-/tirippi(kk)-*, an indication again of the falling-together of the conjugational and suffixal categories.) If the simplex is transitive, the final form may, as Emeneau says, be a double mediative (since the first causative is already mediative), or it may simply be redundant:

cey-/ceyyi(kk)-/ceyyIPPI(KK)- 'do/cause to do/ditto, or cause to cause to do(?).

Verbs with a lexical first causative (in an allomorph other than "change of conjugation") may form a second causative in -I(KK) on this, and then, after operation of the morphophonemic rule, theoretically a *third:*

varu-/varutt-/varutti(kk)-/varuttIPPI(KK)- 'come/summon/cause to summon/cause to cause to summon(?)'.

In the case of verbs with both lexical and morphological first causatives, this leads to a possible total of six forms, including two second causatives and a third causative:

uṇṇ-/uuṭṭ-/uṇṇi(kk)-/uuṭṭi(kk)-/uṇṇIPPI(KK)-/uuṭṭIPPI(KK)- 'eat/feed/cause to eat/cause to feed/cause to cause to eat (?)/cause to cause to feed(?)'.

It is not clear how many of these theoretical categories are actually operational and, if so, in what functions. One thing is clear, however; neither the suffix -I(KK), or even the sequence -IPPI(KK), is unambiguously a marker of a category "mediative" in Malayalam. Such a category exists, somewhat uncertainly on the first causative level, definitely on the second causative level, and possibly on a third causative level (double mediative). However, not all Malayalam verbs participate in it, or participate to the same degree – *although they do participate in the associated morphology.* That morphology does not neatly correspond to semantic-syntactic functions and meanwhile follows purely mechanical rules of its own, which, as it were, cut down certain verbs before they even reach the mediative level. We are once more reminded of Elizarenkova's warning concerning the "asymmetries" of these systems.

The sequence -I(KK) really needs the brackets only because it changes to -ICC in the past tense: *oṭiKKunnu/oṭiCCu* 'break(s)/broke(tr.)' *vs. oṭiyunnu/oṭiññu* 'break(s)/broke(intr.)'. This variability in association with tense is reminiscent of the situation in nearby Indo-Aryan Sinhalese: *hadaWAnawaa/hädeWUwaa* 'has/had made(caus.)'.

Does the use of the sequence -I(KK) in intransitive denominative formations argue against its recognition as even the regular *causative* suffix of Malayalam (forgetting now about mediatives)? If so, the same argument can be made in many other languages. Hindi -AA and especially Bengali -AA, it should be recalled, are also involved in such formations, for example. Denominatives must be treated as a special case.

The system of the third major South Dravidian language, Kannada, has been greatly regularized and simplified. Phonological developments presumably have largely destroyed the old system of derivation based on consonant strengthening. It has been generally replaced by the affix -(I)SU, added to both intransitive and transitive bases:

kuru/kurISU 'sit/seat', *baggu/baggISU* 'bend (intr/tr)', *baru/barISU* 'come/summon', *eeḷu/eeḷISU* 'rise/raise-cause to rise', *nagu/nagISU* 'laugh/make laugh' *naḍugu/naḍugISU* 'shake (intr/tr)', *naḍe/naḍeSU* 'move (intr/tr)', *haaru/haarISU* 'fly (intr/tr)', *teeḷaaḍu/teeḷaaḍISU* 'float (intr/tr)', *beḷe/beḷeSU* 'grow (intr/tr)', *maaḍu/maaḍISU* 'do, make/get done, made', *koḍu/koḍISU* 'give/cause to give', *uṇṇu/uṇṇISU* 'eat/feed', *koḷu/koḷISU*, etc.

"Mediative" significations naturally arise in connection with derivatives from transitive bases and occasionally elsewhere, but there obviously can be no question of a separate mediative category associated with a special morpheme.

The suffix -(I)SU is also the verbalizer in denominative formations: *tayaaru* 'ready'/*tayaarISU* 'make ready, prepare'; *aananda* 'bliss'/ *aanandISU* 'be happy'.

Despite many statements to the contrary (e.g., Andronov 1962:50), -(I)SU may be added to itself, at least in the colloquial language, to produce *second causatives: maaḍISU/maaḍIS(I)SU.*[9] (Cf. -AWAW in neighboring Marathi.)

There survive a very few pairs that appear to go back to overt-phonological and consonant-strengthening allomorphs of **tt.* Subrahmanyam cites, e.g.,

muḍugu/muḍuku 'bend (intr/tr)' and *naanu/naaru* 'get wet/make wet'.

However, if we can believe such dictionaries as Maisale 1957, the first pair are used interchangeably in both (intr/tr) functions, while the second has on the one hand given way to the regular *nane/naneSU* and on the other developed special restricted meaning (*naaru* = 'give off a bad smell'). The closest analogy is therefore with such English pairs as *lie/lay* and *fall/fell.*

There also seem to be vestiges of the mysterious suffix -PU, alternating with (I)SU in a few verbs: e.g., *iḷi/iḷiSU~iḷiPU* 'descend/ lower', *maḍi/maḍiPU* 'die/kill' (*maḍiSU* = 'twist/bend').

Of a change of conjugation device, however, there is no trace at all. Failure to compensate for this in every instance results in items like *oḍe* 'break', where transitive and intransitive are not differentiated. (The form *oḍeSU* means 'cause someone to break something'.) Areally, this is again reminiscent of Marathi, where such items also occur due to lack of – loss or failure to develop – a consistent system of vowel-length contrasts.

The remaining Dravidian literary language, Telugu, is somewhat more complicated. Both "lexical" and "morphological" causatives exist in abundance and are fairly well sorted out as to function.

There are two "lexical" suffixes that turn intransitives and semi-transitives into transitives and double transitives: -CU (variant -NCU) and -PU (variant -MPU). These are in some instances simply added to the base: *kaalu/kaaluCU* 'burn(intr/tr)', *kadalu/kadalCU* 'shake(intr/tr)'. Cf. also *poo/paMPU* 'go/send'. More frequently they *replace a suffix of the base: kaaGU/kaaCU* 'boil(intr/tr)', *aaGU/aaPU* 'stop(intr/tr)', *tuuGU/tuuCU* 'hang(intr/tr)', *leeCU/leePU* ' rise/raise', *cuuCU/cuuPU* 'see/show', *meeSU/meePU* 'graze (intr/tr)', *eḍaYU/eḍaPU* 'separate (intr/tr)', *caCCU/caMPU* 'die/kill'. Some verbs have transitive equivalents in both suffixes: *diGU/diNCU~diMPU* 'descend/lower'. A number of Telugu stems in -/rugu/ and -/lugu/ – both verbal and nominal – have variants in -/nugu/ (including the word /telugu~tenugu/ itself). The latter is sometimes the basis for derived stems: *peruGU (penuGU)/penCU* 'enlarge(intr/tr), *ciruGU(cinuGU)/cinCU~cimPU* 'tear(intr/tr)'.

The "morphological" suffix is -INCU, which is added – after application of a morphophonemic rule (analogous to that of Malayalam) changing /c/ – which is incidentally pronounced [ts] in these suffixes – to /p/, and also of vowel harmony, peculiar to Telugu, changing /u/'s to /i/'s before the front vowel suffix /incu/ – both to derived transitives of the above type (*caccu/campu/campINCU* 'have killed') and to original transitives (*kaṭṭu/kaṭṭINCU* 'build/have built', *pilupu/pilipINCU* 'call/have called'). In the first case the results are technically second causatives and in the second, first causatives, but in both the function is "mediative."

The suffix -INCU is also added to certain intransitive and semi-transitive bases – bases *without suffixes,* it should be noted, to form first causatives. However, a case can be made for most of these also having a "mediative" (indirect, non-"contactive") implication: *navvu/navvINCU* 'laugh/make laugh', *erpu/erpINCU* 'cry/make cry', *ekku/ekkINCU* 'climb/help climb', *ubbu/ubbINCU* 'swell/cause to swell', *puṭṭu/puṭṭINCU* 'be born/cause to be born', *traagu/traagINCU* 'drink/give a drink to'. (Certain semitransitives exhibit a "false" layer of derivation before -INCU: *tinu/tiniPINCU* 'eat/cause to eat', *vinu/viniPINCU* 'hear/cause to be heard'.)

It may well be Telugu rather than South Dravidian proper that turns out to lend the greatest support to the Emeneau hypothesis. To be sure, the "system" is not mechanically perfect or completely intact, but that may be too much to expect. -INCU is also the denominative verbalizer, a process that yields many technically intransitive verbs in Telugu also, so it cannot be called an unambiguous marker of a mediative category – unless we make a special exception of denominatives; but, as we have seen, that appears to be necessary for many languages. Subrahmanyam (1971:26) says that -INCU is "in some verbs in free variation with *-cu* and *-pu.*" This deserves closer examination. Are they really true free variants in all situations, or is some latent semantic difference involved? I say "latent" because there seems to be a tendency in Telugu, as in other Dravidian languages at present, to blur the lines between these derivative categories. Thus Krishnamurti (1961:229) also says that such items as *neerPU/neerPINCU* 'teach/*cause to teach' and *cuuPU/cuuPINCU* 'show/*cause to show' occur "more or less" as free variants. Shivram Sharma (1967:74), Lisker (1968:298), and Arden (1937) seem to disagree. What apparently happens is this: one form this blurring takes in Telugu is the pressing of the second (-INCU) causative into service in place of the first (lexical) causative, which may have lost some of its force. However, the two forms do have their "proper" functions, judging by some work with an informant, which are sorted out in sufficiently clear diagnostic contexts: as

'He lowered a rope' = *oka taaḍu diNCaeḍu* (or *diMPaeḍu*)
vs. 'He had the child lower a rope' = *aa korraḍicaeta oka taaḍu diMPINCaeḍu;* 'Graze the cattle!' = *aavulani meePU vs.*
'Have the cattle grazed (by another person)! = *aavulani meePINCU.*

A search for such contrasts on the first causative level itself would have to be conducted with great care. If even a shadow of a contrast between "contactive" and "mediative" first causatives from the same bases could be discovered, it would be additional strong support for the Emeneau model.

Unlike its analogs in Kannada and Malayalam, Telugu -INCU cannot be added to itself. With its system of lexical derivation more or less intact, it has less need for this. If first causatives in -INCU are indeed mediative, it is appropriate that the process stop at that point. This leaves denominatives in -INCU. That gap is filled by auxiliaries such as *-peṭṭu(beṭṭu), -koṭṭu(goṭṭu),* etc., added to the infinitive in *-a.* These are also used to furnish first causatives for a few simple verbs, especially those somehow left out of the system, e.g., *veḷḷu/veḷḷaBEṬṬU* 'go/chase away'.

There is one further aspect of the Telugu situation that deserves attention. In discussion of Dravidian so far there has been no mention of "anticausatives." There has been no occasion for it; in the South Dravidian languages heretofore examined there are no marked intransitives. This is not the case in Telugu: many intransitive bases, as we have just seen, have distinctive endings in -GU, -YU, -SU, and -CU′, which are dropped when the lexical causative suffixes -CU″ and -PU are added.

What is the function of these base-suffixes? They are, no doubt, not a productive means of "decausativizing" transitives and therefore not properly anticausatives. The simpler line of derivation, if one must be chosen, goes from the four intransitive suffixes to the two transitive ones. (The opposite is true in the Hindi case posited earlier, which is, moreover, regular and productive.) Nevertheless, they are there and do help mark the intransitive/transitive distinction, which is thereby often marked on both sides.

Krishnamurti (1961:146) has pointed out a possible deeper layer of such markers in Telugu: a number of intransitive stems (both with and without the above suffixes) end in -/l,r,y/, now effectively part of the root. He notes that -R has this function actively in Kurukh, the Dravidian language of the Oraons: *kam/kamR* 'make/be made'. Subrahmanyam (1971:48) notes a similar intransitive or de-transitive morpheme for Malto in GR/R: *is/isGR* 'tear/be torn'. Finally, in Emeneau's 1961 account of Kolami, a Central Dravidian language bordering on Telugu, a number of intransitive stems end in -G, -Y, -S, and -L (which give way before the "transitive" suffix -P). In the Telugu case it looks as if we may have another instance of morphemic material losing its force and strengthened by more morphemic material, in this case on the anticausative side.

All these Dravidian tongues are spoken in the neighborhood of the Munda languages, where such simultaneous marking of both transitive and intransitive is characteristic (Emeneau 1971:42). As noted earlier, however, A. Zide (1972) has pointed out that "transitive" and "intransitive" (or for that matter "causative" and "anticausative") are inadequate concepts to deal with these Munda phenomena. It is just possible that some of these considerations may apply also at least in part to these adjacent Dravidian phenomena. The reality of some such category even in Telugu, involving such notions as "reflexivity" or "affectedness of subject" as well as "intransitivity," is argued for by the supplying of one by other means when a verb lacks the marked-intransitive form: *teracu/teracuKONU* 'open(tr/intr)'.

This rather lengthy digression on the major Dravidian languages has been undertaken in order to explore the Emeneau proposal, and because these languages are an important part of the Indian scene. I do not propose to examine every Dravidian tribal language here. What is known about them can be found in Subrahmanyam (1971). However, there is one more Dravidian language that it is important to look at for areal-typological purposes.

This is Brahui, in the far northwest (in Pakistani Baluchistan and extending even into Iranian Baluchistan). The causative suffix, which is -IF, -F, may be added to itself, so that there are first and second causatives:

kah-/kasF-/kasfIF- 'die/kill/have killed'; *xul-/xulIF-/xulifIF-* 'be afraid/ frighten/have frightened'.

On the anticausative side, there is an unexpected (for Dravidian) richness – apparently both a "passive" in -ING (*xanING-* 'be seen') – that can follow the causative suffix (*kas-F-ING* 'be killed') – and a "middle" or derived-intransitive in -ENG

(*hars-/harsING-/harsENG-* 'turn(tr)/be turned, turn (oneself)-intr').

We have observed that such phenomena are well-developed in Indo-Aryan languages of the northwest.

Turning now to neighboring Iranian languages, we find not unexpectedly the closest analogies in the languages nearest to India. The Pashto suffix is -AV, closely resembling that of the neighboring Indo-Aryan languages: *alvoz-/alvozAV-* 'fly(intr/tr)', *lval-/lvalAV-* 'read/ teach'. There is a suffix –ED, found comarking the intransitive (and semitransitive) member of intransitive-transitive pairs, e.g., *lagED-/ lagAV-* 'adhere/affix', *aurED-/aurAV-* 'hear/tell'. It also forms intransitive denominatives (*sherm/shermED-* 'shame/be ashamed') but most -ED bases are not found as independent nouns or adjectives.

The Baluchi system is even more like Indo-Aryan in that there are both first and second causatives; the former comes in what may be called lexical and morphological varieties, and the lexical variety involves vowel shifts analogous to guṇa:

thus-/thoos- 'faint/stun', *suc-/sooc-* 'burn(intr/tr)',
ric-/reec- 'spill(intr/tr)', *prush/proosh-* 'break(intr/tr)'.

The morphological suffixes are -EN and -AEN; the difference in their function is not completely clear, but -EN is added both to most first causatives of the above variety to form second causatives (*soocEN-* 'cause to burn') and to simplex bases to form first causatives (jiih-/jiihEN- 'run away/drive away'). A number of the latter undergo a vowel change analogous to that of the former before adding the suffix: *var-/vaarEN* 'eat/feed', *bhur-/bhoorEN-* 'break(intr/tr)'. (The derivation of the secondary -EN forms from the long vowel stems removes any question of treating the short vowel stems as anticausative derivatives as in Hindi, where the opposite is the case.)

The suffix -AEN is used to form second causatives from forms already involving -EN. The -EN is dropped and the vowel reshortened: *var-/vaarEN-/varAEN-* 'eat/feed/cause to feed'. It is also found where -EN has not intervened, however:

prush-/proosh-/prushAEN- 'break(intr)/break(tr)/cause to break', *khush-/khushAEN-* 'kill/cause to kill'.

Not unexpectedly, -EN is also the Baluchi verbalizer:

badal/badlEN– 'change (n./v.)'.[10]

Persian has a causative in -AAN, added to the present stem:

sukhtan/suzAAN(i)dan 'burn(intr/tr)', *rasidan/rasAAN(i)dan* 'arrive/send', *ranjidan/ranjAAN(ī)dan* 'be offended/offend', *rikhtan/rizAAN(i)dan* 'flow/pour'.

It also extends to some semitransitives and transitives:

fahmidan/fahmAAN(i)dan 'understand/explain', *kashidan/kashAANidan* 'pull, smoke (a cigarette)/cause to pull, offer someone a cigarette'; *dukhtan/duzAANidan* 'sew/have sewn'.

There is no second degree of causativization. However, in the eastern dialectal form of Persian known as Tajik the causative is more highly developed, extending to most transitive verbs in the colloquial language, which is also said to have a second causative, although no examples of this are given (Kholodovich 1969:206-20). The Persian verbalizer, which is not very productive, is -ID. A double marking propensity similar to that of Pashto cited above may be detected, however: e.g.,

fahmID-/fahmAAN- 'understand/explain' (from Arabic *fahm* 'understanding-n.').

Kurdish also has a causative, in -AND. Thence moving westward through the rest of Indo-European, Armenian has both anticausatives (in -V) and first degree causatives (in -EÇN):

gar-/garV- 'write/be written', *poxaadr-/poxaadarV-* 'move(tr)/move (intr)'; *hish-/hishEÇN-* 'remember/remind', *ut-/utEÇN-* 'eat/feed', *kem-/kemEÇN-* 'drink/give drink to'.

There is no second causative, apparently, and first causatives are restricted to intransitives and semitransitives.

There is no morphological causative in Greek, but the passive-middle paradigm (*-omai*, etc.) might conceivably be viewed as an anticausative: it frequently is the device for maintaining the transitive/intransitive distinction as well as the active/passive one and, where both forms exist, can be viewed as derived from the active, insofar as it is typically *longer.* However, it is a question of endings rather than of an identifiable *stem.* (The valiant attempt of Koutsoudas 1962 to disentangle the Greek desinences still leaves us with the valence distinctions inextricably bound up with the aspect distinctions, and even then with the four "morphemes" involved – marking, unfortunately, both the active and the passive overtly – having an average of 6.25 allomorphs apiece, one of which is usually zero, and which, moreover, are often conditioned by particular "tense+mood+person+number" morphemes, or sets of them! Even then there is much left over material to be accounted for: the whole situation is fantastically messy. This hardly meets the regularity criterion Kholodovich sets for "morphological" anythings, causatives or anticausatives.) Therefore, it would have to be an anticausative of a very special type. According to Thumb(1964:112-13), many active verbs are used both transitively and intransitively in Modern Greek. Some semitransitives are also used as double transitives with no augmentation of stem: *mathéno* 'learn/teach'. This reliance on context alone is also characteristic of the neighboring South Slavic languages, Macedonian and Serbian (cf. Gołąb 1968). Albanian has an anticausative of a sort, marked by a suffix (-ET) in the Present, but by a "prefix" (U-) in the Past: *falet* 'he is excused', *u fal* 'he was excused'.

Aside from a few vestiges in Germanic of the *liegen/legen* 'rise/raise' variety, and in Slavic with the suffix -/i/- (the more common use of which, however, is to mark the perfective aspect: cf. Greek above) mentioned earlier, there is no causative morphology whatever in the rest of living Indo-European. The one striking exception is Lithuanian, which (along with Latvian, to a lesser extent) has innovatively developed two degrees of causative, in -IN for V^{in} and in -DIN for V_i^{tr} and V_j^k (Gołąb 1968:78).

Generally, however, the languages of Europe mark even the intransitive/transitive derivation mainly negatively, through *anti*-causatives. This is really *morphological* only in the east and north, where the Russian so-called reflexive -S$\widehat{IA}$/-S' (*lomat's$\widehat{ia}$/*

lomat' 'break (intr/break(tr)') and the Scandinavian 'passive' in -S (Swedish *läkas/läka* 'be healed/heal') may properly be regarded as suffixes – although not *stem* suffixes, since they are added, not to the verb stem, but after the other inflectional endings at the end of the verb. Swedish distinguishes this construction, so curiously similar to the Russian one, from the real *reflexive* with *sig,* etc.:

Dörren öppnades 'The door opened' *vs. Dörren öppnade sig* 'The door (possessed of life, or supernatural powers) opened *itself*'.[11]

Scandinavian, however, does not jealously maintain the distinction between intransitive and transitive by this or any other device, many verbs being used either way: in this it is a halfway house to English. There is a similar and more vigorously applied ending, in -IES(-AS), in Latvian.

In the West Slavic languages, in German, and in the Romance languages, the reflexive construction used to signal intransitivity involves variable and separable reflexive particles and therefore must be regarded as a type of syntactic construction, not strictly part of morphology. It is properly somewhere between the two.

As we move westward, moreover, the reflexive takes on more and more functions (lexical or quasi-aspectual) beside the transitive/intransitive one: e.g., Spanish *comer/comerse* 'eat/eat UP', *dormir/dormirse* 'sleep/go to sleep' (alongside *enojar/enojarse* 'anger/get angry', *oír/oírse* 'hear/be heard', *levantar/levantarse* 'raise/rise', etc.)

In French the marking is sometimes in the other (causative rather than anticausative) direction: e.g., alongside *ouvrir/s'ouvrir* 'open(tr/intr)', *terminer/se terminer* 'end(tr/intr)', etc., there is *cuire/faire cuire* 'cook(intr/tr)', *bouillir/faire bouillir* 'boil(intr/tr)'.

Finally we reach English, where, as we have seen, purely syntactic criteria come to play an important role.

In all the European languages, the intransitive/transitive distinction is indicated also to an important degree by *suppletion,* in contrast with the languages of South Asia. A good example is *die/kill,* the relation between which is indicated by derivational means in almost all the languages of South Asia but is expressed by different verbs in almost all the languages of Europe: cf. German *sterben/töten,* French *mourir/tuer,* Spanish *morir/matar,* Greek *petheno/skotono,* Czech *mříti/zabíti,* Russian *umeret'/ubit'.* Even Persian (in this and some other respects a "European" language) has *mordan/koshtan.* A vestige of an older relation, however, is to be seen in such transitive verbs of related but restricted meaning as Russian *morit'* 'exterminate', Czech *marniti* 'kill(time)', *mořiti* 'torment', French *meurtrir* 'bruise, batter' (cf. Hindi *maar-* 'kill, beat' and Russian *bit'* 'beat', hence *ubit'*), as well as the noun *meurtre* 'murder'.

A much closer analogy to the Indian phenomena is to be found to the north, in the Altaic and Finno-Ugric languages.

In Turkish, which is typical, the causative suffix is -DİR- (= dur/dır/dür/dir/tir/tur/tır/tür), with phonologically conditioned allomorphs (aside from vowel harmony!) -T- and -İT- (= ut/ıt/üt), and lexically conditioned allomorphs -İR- (= ur/ır/ür), -ER(ar), -ZİR, and -TER. There is no special correlation with transitive vs. intransitive bases: *öl/öldür-* 'die/kill', but *ye/yedir-* 'eat/feed'; *otur/oturt-* 'sit/seat', but *anla/anlat-* 'understand/explain'. (It is possible that the affixes -İT, -İR, and -ER happen to be added only to intransitive bases, but this may be only a coincidence.) Sometimes stems with irregular causatives have causatives with the productive affix (or regular allomorph) -DİR as well, with a difference in meaning: *gör* 'see, perform' *göster-* 'show', *gördür-* 'make perform'.

Turkish forms second causatives by repeating the "opposite" allomorph of the causative suffix: i.e., -DİR is added to first causatives ending in -/t/, and -T to those with affixes ending in -/r/. E.g., öl-dür-t 'have someone killed'. Sometimes the second causative (of transitive bases?) is semantically redundant: *de-* 'say'/1. *de-dir* 2. *de-dir-t* = 'make say'. Theoretically this process of alternating causative allomorphs is continuable. To quote Lewis, from whom much of this information is taken: "Causatives of the third and fourth degree are theoretically possible but are rarely if ever found outside the pages of grammar books, e.g., öl-dür-t-tür-t- 'to get someone to get someone to make someone die', i.e., to kill through the agency of three intermediaries" (Lewis 1967:146).

There is also a *passive* suffix in -İL- (= ul/ıl/ül), with the conditioned allomorphs (after vowels and -/l/) -N, -İN (= un/ın/ün):

kır/kırıl- 'break(tr)/break(intr)', *yap/yapıl-* 'make/be made', *gör/görül-* 'see/be seen'; *kapa/kapan-* 'shut/be shut', *bil/bilin-* 'know/be known'.

While this corresponds to some of the intransitivizing and passivizing functions of the European reflexive constructions, it is not a reflexive: there is also a reflexive suffix (-N, -İN (un/ịn/ün) – the two overlap after vowels and -/l/, however – and a *reciprocal* suffix -İŞ (uş/ış/üş) that handle reflexive-reciprocal functions proper. The passive may be formed from causative stems:

K′P K′P
otur-t-ul 'be made to sit (or dwell)', *iç-ir-il-* 'be caused to drink'.

This would seem to argue against the treatment of the passive as an anticausative. However, the same thing is true of Gujarati. It could be said that *anticausative* and *passive* are overlapping functions of the same morpheme. Like the Hindi *analytic* passive, the Turkish passive can also be made from *intransitive* verbs. The result, however, is an impersonal meaning, not an expression of helplessness as in Hindi: *İstanbula nasıl gidİLir* = 'How *does one go* to Istanbul?' (from *git-* 'go').

Very similar patterns are found in the other Turkic languages such as Uzbek, Kirghiz, Yakut, Bashkir, and Chuvash. In the latter language (sometimes described as "Turkicized Finnic") the Kholodovich team has no compunctions about calling the reflexive/passive formation in -ÂN/-ÊN/-ÂL an anticausative (Kholodovich 1969:238-58). In some pairs, both members are marked: *vaN/vaT* 'break(intr)/break(tr)'. The more orthodox Turkic languages sometimes show a regular formation where Anatolian Turkish has developed an irregularity: Turk. *gel-/getir-* 'come/bring' = Kirghiz *kel-/keltir.* Chuvash and Yakut are said (Kholodovich 1969:27) to have meaningful second causatives from transitive bases ($V_i^{tr} < V_j^{k}{}' < V_e^{k}{}''$), meaning, presumably, to have someone have someone do something. This is said to be a typological rarity.

In Mongolian and kindred languages the productive suffix seems to be -UUL (= üül – cf. the Turkish *passive*!):

yav/yavuul- 'go/send', *üz/üzüül-* 'see/show', *bic/bicüül-* 'write/have someone write', *or/oruul-* 'enter/allow to enter'.

But there are other (lexical?) suffixes:

uu/uuLGAA- 'drink/cause to drink', *una/unaGAA* 'fall/upset', *bos/bosGO* 'rise/raise'.

The suffix -AA is said (Kholodovich 1969:33-34) to causativize those V^{in} that denote "involuntary" actions ('dry up', 'perish'). In Buriat, at least, second causatives in -LGA are formed from the "lexical" first causative stems, but -UUL closes the construction (cf. Telugu). Mongolian also has a "passive" in -GD, -D, -T: *ala/alagd* 'kill/be killed', *ol/old-* 'find/be found' (cf. the Turkish *causative* in -T). (This reversal of the significance of segments between Mongolian and Turkish is reminiscent of the case of -AA in Gujarati and Hindi, in which it denotes passive and causative respectively.)

In Hungarian, which belongs to a different language family, the causative suffix is nevertheless also -AT (= et), -TAT (= tet). That is the "morphological" suffix: there are also "lexical" suffixes -ÍT, -T, -ASZT (= eszt), -JT, -LAL (= lel), -AL (= el), and -L. (Cf. the Turkish suffixes -T, İT.) A second causative is formed by adding the suffix -TAT to first causative stems formed with lexical suffixes or with -AT-, never to those formed with -TAT itself:

ég-/éget-/égettet- 'burn(intr)/burn(tr)/have burned by someone',

but *ül/ültet-* 'sit/seat'. There is also an anticausative, also with productive suffixes -ED (= od/ód/őd), -KEZ (= koz/kóz/köz/kőz) as well as "lexical" suffixes -UL (= ül), -L (cf. Turkish -İL), etc.:

zár-/zárkoz- 'close(tr)/close(intr)', *gyűr/gyűrőd-* 'crumple(tr)/crumple(intr)'.

Sometimes both intransitive and transitive members are marked with anticausative and causative affixes (generally "lexical") respectively:

szárAD/szárÍT 'dry(intr)/dry(tr), *gyóggyUL/gyógyÍT-* 'be cured/cure', *nyíL/nyíT-* 'open(intr)/open(tr)', *épÜL/épÍT-* 'be built/build'.

With its anticausative/causative lexical correlates and its second causatives made only from lexical causatives (and "uncanonical" morphological causatives) and only with the "canonical" morphological causative suffix, Hungarian is perhaps even more like some forms of Dravidian, especially Telugu, than Turkish is, and would fit on the same "Japanese" grid. However, the canonical morphological suffix is not the verbalizing suffix also as it is in Telugu and Kannada (and Malayalam), and denominative and de-adjectival stems may therefore be causativized:

egyenes 'straight'/*egyenesÍT-* 'straighten'/*egyenesítTET-* 'have straightened'.

There is also a redundant affix -IK (reflexive?), found in association with anticausatives and some other intransitives, which is difficult to fit into precisely this system:

csuk/csukódIK- 'close/be closed', *alszIK/alTAT-* 'sleep/make sleep'. Cf. *mos/mosaKODIK* 'wash/wash oneself'.

In the Komi or Zyryan language of extreme northeastern European Russia, the productive causative affix is -ÖD – which is the Hungarian *anticausative.*

In Finnish proper, however, the causative regular suffix again involves a /t/ element: -TA (= tta, utta, nta; tä, ttä, yttä, ntä). The allomorphs with the geminate /t/ (-tta, utta, ttä, yttä) appear to be the ones used with transitive bases and for second causative formation:

syö/syöttä- 'eat/feed', *tappa/tapatta-* 'kill/cause to kill', *kulke/kuljetta/kuljetutta-* 'go/bring/bring with someone's help', *tehdä/teettä-* 'do/have done'.

Intransitives have more varied suffixes:

nouse/nosta- 'rise/raise', *naura/narratta-* 'laugh/make laugh', *pala/poltta-* 'burn(intr)/burn(tr)', etc.

It will be noted that the causative suffixes are frequently accompanied by various morphophonemic changes in the base, and that the second causative is not formed by piling up suffixes but by a compound suffix -TUTTA (etc.). In this Finnish could be said to resemble Hindi more than Dravidian. There is an anticausative in -U (= utu/pu/y/yty/py – cf. Hungarian -OD, etc.):

kokoa/kokoutu 'gather(tr)/assemble', *pelasta/pelastu* 'save/be saved', *kääntä/käänty-* 'turn/be turned'.

It may correlate with a marked transitive: *mataloitU/mataloitTA* 'descend/lower'. It may also serve itself as a base for a causative (rather than the other way around as in most of the languages examined):

muista/muistU/muistuTTA- 'remember/be remembered/remind ('cause to be remembered').

There is, however, a separate *passive* in postdesinential -N

(pestää 'washes'/*pestääN* 'is washed'/*pestiiN* 'was washed' – cf. neighboring Swedish and Russian).

The Finnish "causative" also has other meanings (e.g., intensive), often unpredictable, and this together with its somewhat irregular formation causes Kholodovich (1969:34-35) to cite it as an example of a "senile" causative system.

Causative systems are equally well developed at the opposite end of northern Eurasia. The Japanese case, in fact, has been taken here as a model. There is a regular or productive formation in the suffix -SAS- (with a predictable allomorph -S-), as well as lexically conditioned formations. The second causative is formed from the latter only, most of which go back to intransitive bases. The regular suffix is used:

waku/wakaSu/wakasaSeru 'boil(intr)/boil(tr)/ have boil'.

There are, however, a number of complications and points requiring comment:

The Japanese causative suffix is sometimes given (e.g., in Dunn and Yanada 1958:170, and Bloch and Jorden 1964:22-23) as -(S)ASE(ru), but this can be analyzed differently. There are two conjugational paradigms in Japanese, one with an invariable "conjugational stem" in -E or -I, the other with a conjugational stem involving several alternating vowels. In the first, the infinitive or dictionary form ends in -ERU or -IRU (*taberu* 'eat', *ikiru* 'live'); in the second it ends in -U (*naku* 'weep', *nomu* 'drink', *arau* 'wash'), but the stem to which the causative suffix is added is the one in -A (= *naka, noma, arawa-*). Regular first causatives from such variable stems should be analyzed *naka+S-, noma+S-, arawa+S-,* not *nak+as, etc. The remainder of the dictionary form of the causative, -/(as)eru/, is the invariable conjugation-vowel -E, added again, + the infinitive ending -(R)U. *nomaseru* 'cause to drink' is therefore to be analyzed *noma+s+e+ru* (or *nom+a+s+e+ru*). With primary verbs having the invariable conjugation-vowel -E, the causative suffix has its "canonical" form, -SAS-, with again the conjugation-vowel and infinitive ending added +E+RU: *tabe+sas+e+ru* 'feed, cause to eat'. A regular causative stem has two conjugation vowels, with the choice of causative suffix allomorph dependent on the first, which is lexically determined. The second (following the causative suffix) is always -E in the standard dialect. Citing Japanese verbs in the dictionary form obscures these relationships: they are brought out by citing the conjugational stems (the -A variant in the case of variable stems): i.e., *waka/wakasa-/wakasaSe-*. (Because of the syllabic nature of the Japanese *kana* script, there has been a reluctance on the part of some writers to analyze Japanese in terms of vowels apart from the preceding consonants, since they cannot be written separately, but such analysis is essential if the system is to be understood.)

Some lexical causatives are formed by changing the conjugation stem only, i.e., with no suffix. However, this may go *either way,* i.e., from -A to -E or from -E to -A, so that neither stem vowel may be itself associated with any "causative" meaning content: *aka-/ake-* 'open(intr)/open(tr)', *yama-/yame-* 'stop(intr)/stop(tr)', but *yake/yaka-* 'burn(intr)/burn(tr)', *ore-/ora-* 'break(intr)/break(tr: long things)'. (Dictionary forms: *aku/akeru, yamu/yameru, yakeru/yaku, oreru/oru.*)

All other lexical causatives make use of *suffixes* – causative, anticausative, or both. They may or may not concurrently involve changes in the paradigmatic vowel. (From various combinations of these variables, Kholodovich – who is personally responsible for this section of his book – distinguishes fourteen subtypes of lexical causative exclusive of the purely paradigmative ones described in the preceding paragraph.) The "lexical" causative suffix is also -S- (cf. Telugu -C-, -NC-, alongside -INC), distinguished from the "regular" -S- by being added after a change in stem-vowel (*ik-i-/ik-a-S-* 'live/enliven', *nig-e-/nig-a-S-* 'run/let run', *d-e-/d-a-S-* 'emerge/take out'), or in place of an anticausative element (*hita-R-a/hita-S-a-* 'get wet/immerse'), and – or sometimes exclusively by – being *followed* by the *variable* conjugational vowel, here represented by "A", rather than by invariable -E (the dictionary form ending in -/su/ rather than -/seru/).

The anticausative suffixal element is -R-, again either added to an unmarked transitive stem (*um-a/um-a-R-e* 'give birth to/be born'), without or with a change of stem-vowel (*mag-E/mag-A-R-a-* 'bend(tr)/bend(intr), or correlating with a causative -S- (*kowa-R-e/kowa-S-a* 'break(intr)/break(tr)'). This element is also a "lexical" version of a *regular* anticausative/passive suffix -RAR-/-R- (with -E endings), which may be added also to causativized stems: *tabe-RAR-e-* 'be eaten', *tabe-sas-e-RAR-e-* 'be fed'. With intransitive verbs and in the negative especially it often has the "potential" meaning typical of the Hindi or Gujarati passive: *oyog-a-R-e-(masen)* = 'It cannot be swum'.

Some verbs have both lexical and regular first causatives (cf. Malayalam): *tat-a* 'stand; be built'/*tat-e-* (paradigmatic-lexical) 'build, erect'/*tat-a-S-e-* (regular) 'make (a person) stand'. (There is a second causative *tat-e-SAS-e-* 'cause to build'.) Cf.

de- 'go out'/*d-a-S-e-* 'take out'/*d-e-SAS-e* 'cause to go out'/*d-a-S-a-S-e-* 'cause to take out'.

Periphrastic expressions do play a role at the level of indirect causative, however. The standard one is "gerund" (-TE form) + *morau* 'receive':

aratte morai nasai 'Better have it washed' (= *araw-a-S-e- nasai*).

Korean has a quite widespread but apparently "lexical" and no longer productive formation with a suffix that has allomorphs -I, -HI, -LI, -KI, -U. The interesting thing is that with transitive bases the result may be sometimes causative, sometimes "passive" (anticausative) – sometimes either. That is, *the causative and anticausative formations overlap or are the same:*

po-/poi- 'see/show *or* be seen', *jap-/japhi-* 'catch/have s.o. catch *or* be caught'.

With intransitive and "descriptive" bases the result is, of course, causative (transitive): *anj-/anjhi-* 'sit/seat', *mal-/malli-* 'be dry/ make dry', *juk-/juki-* 'die/kill'. One is tempted to see a tendency (with transitives) toward a specialization of -I for causative and -HI for anticausative, as in, e.g., *mϕk-/mϕki-/mϕkhi-* 'eat/feed/be eaten', or *ssu-/ssui-/ssuhi-* 'spend/make spend/be spent', but according to Martin and Lee (1969:435-438, 288-89), who presumably have tried,[12] "the shapes and meanings are largely unpredictable." Chang Hei Lee (1955:109-112) indicates that a distinction here, e.g. between *poi-* 'show' and **pohi-* 'be seen', is often carelessly lost through the elision of /*h*/. In any case, -HI does causativize intransitives.

Causatives are supplied periphrastically in Korean where this formation does not operate, and also in substitution for it, e.g., *mϕkKE HAE YO* 'cause to eat'. There is no analogous regular method for supplying an anticausative.

To the northeast, Gilyak follows the familar pattern: it causativizes both V^{in} and V^{tr}, has regular *vs.* "lexical" devices (-GU *vs.* -U, correlated *an*lauts – stop to fricative, or both), and uses the former with the latter to produce second causatives:

kez-/ġez-/ġezgu- 'trickle/strain/make someone strain' (also *kezgu-* 'allow to trickle').

Chukchi and Kamchadal, on the other hand, causativize mainly intransitives, and by complicated "confix" devices that bear little resemblance to the suffixation devices we have been discussing –

except that the Gilyak anlaut-change + suffix is a step in that direction. Kamchadal, like Japanese, also distinguishes otherwise homonymous intransitive and transitive verbs by *conjugation* alone.

To the south in eastern Asia, Chinese has no causative morphology. The distinctions are conveyed contextually, by suppletion, or where necessary by auxiliaries, but principally by the first of these: e.g., *sž̂* = 1. 'die', 2. 'kill'; *kāi* = 1. 'open(tr)', 2. 'open(intr)'. Vietnamese uses the auxiliary (or "sequential construction" [Thompson 1965:331]) *làm* ('make') + V: *Tôi làm dau con mèo* 'I made hurt the cat'. Thai is similar, relying on context or employing the auxiliary *hai* 'give': *vaikum* 'hide'/*hai vaikum* 'conceal'. However, there do exist in Thai nonproductive vestigial *prefixes* (PRA/PA/BAṄ/P-) that causativize a few verbs (and verbalize adjectives):

lug/plug 'wake up/awaken someone', *loṅ/ploṅ* 'go down/bury'.

This brings us back to the Austroasiatic languages, for the Thai prefixes look suspiciously like the productive causative /p/-element prefixes of Cambodian and other Mon-Khmer languages (allomorphs /p/baṅ/pɔṅ/bañ/ban/pɔn/bam-): *ḷeañ/pɔnḷeañ* 'perish/ruin' – said to be in these languages "the only prefix which has quite definite functions" (Gorgoniev 1966:93ff). And with this we are back to the PN- of Khasi and the AB/OB- prefix of the Munda languages.

This /p/ element appears again in some of the more obscure Tibeto-Burman languages (Angami-Mikir PE-, Dimasa PU-, Boro FI-: *thi/pethi* 'die/kill', *ngu/pengu* 'see/cause to see'), where it is connected by Grierson with the verb 'give' (Mikir PĪ), which itself is suffixed (Thado) or prefixed to verbs to form causals in other dialects. (Cf. Thai *hai* 'give' + V.) Other languages (Tipura) suffix other verbs meaning 'give'.

Another common prefix (in Kachin, Thado, Balti, Ladakhi) is SI-/S-/SU-: Lad. *gangches/sgangches* 'be full/fill', written Tibetan *gabpa/sgabpa-* 'hide/conceal'. The Kachen SI- is prefixed to form first causatives and suffixed to form second causatives. A similar element SEI(zei) is suffixed to form the Burmese causative:

pya./pya.zei 'show/have shown'.

Most Tibeto-Burman languages seem to hesitate between (older) prefixing and (newer) suffixing modes of causative formation and employ both. In many the prefix, originally a separate syllable, has first lost its syllabicity, then becomes only a modification of the initial consonant of the root, or even of the tone of the root. Thus, beside the suffix SEI (for *indirect* causation?) Burmese forms transitives (first causatives) by aspirating the initial consonent (*pyet/ hpyet* 'be destroyed/destroy') as do Limbu (E. Nepal: *peemaa/ pheemaa* 'fly/cause to fly') and Gurung (Nepal: *chaba/chhaba* 'eat/ feed'). Lepcha (Sikkim) palatalizes the consonant (*thór/thyór* 'escape/ cause to escape'), while Khambu (Nepal) and Newari harden it (*dae/ tae* 'be/make', *bokko/pokko* 'rise/raise'). In Central Tibetan all that remains is often a high tone (in contrast with the western dialects, Balti and Ladakhi, where, as we have seen, the prefix is still alive). In many verbs, there seems to be no distinction left between tr/intr; suppletion is resorted to in other cases: *che̱* = 'open(tr/intr)'; *thḕè/kap* 'close(intr)/ close(tr)'.

In Indonesian the suffix -KAN could be called a causative of sorts (*merebah/merebahkan* 'fall down/knock over', *memerah/ memerahkan* 'become red/make red') but it has a number of other meanings ('benefactive', 'directive') and is part of an essentially rather different set of distinctions. There is a "passive" made by substituting the prefix DI- for the "active" prefix ME(N); it can also be made from "causatives":

mendatang/medatangkan/didatangkan 'arrive/import/be imported'.

Related languages have affixes with similar functions (Javanese DI-, -AKĒ). Whereas causativization with -KAN, etc., appears confined to intransitive stems (applied to transitive stems the 'directive-benefactive' rather than the causative meaning emerges:

membuat/membuatkan = 'make something/make something for someone',
membatja/membatjakan = 'read something/read something to someone')

some related languages have a definite causative prefix PA-, which makes causatives from transitives as well (Madurese

ṇtabur/paṇtabur 'sow/have someone sow'; Cebuano Visayan *kawus/ pakawus* 'fetch water/have someone fetch water'; *bayad/pabayad* 'pay/have someone pay').

Cebuano also forms transitives from some intransitives by adding the "active" prefix MA- (Indonesian MEN-): *kamatáy/makamatáy* 'die/kill', *kahúlug/makahúlug* 'fall/drop'. Any analog to this PA- in Indonesian has eluded me (unless it is PER- with different functions), and Indonesian ME(N) does not appear to have this function. In the Polynesian languages, especially Samoan and Maori, it is the anti-causative-passive that is developed (through suffixes, however, not prefixes: -INA, -A, -MIA, -IA, -TIA, -KIA, etc.) at the expense of the causative, which is vestigial or absent.

Form II of the Arabic verb (with doubling of the second consonant of the root: *fa“ala*) is sometimes called a causative

(jamad/jammad 'freeze – intr/freeze – tr', *birik/birrik* 'kneel/force to kneel', *fihim/fahham* 'understand/make understand')

but it is as often or oftener an *intensive* (*kasar/kassar* 'break/smash') and "these are by no means the only possibilities" (Mitchell 1962:66). The causative meaning emerges as often from Form IV (*'af'ala*): *jalasa/'ajlasa* 'sit/seat', *sami'a/'asma'a* 'listen/allow to listen', *xaraja/'axraja* 'emerge/take out', *sakata/'askata* 'be quiet/cause to be quiet'.[13] While by no means excluding transitives, Arabic causatives are confined to the ingestive subclass among them. There is also a passive-anticausative-reflexive, made by prefixing TA-, frequently to Form II stems:

'alim/'allim/ta'allim 'know/teach/learn (= 'be caused to know')',
baddal/tabaddal 'change (tr)/change(intr).

Sometimes the undoubled root is not itself in use. There is no second causative.

Georgian has causative *confixes* – A . . . EB for intransitives and A . . . INEB for transitives, generally speaking, including derived transitives:

duġ/AduġEB/AduġINEB 'boil(intr)/boil(tr)/have someone boil', ts'er/Ats'erINEB "write/have someone write'.

A "lexical" confix A . . . EV on a few "ingestive" verbs allows second causatives to be formed from a few (semi)transitives also:

ch'am/Ach'mEV/Ach'mevINEB 'eat/feed/cause to feed'.

In token again of the close relationship we have noted so often between causative and passive (anticausative) in many languages, Georgian has also an *anticausative* confix of very similar shape, namely I . . . EB: Its'erEB 'be written'.

There is also a causative system in full vigor to the south, in Ethiopic Semitic. There are two causative *prefixes*: A- and AS-, applied to intransitive and transitive bases respectively: *fälla/afälla* 'boil(intr)/ boil(tr)', *ayyä/asayyä* 'see/show'. The A- prefix is also used with "ingestives": *ballä/aballä* 'eat/feed', *ṭäṭṭa/aṭäṭṭa* 'drink/give to drink', but the AS- prefix may also be applied, with different results: *asballä-* 'force to eat'. There is also an anticausative or passive prefix TÄ-: *tägäddälä* 'be killed', *täqammätä* 'sit down'. The AS- prefix may be substituted for the A- prefix to produce second causatives, and for the TÄ- prefix to produce first causatives:

läffa/aläffa/asläffa 'be soft/soften/cause to soften',
täqämmätä/asqämmätä 'sit down/seat'.

Presumably there is no second causative from transitive bases already taking the AS- prefix once.

The Cushitic languages have causative *suffixes*. In Southern Agaw, a language probably closest to what may be regarded as the specific substratum of Amharic, there is a suggestion of a four-term causative system:

zur-/zurC-/zurəCC-/zurəCCəCC- 'return(intr)/return(tr)/send back/ make send back'

(Hetzron 1969: 60-69). That is, we seem to have, in Kholodovich's terms *base/lexical causative/morphological causative/second causative* – conceivably analogous to the Emeneau Dravidian model ("simplex/ contactive-causative/mediative of simplex/mediative of causative"). The only problem is, the second causative seems to be built on the morphological rather than on the lexical causative, but there may be a phonological explanation for this. In any case, like the Dravidian systems, it would seem to be incomplete for many verbs. It seems to be the lexical-transitive term (sometimes in -C, sometimes in -S) that is often missing, and the fourth term is rare. This language also possesses productive "passive" (*ku-/kuST* 'kill/be killed') as well as "reciprocal" formants, and the latter can be causativized (*kutŋ-* 'kill each other', *kutəŋC-* 'cause to kill each other). The "passive" is apparently not compatible with causative formations, and may therefore be a true anticausative; on the other hand, it does not produce the typical intransitives characteristic of anticausatives, e.g., *kuST* = 'be killed', not *'die' (which is *kər-*).

From F. R. Palmer's rather thorough analysis of the verb in a language at the opposite (northern) end of the Agau subgroup of Cushitic, the Bilin of Eritrea (1957), it does not appear that the causative element (-IS-, -əD/D-, -S-) can be repeated, resulting in just a two-term system:

qʷal-/qʷalIS- 'see/cause to see', *gáŋ-/gáŋS-* 'run/cause to run'.

However, there are also "passive" (-əST-, -S-) and "reciprocal" (-əŋ-) formants analogous to those of Southern Agaw – except that the reciprocal is *added* to the passive: *qʷal-/qʷaləSTəŋ-*. There is also a reciprocal causative, the reciprocal being added to the causative rather than the reverse as in Southern Agaw (*qʷal-/qʷal-IS-əŋ-* 'see/ cause to see each other'. In passing, the partial overlap of passive and causative (one of the allomorphs of each being -S-) should be noted.

The Somali system appears to contain only one layer of causatives also (in *-I,* sometimes with root vowel and consonant modification):

dilaᶜ-/dilaᶜI- 'tear (intr/tr)', *deg-/dajI-* 'descend/lower', *jab-/jebI-* 'break (intr/tr)', *joog-/jooji-* 'wait/cause to stop', *baĝ-/bajI-* 'be afraid/frighten'.

Another suffix, *-SII* (cf. Bilin *-IS-*, *-S-*), may contrast with this:

ᶜabb-/ᶜabbSII- 'drink/give to drink', *ᶜaddee-/ᶜaddeySII-* 'apply whiteness/cause to apply whiteness', *ᶜayyaar-/ᶜayyaarSII-* 'play/drill soldiers'.

If so, it is not clear just how. There are two suffixes of the anticausative type in Somali, however. According to Warsama and Abraham (1951:339), *-M* is an "intransitive suffix", while *-AN* (pp. 342-47) is a "middle" meaning "for oneself": *fur-/furM-* 'open(tr/intr)'; *dub-/dubAN-* 'roast/roast for oneself'. In most of the examples they give, however, *-M* seems to have a quasi-passive function (*dil-/ dilM-* 'kill/be killed', *abuur-/abuurM-* 'create/be created') and *-AN* an intransitivizing one (*ĝub-/ĝubAN-* 'spill-tr/intr', *gub-/gubAN-* 'burn-tr/ intr', *waal-/waalAN-* 'madden/go mad'. Bell 1953 says that -AN verbs mean 'be in the state of' and cites as an example of this *ḍis-/ ḍisAN-* 'build/be built'. Clearly, glosses are confusing, as is usual in these matters. According to Bell, the 'reflexive' (= 'middle') suffix is

-O/SO: gub-/guBO- 'burn(tr/intr)', *mayḍ-/mayḍO-* 'wash/wash oneself', *bar-/barO-* 'teach/learn'.

This may be only a matter of transcription and segmentation. The Somali causative is occasionally found paired with one or the other of the anticausatives in a situation of double marking:

maḍAN-/maḍI 'become empty/make empty', *dirsAM-/dirI-* 'become warm/make warm'.

According to Warsama and Abraham (p. 343) certain verbs occur only in the 'middle': *deserve, recover, sit down, curdle.* The foregoing account is based mainly on a crude attempt to reconcile Bell 1953 and Warsama and Abraham 1951. With more data, a better analysis would no doubt be possible.

Away to the south, the Bantu languages of eastern and southern Africa also have well-developed systems of causative suffixes (this despite the fact that they are largely prefixing languages), e.g., Swahili (productive) -ESHA(ISHA/SHA) and (unproductive) -(I)ZA,YA: *enda/endESHA* 'go/drive', *fanya/fanyIZA* 'do/cause to do', *pona/ponYA* 'get well/cure'. To these correspond Luganda /-esa, isa, sa, za, ya/, Tswana (Bechuanaland) /-isa, tsa, ya/, etc. Both intransitives and transitives may be causativized, and second causatives are possible – perhaps from unproductive (=lexical) types only: e.g., Tswana *tlala/tlaTSA/tladISA* 'become full/fill/cause to fill'. In Swahili it is not clear whether this results in a regular category, or merely scattered synonymous or lexicalized alternates: *pona/ponYA=ponYESHA, ona/onYA/onYESHA* 'see/warn/show' (Perrott 1957:120-123). There are also anticausative formations – in Swahili, in EKA(IKA) "stative" and in -WA "passive":

vunja/vunjIKA/vunjWA 'break(tr)/break(intr-no agent)/be broken (by an agent)'.

In West African languages, causatives are either not well developed or not well described. There is no mention of them in descriptions of Twi (e.g., Christaller 1875:55); on the contrary, "many verbs are used both transitively and intransitively." Likewise in Yoruba, Mende, or Nuer, but Mlle Homburger (1941) cites a few stray forms from Wolof (Guinea/Senegal) and Fulani (Cameroons) that may or may not be representative of wider systems. References to causative formations in Hausa (e.g., in Kholodovich) seem to err in attributing the "relater particle" DÀ, which properly goes with a following direct object, to the preceding verb (cf. Kraft and Abubaker 1965: 131-32, 181, 360).

Summary and Areal Implications

Any conclusions here are of course tentative, subject to correction or modification on the basis of information on languages not included in the foregoing survey, or better information on languages that were included. Gaps in both respects in the accompanying maps and tables should be plain enough. Nevertheless, it is hoped that the survey has been representative enough to give some ground for making the following statements regarding causative distributions in relevant areas of the Old World.

First, they show no simple correlation with language relationship or with general language "type." Some language families, to be sure, such as the Altaic and Uralic, show a generally strong development of causative morphology. Others, however, including Indo-European, Austroasiatic, Sino-Tibetan, and to some extent Semitic, are split over the question. Similarly, while the distinction between "context-creating" and "context-created" grammars (Gołąb 1968) is appealing, it does not really fit the causative situation. Highly inflected languages, such as Russian or Greek, have no active causative morphology, while predominantly "analytical" languages such as Persian or Hindi have respectable or even large amounts of it. Relatively inflected German has a semi-analytical anticausative; relatively uninflected Swedish has a morphological one. The case of Chinese may appear to fit better, but even Chinese has sublexemic particles, while Thai, which some consider to be more "isolating" than Chinese, accommodates even causative prefixes, as we have seen. Anomalously again, there are *right*-branching languages with causative *suffixes,* such as the Bantu group, and *left*-branching languages, such as Burushaski and Classical Tibetan, with causative *prefixes.*

At the same time, the distribution of causatives is hardly random: it manifests quite definite *areal* correlations. It should be clear from the map that the Indian subcontinent is one of the main centers for the development of causative morphology in the Old World. The others are northern Eurasia, which might be called the area of causatives *par excellence,* and eastern and southern Africa. A weaker center exists in Indonesia, connected with India via the Austroasiatic languages. Europe, China, and West Africa, on the other hand, are areas without causative morphology, except for the intrusive Hungarian and marginal Finnish, and the innovations of Lithuanian-Latvian.

TABLE 7
Causative and Anticausative Morphology: Categories and Domains

Key:

First Causatives	Second Causatives	Anticausatives
$1 = V_i^{in} > V_j^{k\,'}$	$4 = V_i^{in} > V_j^{k\,'} > V_e^{k\,''}$	
$2 = V_i^{tr\frac{1}{2}} > V_j^{k\,'}$	$5 = V_i^{tr\frac{1}{2}} > V_j^{k\,'} > V_e^{k\,''}$	$7 = V_i^{tr} > V_j^{ak}$
$3 = V_i^{tr} > V_j^{k\,'}$	$6 = V_i^{tr} > V_j^{k\,'} > V_e^{k\,''}$	

Probably all languages express the above *semantic* relations. This table merely indicates whether they do so *morphologically*: + = "yes, regularly," – = "almost never," ÷ = "vestigially." Problems in demarcation of *word* vs. *affix*, however, occur in some Sino-Tibetan and Austroasiatic languages as well as in the case of European "reflexives." They are marked (+).

Language	1	2	3	4	5	6	7
Hindi-Urdu	+	+	+	+	+	[+]	+
Panjabi	+	+	+	+	+	[+]	+
Nepali	+	+	+				+
Kashmiri	+	+	+	+	+	–	–
Gujarati	+	+	+	+	+	[+]	+
Marathi	+	+	+	+	+		
Sindhi	+	+	+	+			+
Bengali	+	+	+	–	–	–	–
Oriya	+	+	+	–	–	–	–
Assamese	+	+	+	–	–	–	–
Sinhalese	+	+	+	–	–	–	+
Shina	+	+	+				+
Pashto	+	+	+				?
Balochi	+	+	+				
Persian	+	+	+	–	–	–	–
Armenian	+	+	–	–	–	–	+
Greek	–	–	–	–	–	–	(+)
Albanian	–	–	–	–	–	–	+
Serbo-Croat	.	.	–	–	–	–	(+)
Bulgarian	.	.	–	–	–	–	(+)
Russian	.	.	–	–	–	–	+
Polish	.	.	–	–	–	–	(+)
Czech	.	.	–	–	–	–	(+)
Lithuanian	+	+	+	+			
Latvian	+	+					+
Swedish	.	.	–	–	–	–	+
Norwegian	.	.	–	–	–	–	+

TABLE 7 – *Continued*

Language	1	2	3	4	5	6	7
German	·	·	–	–	–	–	(+)
Dutch	·	·	–	–	–	–	–
English	·	·	–	–	–	–	–
French	–	–	–	–	–	–	(+)
Spanish	–	–	–	–	–	–	(+)
Portuguese	–	–	–	–	–	–	(+)
Italian	–	–	–	–	–	–	(+)
Rumanian	–	–	–	–	–	–	(+)
Arabic	+	+	–	–	–	–	+
Amharic	+	+	+	+		–	+
Georgian	+	+	+	+	+	–	+
Finnish	+	+	+	+	?	?	+
Hungarian	+	+	+	+	?	?	+
Turkish[a]	+	+	+	+	+	+	+
Mongolian[a]	+	+	+	+	?	?	+
Korean	+	+	–	–	–	–	+
Japanese	+	+	+	+	+	–	+
Telugu	+	+	+	+	[+]	–	·
Kannada	+	+	+	+	+	+	
Tamil	+	+	(+)	(+)	(+)	–	–
Malayalam	+	+	+	+	+	+	–
Santali	(+)			–	–	–	+
Sora	+	+		–	–	–	+
Khasi	+	+		–	–	–	
Cambodian	+	+		–	–	–	
Vietnamese	–	–	–	–	–	–	–
Indonesian	+	–	–	–	–	–	+
Javanese	+	–	–	–	–	–	+
Madurese	+	+	+	–	–	–	+
Cebuano	+	+	+	–	–	–	
Tagalog	+	+	+	–	–	–	
Samoan	–	–	–	–	–	–	+
Thai	·			–	–	–	–
Chinese	–	–	–	–	–	–	–
Tibetan(C.)	·	–	–	–	–	–	–
Tibetan(W.)	+			–	–	–	
Newari	+						
Limbu	+						
Lepcha	+						
Burmese	+		(+)				
Kachin	+	–	–	–	–	–	–
Gilyak	+	+	+	+	+		
Chukchi	+		–	–	–	–	

TABLE 7 – *Continued*

Language	1	2	3	4	5	6	7
Swahili	+	+	+	+			+
Luganda	+	+	+	+			+
Tswana	+	+	+	+			+
Hausa	–	–	–	–	–	–	–
Yoruba	–	–	–	–	–	–	–
Mende	–	–	–	–	–	–	–
Twi	–	–	–	–	–	–	–
Southern Agau	+	+	+	+	?	?	(+)

[a]And related Turkic and Mongolic languages.

The several centers are connected to form essentially one loosely continuous zone of causatives, bounded by zones lacking causatives. The Austroasiatic bridge to Indonesia has been mentioned: on the other side, the Indian, East African, and Northern Asian concentrations are mutually connected by Arabic and Persian, which have a less elaborate development of causatives, but nevertheless do have causatives.

Suffixation predominates in the three main centers as the mode of marking, while prefixation and more aberrant phenomena tend to occur at the margins: 1) at the western margins, in Arabic, Georgian, and Ethiopic (not in Cushitic, which is an extension of the East African area of suffixation); 2) at the southeastern margins, in many Indonesian languages (though not Indonesian itself), Austroasiatic languages, and extending through Khasi and Tibeto-Burman as far as Burushaski and Munda into the eastern and northern margins of India itself; 3) at the far northeastern margins, in Paleosiberian languages.

Zones of transition can be identified, not only in terms of aberrant modes of marking, as with the marginal areas of prefixes, infixes, and confixes noted above, but also in terms of elaboration of the causative categories themselves. That is, development of *second* causatives correlates with the cores of the three primary centers and gives way at their margins to one layer of causatives, which also characterizes the secondary "Austric" center and the areas connecting the centers. The Indian subcontinent itself is not uniformly strong on causatives. They are weaker in the east, stronger in the west and south – though weaker again in Tamilnad and Ceylon. The marginal zone of one layer of causatives only thus includes northeast Siberian languages, Korean, western Tibetan and Burmese and related languages, Khasi, Munda languages, Eastern Indo-Aryan (Bengali, Assamese, Oriya), Nepali, modern Tamil, Sinhalese, Indonesian and Philippine languages, Cambodian and other Mon-Khmer languages, Somali and Bilin, Arabic, Kurdish, Armenian, Persian, apparently Pashto, Shina, and Burushaski – neatly forming a membrane around and between the centers of more intense development. (The respective centers would contain: 1) Malayalam, Kannada, Toda, Kota, Telugu, Marathi, Gujarati, Hindi, Punjabi, Kashmiri, Sindhi, Baluchi, and Brahui; 2) Turkic, Mongolic, and Uralic languages, including Finnish and Hungarian: Japanese, Lithuanian, and Georgian; 3) Amharic, certain Cushitic languages, and at least some Bantu languages.)

The only abrupt transition would seem to be on the northwest, between Uralic-Turkic and the Indo-European languages of eastern and northern Europe. This may in part be illusory, however, born of the oversimplifications of mapmaking. We have noted in the foregoing discussion that, on the one hand, Baltic Finnish causatives exhibit a certain "senility," and on the other, that Slavic languages – at any rate, Polish and Russian – do exhibit rather considerable vestigial causative morphology (Gołąb 1968), although not enough to constitute an active "system." Such details could not be included in our general definitional criteria. (More such details might be revealed by a detailed investigation of the Volga Finnic languages.) The presence of active causatives in the Baltic languages (Lithuanian and Latvian) further blurs this boundary.

West of this boundary, however, is the strongly marked European area of *anticausatives.* Although they are not confined to Europe, and pose in the wider context acute problems in their very definition (see chap. 7), it is essentially in Europe that anticausatives, in the narrowest (and perhaps in the end most useful) sense of one-sided negative marking of the intransitive/transitive distinction, prevail. Their function elsewhere, which is generally in the presence of causative systems, is less clear, since that distinction already has a means of being marked. In certain transitional languages, such as Arabic, the two modes of marking may split the task between them, some verbs going one way, some the other.

Within the European anticausative area, the consistency of anticausative marking – in terms of always making the distinction, of making it with a particular device, and of use of this device for this and not other purposes – is strongest in the east (in Russian, Polish, Slovak, Rumanian, Latvian), closest to the boundary with causatives. Thence it diminishes steadily across Europe to disappear in Holland and Britain.

Outside of Europe, anticausative morphology (or phenomena that we have lumped together under that heading) generally occurs within the greater area of causative morphology, but not coextensively with it. It really breaks into two areas, with the break coming precisely in India. One area takes in northern Eurasia, with extensions to the southwest through the Caucasus, Semitic, Cushitic, and Bantu. The other is Indonesian and Austroasiatic. The Indian subcontinent lies between

TABLE 8
CAUSATIVE AND ANTICAUSATIVE MORPHOLOGY: MANNER OF MARKING

( ) = supplementary device

	Causatives	Anticausatives
English	--	--
Dutch	--	--
French	--	reflexive particle
Spanish	--	reflexive particle
Italian	--	reflexive particle
Rumanian	--	reflexive particle
Hungarian	suffix	suffix
German	--	reflexive particle
Czech	--	reflexive particle
Polish	--	reflexive particle
Swedish	--	postinflectional suffix
Russian	--	postinflectional suffix
Lithuanian	suffix	
Latvian	suffix	postinflectional suffix
Finnish	suffix	postinflectional suffix
Turkish, etc.	suffix	suffix
Mongolian, etc.	suffix	suffix
Korean	suffix	suffix
Japanese	suffix + (paradigmatic)	suffix
Gilyak	suffix + initial cons. str.	
Chukchi	confix	
Georgian	confix	confix
Albanian	--	prefix + (paradigmatic)
Greek	--	paradigmatic
Arabic	middle cons. str. + (prefix)	prefix
Amharic	prefix	prefix
Agau	suffix	suffix

TABLE 8 – *Continued*

	Causatives	Anticausatives
Somali	suffix	suffix
Swahili, etc.	suffix	suffix
Armenian	suffix	suffix
Kurdish	suffix	
Persian-Tajik	suffix	(suffix?)
Pashto	suffix	(suffix?)
Baluchi	suffix + vowel str.	
Brahui	suffix	suffix
Burushaski	prefix	
Shina	suffix	suffix
Kashmiri	suffix	
Punjabi	suffix	
Sindhi	suffix	suffix + (final cons. mod.)
Gujarati	suffix	suffix
Hindi	suffix + vowel red.	vowel reduction
Marathi	suffix	
Oriya	suffix	
Bengali	suffix	
Assamese	suffix	
Nepali	suffix	suffix
Sinhalese	suffix + final cons. str.	suffix + vowel change
Malayalam	suffix / final cons. str.	--
Tamil	suffix / final cons. str.	--
Kannada	suffix	--
Telugu	suffix	(suffix?)
Kurukh	suffix	suffix
Sora	prefix/infix	suffix
Santali	(suffix)	suffix
Khasi	prefix	
W. Tibetan	prefix	
Newari	initial cons. str.	
Limbu	initial cons. str.	
Lepcha	initial cons. str.	
Kachin	prefix	
Burmese	suffix / initial cons. str.	
Thai	(prefix)	
Cambodian	prefix	
Indonesian	(suffix)	prefix
Javanese	suffix	prefix
Madurese	prefix	prefix
Cebuano	prefix	
Samoan		suffix

them, with important parts of it – eastern Indo-Aryan, the greater Dravidian languages of the south, probably Marathi – outside any area of anticausative morphology. The phenomena in northwest Indo-Aryan as far as Gujarati, along with Shina, Pashto, Tajik-Persian, and Brahui, may be viewed as an extension of the northern Eurasian zone. Those in the Munda languages, the north and central Dravidian languages (with the traces in Telugu), and Sinhalese may perhaps be connected with the Indonesian zone as outlying fragments.

There are again interesting areal correlations in terms of manner of marking. The center of the northern Eurasian area uses regular stem-suffixation (as does the subcenter of its East African extension). On the margins, however, we have, in the northwest, first the *postinflectional* suffixes of Russian, Finnish, Latvian, and Swedish, then the *semisyntactic reflexive particles* of West Slavic, German, and the Romance languages. On the southwest, Arabic, Amharic, Georgian, and Albanian use *prefixes*: Greek uses *paradigmatic* differences, as do in part Japanese and Kamchadal on the northeast. Then, on the southeast, we have the *reduced-vowel-grade* phenomenon of borderline Hindi that has given occasion for so much discussion earlier in this chapter. The other area, that centering in Indonesia, is prefixing.

4

CONJUNCTIVE PARTICIPLES

Problems of Definition and Delimitation

South Asian languages also typically use a special nonfinite verbal form to subjoin sentences (usually with the same subject) to the left of the main finite verb in a sentence: e.g.,

Hindi *usne uskii ããkhõ mẽ dekhaa* 'He looked into her eyes' + *usne darwaazaa band kar diyaa* 'He closed the door' = *usne uskii ããkhõ mẽ DEKHKAR darwaazaa band kar diyaa* 'He looked into her eyes and closed the door/Looking/having looked into her eyes he closed the door'.

This process is often referred to as one of *conjunction,* as the sentences involved might often well be linked by *and* in a language like English, but grammatically and often semantically it would seem to involve *subordination* in some sense. (A "conjunction" in the sense of a linking "part of speech" in traditional grammar can, of course, be subordinating as well as coordinating, but in contemporary linguistic discussion[1] *conjunction* seems to imply coordinate linking only. That is to say, the sentence(s) represented by the nonfinite verbal form(s) in question are in some sense subordinate to the sentence represented by the finite verb.) It should not be assumed at this stage of linguistic science that the semantic implications of various linking devices used in similar situations by different languages are necessarily identical. South Asian languages generally also possess conjunctive particles or affixes that can be used instead of the nonfinite verbal, and indeed must be used in most cases where the subjects of two sentences are different. The use of the nonfinite verbals in question implies some *closer* semantic relationship between or among the sentences involved than mere juxtaposition would imply: at the very least, as sequential parts of a process or larger activity, or perhaps as cause, manner qualification, or instrument of the activity named by the finite verb.

The special nonfinite verbal forms used to "conjoin" underlying sentences in the manner described are given various names by different writers on South Asian (and other) languages. To take terms used in English:

"Conjunctive Participle" is the term used by Grierson (1903-1928) in the *LSI* with reference to all the languages of India. It is commonly used by writers on Hindi (e.g., Bailey 1933, Greaves 1933, Scholberg 1940, Kellogg 1938, Phillott 1918, Saihgal 1958, Harley 1944, S. N. Sharma, Forbes 1855), and increasingly by writers on other Indian languages (e.g., Kakati 1962 on Assamese).

Writers under the influence of European, especially German, traditions of description (Pořízka 1963, Garusinghe 1962, A. Sharma 1958, Bloch 1934; but also Master, McGregor 1968, Turner 1966) call the forms in question "Absolutives." This is misleading. While there are a few exceptions, mostly involving expressions of time, as a general rule there is nothing "absolute" about the constructions of these verbals, in the usual sense of not being dependent on the subject or other noun of the main sentence to which they are attached. As we have seen, they are not independent of the main sentence generally, but are closely linked up with it, implying the same subject and tense.

"Past Participle" (sometimes qualified as Past Active Participle) is the term favored, with some justification, by writers on Bengali and Nepali (MacLeod 1967, Sutton-Page 1934, Morland-Hughes 1947, Dimock 1964; Hudson 1965, however, uses "Perfect Participle") as well as to some extent by writers on Tamil (Jothimuththu 1963) and Telugu (Krishnamurti 1968). The justification is that in these languages the same form serves as a basis for the perfect tenses (Beng. *kOre* 'having done', *kOrechi* 'I have done', *kOrechilam* 'I had done'; Tam. *ceytu* 'having done', *ceytirukkireen* 'I have done'). Fairbanks and Misra (1966), however, use it also for Hindi where this is not the case (H. *karke* 'having done', *kiyaa hai* '. . have done', *kiyaa thaa* '. . had done'). The base of the perfect tenses they call, not illogically, the "perfect participle" – although this, as we just noted, is what Hudson (1965) calls (in Bengali) the analog of what they call the "past participle"!

"Verbal Participle" is otherwise the term favored by writers on Dravidian (Arden 1937, 1942, Ziegler 1953, McCormack 1966, partly by Krishnamurti 1968) – except that writers on Malayalam (Frohnmeyer 1913, Wickremasinghe and Menon 1927, Chandra Sekhar 1953), as well as Pope (1904), for some reason prefer "Adverbial Participle." The latter term is also used by many writers for analogous forms in Russian and Hungarian.

"Indeclinable Participle" is used by Monier-Williams (1899) and partly by Macdonell (1927) in reference to Sanskrit.

"Gerund" is, however, the term employed by Whitney (1885) and Lanman (1884-89), Perry (1885/1936) and generally Macdonell (1927), even by Gonda (English version 1966), as well as by Bender (1967) for Hindi, Beschi (1843) for Tamil, and Geiger (1938) for Sinhalese. It is no doubt the most common term for analogous or partly analogous forms in languages outside of India ("conjunctive participle" seems never to be used), e.g., in Turkic languages and Mongolian (cf. Lewis 1953, 1967, Sjöberg 1963, Whynant 1926), in Slavic languages (cf. de Bray 1951, Unbegaun 1957), in Persian (cf. Boyle 1966), in Japanese (cf. Miller 1967), in Tibetan (cf. Jäschke 1954), and in Romance languages (cf. Agard 1944, Nandriş 1945). However convenient, the term "gerund" is certainly confusing in that it properly refers to a verbal *noun* – and neither the Sanskrit forms, those of modern Indian languages, or those of the various extra-Indian languages mentioned above (except Persian) can be used as nouns (or for the most part, even as adjectives). As Lewis points out (1967:174), the usage in question seems to be drawn from a parallelism with certain uses of the Latin gerund in the *ablative case* – i.e., adverbially. Although the parallelism is not really with the most typical (i.e., conjunctive) function of these forms, especially in Eastern languages, in the Romance field this is offset by the obvious etymological relationship of, e.g., Port. *fazendo,* Sp. *haciendo,* etc., to the Latin gerund-in-the-ablative, *faciendō*. At the same time, grammarians of English (cf. Zandvoort 1966, Ganshina and Vasilevskaya 1945) take great pains to distinguish the "gerund" in -ING from the "present participle" in -ING, ascribing to the former a purely nominal function and to the latter those adverbial functions characteristic of the "gerunds" under discussion here. The term "gerund" is also sometimes used to indicate a verbal noun rather than an adverbial participle in languages that have both, e.g., by Anderson (1920) in Bengali (for the verbal noun in *-iba*) and Vaccari (1954) in Japanese (for the locution *Pres + koto: iru koto* 'being'). Similarly Grierson (1927), generally.

Similar confusion prevails regarding the related term "Gerundive." Originally applied to a (future passive) verbal *adjective* (in Latin), it has come to mean in French grammar the verbal adverb (*en faisant*) *rather than* the verbal adjective (= "present participle": *faisant(e/s)*) – both having present active value. Presumably following this French usage, Lazard (1957) uses the term *gérondif* to distinguish the conjunctive (and active) function of the Persian *past* participle in -È from its adjectival (and passive) function, and Leslau (1968) the term *gerundive* for the conjunctive participle of Amharic. (Elwell-Sutton 1941, on the other hand, reserves the term for the Persian "participle of obligation" in -ANI – a future passive *adjective* close to the Latin prototype.) As a final irony, it may be noted that, in terms of the formal distinctions insisted upon by the French grammarians themselves, it is the French *participe présent* (that is, the form without *en*) *rather than* the *gérondif* with *en* that actually corresponds to the function of these "gérondifs" in Persian, Amharic, and other languages: *Voyant la porte ouverte, je suis entré*, etc.

Finally, and not surprisingly in view of the above-detailed confusion, there is no dearth of ad hoc "functional" terminology, especially from the quarter of the Bloomfieldian linguists. Frequently the construction is designated merely by the marker involved, e.g., "the -KAR construction," "the -TE construction." Lisker (1963) simply calls it (in Telugu) the "Past Nonfinite." The term "Converb" seems to be in vogue with the Indiana school of Altaic description, but Alo Raun (1969) and Hangin (1968) employ it in different senses, the former to designate the whole verbal form, the latter to denote the ending only ("perfective converb"). Paresh Chandra Deva Sarma (1962), in his little bazaar handbook on Assamese, comes up with the original and not inappropriate term "Incomplete Verb."

In any case, it is once again clear that, as we go about our stated business of tracking down the geographic distribution of this phenomenon, we cannot rely on names, but must examine functions. The feature in question goes by many names, some of unclear signification or other possible significations, or it may not be named at all. A language may have "gerunds," but in a nominal sense only, or "past participles," but without the capacity to function actively as conjoiners of sentences. "Adverbial participles" may be just that again without the capacity to represent a succession of events. "Conjunctive participle" is perhaps the least ambiguous term – granted that "conjunctive participles" may shade off into other functions for which the term is not quite appropriate.

The several terms that have been used for *Indian* languages might be held to suggest collectively at least the following characteristics:

a. ("verbal," "adverbial" =) inability to function as an adjective.

b. ("past" =) in conjoining events in sequence, implication of time prior to that of the finite verb. In some contexts, to be sure, where the function has become one of *characterization* of the action of the finite verb, this does not apply, the time implication then being one of simultaneity.

c. ("conjunctive" =) at least one main function the conjoining of underlying sentences.

d. ("participle," "nonfinite," "incomplete verb" =) lack of such features of the finite verb as personal endings – attribution of subject and also absolute tense deriving from the finite verb on which it is dependent.[2]

e. ("indeclinable" =) lack of agreement with any NP in the sentence.

f. ("gerund" =) correspondence to at least some functions of the English -ING form – although, unfortunately, to certain of its present participial functions rather than to its gerundial functions, if we accept, e.g., Zandvoort's demarcation of the two.

g. ("absolutive" =) not much can be said for this term, unless it merely means "indeclinable," or perhaps "separated from the rest of the sentence by a clear break." It *should* mean "not dependent on the subject of the finite verb," but it clearly does not mean that.

h. ("gerundive" =) not much can be said for this term.

The different terms in some cases, however, can denote real differences among the languages to which they are applied. Thus the verbal used for conjunctive purposes in Bengali and Tamil, but not in Hindi and Assamese, is also the past active participle used in forming compound perfect tenses. In Dravidian languages, but not in Bengali, it is also overtly *marked* as past, not merely given past implication. (It is, of course, questionable whether the terminology as applied succeeds in bringing out these differences, but the possibility of using it to do so is there.) Let us return to these particular points later. The point is, there are some real, albeit minor, differences among Indian languages in these matters.

The question therefore is, how far do these forms have to be alike in order to merit discussion together? There are some differences even between Hindi and Bengali. When we come to look at extra-Indian languages, we shall find that nonfinite verbal forms of similar conjunctive function sometimes lack one or more of the attributes listed above for Indian languages. They may be able to function as adjectives or nouns (e.g., in Persian). They may agree with some NP in the sentence in gender, number, and even case (e.g., in Hellenistic Greek). They may even be marked for person, thus obviating any requirement that the subjects of the two sentences be the same (e.g., in Amharic). Are such forms comparable?

I hold that they are, at certain levels. At that level of abstraction, all the languages concerned may be said to contrast collectively with languages, of which there are many, that do not have nonfinite verbals that function in this way. The solution would seem to be to avoid a definition of the subject of our investigation that might arbitrarily exclude relevant phenomena and attempt rather to establish a hierarchy of successively narrowing criteria.

It might be asked, why not attempt to survey the distribution of nonfinite verbals in general? Greenberg, for example, has remarked that the use of "participles" or nonfinite verbal forms (i.e., not only conjunctive and adverbial, but also adjectival, conditional, adversative, etc.) instead of subordinate clauses appears to be a characteristic of SOV languages (1966:83). Such an investigation would no doubt be interesting, but it poses problems, particularly in the analysis and taxonomy of forms, that are quite beyond the present writer's capacity at the moment. (Playing such a game as, for example, "Who has the most – the greatest variety of – nonfinites?" involves decisions as to what is a form in its own right and what is merely a subvariety of another form, or what is a nonfinite verb form as against a noun with a case-ending, which I am afraid would be as arbitrary as they would be ill-informed.) It might well be claimed, however, that the conjunctive participle is really the most interesting of these from an Indian-areal point of view: it represents a phenomenon at once more limited and yet pan-Indian; participles used, e.g., adjectivally, on the other hand, are a rather widespread phenomenon, and *uniquely* adjectival participles are confined in India to the Dravidian languages.

In opting to consider conjunctive participles alone, we come up against a special problem, however. Often the Indian conjunctive or verbal *past*-active participles are equivalent to *present* adverbial participles in languages that have both present and past adverbial participles (e.g., Russian), and to present participles used adverbially in languages that use both present and perfect participles (or "gerunds"?) adverbially (e.g., English, French, Spanish *doing, faisant, haciendo* vs. *having done, ayant fait, habiendo hecho*). This is partly the fault of the Indian "past" participles, as they develop manner-adverbial functions with "simultaneous" time-implications, and partly the fault of the latter languages, as they loosely use their present participles ("incorrectly," we are sometimes told e.g., Semeonoff 1962:217) in sequential situations where a past or a perfect participle is called for according to some rather tedious canon of logic. I am not about to attempt to sort out "adverbial" from "sequential" usages in Indian languages (in a sense they are all "adverbial," so it would be a matter of "manner" *vs.* "time" adverbial, except that there are a number of other possibilities), nor to oppose "logic" to usage in Western languages. I am forced to include in this study the "present" participles – adverbial in essence or merely used adverbially – of other languages that are equivalent in function to Indian conjunctive participles in their central function, as well as to the manner-adverbial functions of those participles, which we do not wish to exclude.

In a way this opens a Pandora's box. The present participles in question typically have a number of other functions besides the ones immediately equivalent to Indian conjunctive participles. Some Indian languages also have present participles, some of whose functions correspond to some of these other functions of extra-Indian present participles. Some of these "other functions" are adjectival, some adverbial, some are of an unclear status between the two – unclear in that languages as well as grammarians disagree as to their exact status: grammarians, even of the same language, perhaps because different analytical criteria yield conflicting results; and languages, in that they treat the same "function" differently.

When adjectival *vs.* adverbial functions of nonfinite verbals are not uniquely identifiable through surface form, it becomes necessary to sort them out on some other basis. With past participles this does not present much of a problem. Such cases are fewer to begin with (Persian being our main example), and fewer functions (positions in the sentence) seem to be involved. They essentially amount to (a) embedding in the NP (equivalent to a relative clause, and best derived by reduction of the latter), and (b) embedding as a sentence adverb (or possibly in the VP). Transitive verbs ordinarily have a passive sense as adjectives, but retain an active sense as verbal adverbs. (They also retain an active sense in a third function that is not under discussion here, although it may be said to be closely allied to function [b], namely, as a component of the finite verb phrase.)

Present participles, on the other hand, more often have the same or confusingly similar forms as adjectives and as adverbs (for example, in Hindi, in Greek, in English, and, I might add, in spite of the grammarians, in French) and occur in varied and complicated sentence environments. Some of these, such as the attributive adjectival slot ("the laughing boy"), offer no difficulty, as a rule. Others, such as the one (called "free adjunct" by Zandvoort) equivalent in function to the Indian conjunctive participles perhaps should not be controversial either, but nevertheless they seem to be. The verbals in, e.g., *Coming into the room . . .* or *Venant dans la chambre . . .*, are called "present participles" (i.e., *rather than* "gerunds" or *gérondifs* – therefore, they are presumably "adjectives") by Zandvoort (1966:35-36) and the French grammarians respectively (e.g., Chevalier 1964:374-76)[3]. Yet the former would seem to be derivable by reduction from **On coming into the room* (cf. *on arrival*), hence plausibly a noun (gerund in its original sense), and the latter would seem to differ from the "gérondif" *en venant* only in implied time relation to the main verb (priority *vs.* simultaneity),[4] not in sentence function.

From there on, present participles get worse. Even manner-adjuncts to the verb phrase turn out to be not quite as simple as they seem. For instance, certain verbs of motion, such as *come*, may be understood as "quasi-copulas" in certain contexts – e.g., *He came running*, and the participle therefore as predicative-adjectival. Introduction of a pause, or the possibility of a pause, changes the whole picture: *He came, running.* Certain languages (e.g., Swedish), which are generally averse to the use of the present participle "adverbially," permit it in the former case (and nowhere else). The problem in English, as Ganshina and Vasilevskaya (1945:125) point out, is that the participle

> . . . often remains attached to both verb and noun. Therefore in such sentences as *He came in laughing loudly, laughing* may be considered as an adverbial modifier of manner to the predicate *came in* and at the same time as a predicative to the subject *he*. . . . In English there being only one form . . . the question of its syntactic function is often complicated and ambiguous.[5]

The problem is by no means confined to English. In older Greek also, the participle is often "attached to both verb and noun," moreover perforce agreeing with the latter. Goetchius (1965:136) momentarily raises our hopes by stating that "circumstantial" (= adverbial) participles *lack the article,* but dashes them again in the next line, observing that "some anarthrous participles may, however, be understood as attributive. . . ." In Hindi and Urdu the ambiguity (or multiplicity) of function is reflected in a hesitancy between adjectival and adverbial forms in some of these contexts:

yah kahtaa huaa bandar peṛ ke uupar caṛh gayaa 'Saying this, the monkey climbed up the tree' *vs. yah socte hue usne zor se laat maarii* 'Thinking this, he kicked hard'.

(Here as elsewhere in Hindi-Urdu the question is further muddied by the fact that the so-called adverbial present participle, ending in *-te(hue),* is identical in form with the oblique case of the masculine adjectival present participle, which might be held to be called for on other grounds. In the second example above, one could perhaps argue that *socte hue* is in the oblique form because it refers to the subject pronoun in the agentive case, *usne.*) Further ambiguity is afforded by the fact that the masculine *plural* form of the adjectival participle is also *-te (hue).* In other words only sentences with feminine or nonoblique masculine singular subjects can be truly diagnostic. The hesitancy remains, although grammarians with a prescriptive bias sometimes seek to rule it out of order – generally in favor of the adverbial form. Further selectional restrictions may operate. It is significant that in Gujarati the present participle remains fully concordant in all these functions (Cardona 1965:136).

One of the knottiest problems involves predicative adjuncts (of the type exemplified by *He saw Mary coming down the stairs*). Transformational grammar, which perhaps could be of some help here, has, to my very limited knowledge, so far probed this area very little. We may agree that such sentences go back to an underlying **He saw Mary* + **Mary was coming down the stairs* (ignoring for the moment a possible ambiguity involving an underlying **He was coming down the stairs* – which is usually avoided in other languages). But what has the latter sentence actually *become* in the final sentence, and how did it get there? Such constructions can often plausibly be viewed as reductions *either* of a relative clause (**who was coming down the stairs,* hence "adjectival") *or* of an adverbial clause (**as she was coming down the stairs,* hence "adverbial"). A possible source of help in such matters, namely the analogy of languages with unambiguously marked forms, is similarly rendered equivocal by the fact that such languages disagree in their treatment of this function. It might be worth a slight digression to illustrate this point more graphically. Let us take three sentences involving such adjuncts (from the Bible, a convenient source for such games) and look at their equivalents:

1) "And he cometh, and findeth them *sleeping* . . . [Mark 14:37]."
2) "And then shall they see the Son of man *coming* in the clouds . . . [Mark 13:26]."
3) "And one of the scribes came, and having heard them *reasoning* together . . . [Mark 12:28]."

These are perhaps not too well chosen: the third example lends itself to rendering as a lexical noun ("their discussion" or the like) and this is in fact the option taken in the new Hindi, new Bengali, Gujarati, Marathi, Persian, Turkish, Russian, and Hungarian versions. The participle is kept in the Revised Version, however ("heard them *disputing* with one another"), and is found in the Greek original:

1) "Kai erchetai kai euriskei autous *katheudontas*. . . ."
2) "Kai tote opsontai ton hyion tou anthrōpou *erchomenon* en nephelais. . . ."
3) "Kai proselthōn heis tōn grammateōn, akousas autōn *syzētountōn*. . . ."

Since all three of the above participles lack the article in Greek, one might be tempted to pronounce them all "adverbial" forthwith, but remember, "*some* anarthrous participles may . . . be understood as attributive."

Russian, which has a clear demarcation between adjectival and adverbial participles in form, clearly understands them that way, that is to say, as adjectival: . . . *i nakhodit ikh spi͡ashchimi;* . . . *uvidi͡at Syna Chelovecheskogo, gri͡adushchego na oblakakh.* Other languages with adjectival forms here include Gujarati (*teone ũũghtaa joiine; diikraane . . . vaadaḷããmãã aavto joshe*). In the first example, French and Italian employ past verbal adjectives (= "asleep": *endormis, addormentati*), and German and Swedish employ their essentially adjectival present participles (*fand sie schlafend, fann dem sovande*).

On the other hand, a number of other languages understand the contexts as adverbial: Hungarian uses its adverbial participles in *-va* (*aluva* 'sleeping'), Arabic uses *masdars* with the adverbial-accusative ending (*niyaaman, aatiyan*), Persian and Turkish adverbial phrases (*dar khvaab* 'in sleep', *uykuda* 'in sleep'), and certain of the Romance languages employ their present gerunds, which are essentially adverbial or in any event cannot otherwise be used adjectivally, e.g., Spanish *durmiendo* in the first case. Rumanian, which has a verbal adjective in *-tor, -toare,* etc., uses the gerund in all three cases: *dormind, venind, vorbind.*

Hindi fluctuates between adverbial and adjectival forms, adverbial (with the reservations noted above) in the older version (so also in Urdu): *unhẽ sote paakar . . . ; . . . putr-ko . . . aate dekhẽge; . . . unhẽ vivaad karte sunaa;* some adjectival forms in a newer version: . . . *putr-ko . . . aataa huaa dekhẽge.* French has the form of doubtful status *venant* in the second example, but this is probably to be understood as adverbial, parallel to cognate forms in other Romance languages. The diagnostic inflection of the participle, i.e., *venants,* no longer occurs in modern French (Chevalier 1964:376n.), but it is doubtful that it would be used in this context even in older French, thus marking it as adverbial.

This by no means exhausts the possibilities. The most common West European equivalent is the infinitive: in example 2, Ger. *kommen,* Ital. *venire,* Hung. *eljönni*; in example 3, Span. *disputar,* Fr. *discuter.* Similarly in other examples, e.g., Mark 6:49:

> ". . . they saw him walking on the sea . . ." = Fr. . . . *ils le virent marcher sur la mer,* Ital. . . . *avendolo veduto camminar sul mare. . . .*

Nominal expressions (i.e., rather than the available participles) of a different kind are also used regularly by the Dravidian languages and Japanese:

Malayalam:	. . . avar uṟaṅṅunnatu. . . .
	. . . putran . . . varunnatu. . . .
	. . . avar tammil takkukkunnatu. . . .
Telugu:	. . . vaaru nidrinc̄uc̄unḍuṭa. . . .
	. . . kumaaruḍu . . . vac̄c̄uṭa. . . .
	. . . vaaru tarkinc̄uṭa. . . .
Kannada:	. . . avaru niddemaaḍuvadannu. . . .
	. . . kumaaranu . . . baruvadannu. . . .
	(example 3 = lexical noun: avara tarkavannu)
Tamil:	. . . avarkaḷ nittiṟaipaṇṇuukiṟatai. . . .
	. . . kumaaran . . . varukiṟatai. . . .
	. . . avarkaḷ tarkkampaṇṇukiṟatai. . . .

Japanese: . . . nemutte ita no de. . . .
. . . ko ga (kumo ni) notte kuru no o. . . .
. . . karera ga tagai ni ronji atte iru no o. . . .

For the most part these are really nominal*ized* present participles, which themselves serve as the head of the object-phrase, with the noun or pronoun as a kind of adjunct (not, however, put into the genitive case), rather than the other way around as in most of the constructions considered above. In Tamil, Kannada, and Japanese this verbal noun has the accusative marker. In the Turkish construction, the genitive of the subject of the verbal noun is actually used:

. . . İnsanoğlu*nun* . . . bulutlarda geldiği*ni* göreceklerdir (= "the son-of-man'*s* . . . in-the-clouds *his*-coming-acc. they-will-see")

This suggests a third hypothesis for the intermediate stage in the derivation of the first example sentence: what he saw was not *Mary,* but **Mary-coming,* or **Mary's coming, coming* being taken here as a noun. It may be less appropriate in the English case than in the Japanese, Dravidian, and Turkish cases, however, and is clearly impossible in some of the other languages, where the participle cannot function as – or be made into – a noun.

There is a fourth possibility: use of a finite predication, or one reduced in some way but still finite rather than participial or nominal. This is found in Modern Greek in all three cases: . . . *ke tus vriski na kimunde; . . . ton yon tu anthropu na erchete . . . ; . . . tus akuse na sizitun. . . .* It is also found in Arabic and German for example 3 (*wa-samiᶜahum yataḥaawaruuna; ihnen zugehört hatte, wie sie sich mit einander befragten*), in Persian and Spanish for example 2 (*binand ke . . . bar abr-haa mi-aayad; verán . . . que vendrá en las nubes*), and in Bengali and Marathi for example 1 (*dekhilen, tãhara ghumaiya achen; paahto tõ te ǰhopĩigele aahet*). This avoidance of the predicative adjunct may be dictated by structure, or by stylistics, or by something between the two: sometimes things are impossible; other times things are claimed to be possible but are somehow "never used." This problem will be taken up in the following section.

Thus we see that there are (at least) four different modes of expression that these "predicative adjuncts" may assume: (1) the adjectival, (2) the adverbial, (3) the nominal, (4) the finite verbal in a subordinated or merely juxtaposed clause. (No. 3, of course, is no longer an "adjunct.") These modes of expression may perhaps exemplify different phases of transformational development. (It should also be noted that seemingly analogous sentences, and even the same sentence at different times, are often treated differently by the *same* language.) A more detailed study, involving many more examples compared in at least the languages mentioned here plus some others, and employing transformational theory, would doubtless throw more light on sentence combination in what seems to be an area of considerable general theoretical interest. That is not a part of our purpose here. It is sufficient for the time being to know that this is an uncertain area, the value of which for typology, especially areal typology, is unclear until we can better define what is involved. The differences exhibited among languages here form no clear areal pattern (although perhaps fragments of one may be discerned in the West European use of the infinitive). It impinges on the focus of this study only marginally in that Indian conjunctive participles are never used in such constructions, but their present participle or gerund equivalents in Western languages sometimes are. The focus of this chapter is the use of participles as quasiconjunctives, or, it might be said, as free adjuncts pertaining either to the *subject* of a sentence, or marginally, to nothing (absolute constructions). Predicative adjuncts pertain rather to the *object* of a sentence, and this is somehow far more troublesome.

In addition to the use of the participle + auxiliary as a component of perfect or continuous finite tense formations (Eng. *I am speaking,* Sp. *estoy hablando,* Tel. *matlaaḍutunnaanu,* Jap. *itte imasu;* Beng. *bọlechi,* Pers. *gofte-am,* Tam. *collirukkireen,* etc.), also specifically excluded from the subject matter of this chapter – although it is in fact closely related to it – is the use – typical of India – of these participles with another set of auxiliaries sometimes mislabeled *"intensifiers,"* and usually including *give, take, go,* etc. These will form the subject of chapter 5.

Hierarchical Survey of Conjunctive Participial Devices in Languages

Let us now turn to a classification of languages, or at least of a sampling of those languages relevant to our areal focus, in terms of the participial equipment they possess for conjunctive purposes, starting with the broadest and most inclusive definition of such equipment. We could perhaps still follow our usual practice of first establishing the characteristic *Indian* pattern (combination of criteria) and then working our way outward through successive sheddings of criteria, but let us try it the other way for a change, establishing the broadest area first and seeing if and on what basis an "Indian" area emerges within it.

As always, the data collection rests on the assumption that such an important feature will at least find *mention* (and recognizably) in grammars of a language if it exists.[6]

The first discrimination is between languages that have conjunctive participial equipment and those that do not. There are many languages that do not possess such devices, relying instead on subordinate clauses introduced by conjunctive particles (conjunctions), or even on the loose stringing together of independent clauses (parataxis). Some languages do have such devices, but prefer not to employ them very often: this problem is taken up in the following section. What, in the most general sense, are these devices? Essentially, nonfinite verbal forms through the substitution of which for finite forms one sentence is attached to and made dependent on another *as a "free adjunct" or general adverbial element.* The last part is important. One sentence is attached to another *sentence* not, for example, to an NP within that sentence. Excluded here are more specialized elements such as conditionals. (It may be guessed, however, that nonfinite elements of more specific function will not occur in a language unless the more generalized nonfinites under discussion also occur.) Typical functions of these verbals must be equivalent, more or less, merely to *and,* to sentence introducers implying sequence such as *then, when, after,* or merely to sentences in sequence.

We should probably add the qualification *morphologically* (positively) *marked* to the definition "nonfinite verbal forms," to exclude such phenomena as the possibility of occurrence of any Santali verb form in quasiparticipial function merely by dropping the "finitizer" -A (i.e., with all indications of tense, mood, subject, object, etc., intact), or the occurrence of Chinese verbs with the "change-of-status" particle *-le* with "nonfinal" intonation:

woo chy-wanle nii chy '(After) I eat, you eat'

(Chao 1968:120). As usual in Chinese, the syntactic relations here are only implied by position (+ intonation), not overtly marked. It must be admitted, however, that the line between this and the coincidence in form of a number of conjunctive participles in Malayalam with the finite past (*pooyi* = 'went' or 'having gone', depending on position and intonation) – and the *near*-coincidence of the others (a slight change of vowel quality being the only difference) – is rather tenuous. The

Malayalam problem is unique in India, however, and it is significant that the Malayalam conjunctive participle is frequently "reinforced" by the suffix (originally auxiliary verb) *-iṭṭu.*

With these qualifications, then, it may be said that nonfinite verbals with conjunctive functions are present in English, Romance languages, Slavic languages, Latvian, Greek, Finno-Ugric, Altaic languages, Persian, Indo-Aryan, Dravidian, Japanese, Korean, Tibeto-Burman, Munda languages, and Amharic, and are lacking in Arabic, Hausa, Swahili, Georgian, Chinese, Thai, Vietnamese, and Indonesian.

They are also lacking for practical purposes in Germanic languages outside of English, with one exception. German *-end*, Swedish *-ande*, Norwegian *-ende*, etc., are essentially adjectives and may be pressed into service as sentence-adverbs only with difficulty and a certain amount of artificiality. English "abbreviated sentences" involving *-ing*, we are told, have to be rendered in Swedish by two full clauses:

Being a member of the government, . . . = Eftersom han är medlem av regeringen, . . . ; Having walked the whole way, . . . = Efter att ha gått hela vägen . . . (Beite 1966:116).

The elaborate participial syntax of German is entirely a property of the NP, involving past and present *adjectival* participles (*die an früherer Stelle kurz erwähnten und hier eingehender zu besprechenden ausserordentlich wichtigen Entdeckungen*) (Bergethon 1950:85).

MAP 4. Conjunctive Participles ("Gerunds")

Key:

● ● ● ● 'Past' Gerunds dominant

○ ○ ○ ○ 'Present' Gerunds dominant

○● ○● ○● 'Past' and 'Present' gerunds both important

\+ + + + Gerunds (usually 'Present') exist but unimportant syntactically

– – – – no true gerund forms or usages

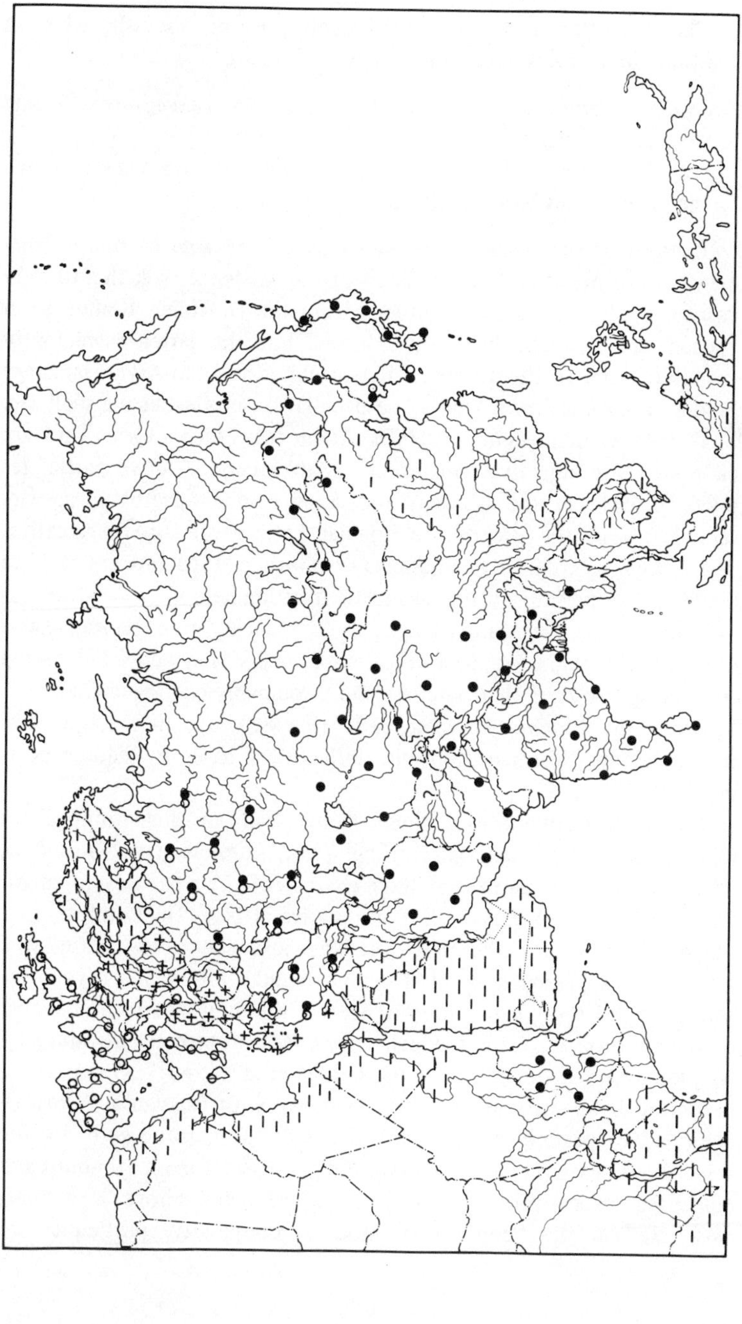

The exception turns out, significantly, to be Yiddish, where a "gerund" in *-endik* is in common use:

Zeyendik az kayner iz nito in der heym, bin ikh avekgegangen 'Seeing that nobody was home, I left':
Geyendik oyf der gas, hob ikh getrofn Moyshen 'As I was walking down the street, I met Moyshe' (Weinreich 1965:251).

In the materials available to me, I have been able to find neither mention nor evidence (i.e., in texts) of the existence of such a form in Pashto. It also seems to be missing from the Dravidian Brahui. Both Persian and Balochi have such forms, but the latter suspiciously resembles one of the forms in the neighboring Indo-Aryan language Sindhi, while the former has some peculiar properties, as we shall see.

Despite its richness in participles, Arabic lacks such a form. They are all nouns and adjectives. In literary Arabic, certain active participles may be used in the accusative case as manner-adverbs in a way reminiscent of the use of the original Latin gerund in the ablative. These occur as predicative adjuncts (see above, p. 116), but not as "free adjuncts" to the subject, the diagnostic function here.

Although all the Munda languages have such forms (Santali *-kate,* Mundari *-chi,* Juang *-ja,* Sora *-le*), their diversity is evidence (according to Pinnow 1960) of their lateness and presumably borrowed character. Speaking of Mundari, Grierson (1927IV.1:86) says that conjunctive participles are "formed from the inflectional bases by adding post-positions."

In Tibeto-Burman also, these forms seem in their multiplicity (Tibetan *-te, -cing, -nsa, -la;* Gurung *-iibirii;* Burmese *-ywe', -pi, hlyin, -tho,* etc.) and certain lack of fixed character to be a late development. St. John (n.d.:119) speaks of "continuative affixes" (in Burmese) that "take the place of the participle and join clause to clause in a sentence." Yet, speaking of Tibetan, Jäschke (1954:55) says these forms are "of the greatest importance . . . the only substitute for most of the subordinate clauses which we are accustomed to introduce by conjunctions." Maun Maun Nyun, Orlova et al. (1963:72-73) have no hesitation in identifying the Burmese forms with Russian adverbial (= conjunctive) participles. (In his account of the Gurung verb, by the way, Glover uses the terms *gerund* and *gerundive* for verbal nouns and adjectives respectively; the form in *-iibirii* listed above is a "past participle" in the "conditional mode.") Conjunctive participles are affirmed by Mainwaring (1876:49) for Lepcha and in the LSI (3.3:30, 134 etc.) for Manipuri, Lushai, and other languages.

There is in Swahili a form with the marker *-ka-* that indicates an action *subsequent to* (rather than prior to) another action and (naturally) follows the main verb. It would be tempting to call this the direct opposite of the Indian conjunctive participle, its mirror image as it were – like everything else in Swahili. Unfortunately, this seems to be a finite verb form, a "tense," like any other, complete with subject-prefixes:

> *Ni*likwenda sokoni *ni*KArudi 'I went to the market and came back'
> *Tu*likwenda mjini *tu*KAmwona Ali 'We went to the village and saw Ali'

Its only peculiarity is in its meaning, and perhaps its syntax – although it is paralleled, interestingly enough, by another "tense" in *-ki-* which indicates simultaneous action: *Nilimwona akilia* 'I saw him crying' (Perrott:1957).

Although we did not posit absence of any mark of subject-concord as a necessary characteristic of these participles in the most general sense, it is in fact characteristic of most of them. Exceptions to this rule accordingly constitute a special subgroup, which includes the participles of Amharic, Czech, and older Greek as well as past participles in Spanish and Italian, and, if I am not mistaken, certain forms in Finnish (*syötyämme* 'when we had eaten', *syötyään* 'when he had eaten', etc.). It may or may not include the present participles of Indo-Aryan languages (that is, of the Western Indo-Aryan languages – Hindi, Panjabi, Marathi, Gujarati, etc. – concord not being a possibility in the eastern group consisting of Bengali, Assamese, and Oriya). When these exhibit concord, their function is ordinarily either clearly nonadverbial or a matter of controversy. But as we have seen, they sometimes (aberrantly?) exhibit concord even in a type of adverbial adjunct similar to those at the center of our discussion:

yah kahtaa huaa bandar peṛ ke uupar caṛh gayaa 'Saying this, the monkey climbed up the tree'.

The concord exhibited may be of different sorts: gender-number-case in Greek and perhaps in Indo-Aryan, gender-number in Czech, Italian, and Spanish, person in Amharic and Finnish.

Presence of gender-number concord does not make a participle necessarily *adjectival.* All participles, as verbs, must refer to some subject, overt or implied. Marking of this reference, through concord of some sort, does not affect the status of the participle and should not be confused with *modification.* The participle may still be predicative rather than attributive, and if the predication is not a finite one, it becomes in a sense adverbial. In practice, agreeing participles functioning predicatively to form adverbial adjuncts are set off from attributive participles by some additional mark, however. In Greek, as we have seen, it was by the absence of the article. In Romance, there is the abnormal order – participle first:

It. *Fatte le visite,* . . . 'Having made the calls (lit. 'the calls having been made');

Sp. *Y tomados los cinco panes* . . . 'And having taken the five loaves (lit. 'and being taken the five loaves'). . . .'

Or alternatively, especially with intransitive verbs, a pause:

Or, i farisei, avvicinatisi, gli domandavano, per tentarlo . . . 'Then the Pharisees, having drawn near, asked him, in order to tempt him. . . .'

Another general characteristic of these participles unmentioned in our initial definition is *dependence on the same subject as the finite verb.* There are exceptions to this rule in probably all the languages concerned. Some are not really exceptions, but involve difference in surface subject only, while the deep subject is the same (see chapter 5 on the dative construction). There remains a residue of truly "absolute" or unrelated-participle constructions, however, which cannot be explained away in this manner. For the most part, they consist of expressions of time and the weather, e.g., in English, *It having rained* . . . , *Night having fallen* . . . , etc.

It might be wondered whether the presence of subject-concord might lead to greater flexibility in this regard. To a limited extent this is the case: there certainly seem to be more absolute constructions in this sense in Spanish and especially in Italian than in English, for example, and the same seems to be true to an even greater degree of Amharic, where the person-marking makes possible nonidentity of pronoun as well as of noun subjects. I am not aware of any special exploitation of the possibilities in Czech. (In Greek, such constructions were thrown into a special case, the genitive.) Nevertheless, it seems to be true of these languages also that identity of subject predominates, and that a good part even of the remainder is covered by identity of "deep" subject. Cf. . . . *presi i sette pani, rendendo grazie, li spezzò e li diede ai suoi discepoli* . . . (surface subjects: *pani* ≠ *Egli*). This possibility appears also in the example given by Leslau (1968:289) to illustrate nonidentity of subjects in Amharic: *särk'O yazuT* 'He having stolen, they captured him'. Here the subject of the gerund is identical with the object of the main verb.

Telugu uses a special form, an infinitive with the adverbial suffix *-gaa*, in place of a conjunctive participle (but reminiscent of the Latin gerund in the ablative) when there is nonidentity of subject:

aayana akkaḍanunḍi bayaludeeri, svadeesyamunaku RAAGAA, aayana syisyulu aayananu vembaḍinciri. 'He, setting off from there, came to his own country *and* his disciples followed him'.

I do not know the extent to which this has parallels in other Dravidian languages.

The first real dichotomy, however, is between forms that can also be used as nouns or adjectives and forms that cannot be so used. This is not the same as having *vs.* lacking concord, being broader than the former: there are forms, such as English *-ing* forms, that do not exhibit concord but may be used as nouns and adjectives (or at least, are formally identical, at the word-level, with forms that may be). On the other hand, neither the concordant forms of Amharic and Finnish (which are concordant in *person*) nor those of Czech (in which separate adjectival participles exist) may be used as nouns or adjectives.

Usable in adjectival and nominal functions are the English *-ing* forms (and other Germanic present participles), French *-ant* forms, Spanish and Italian past participles, older Greek participles, and Persian past participles. (Western Indo-Aryan present participles are usable in adjectival but not in nominal functions.)

Nonusable in adjectival or nominal functions are the Dravidian verbal participles, the Indo-Aryan conjunctive participles, the Russian (and other Slavic) adverbial participles, the Modern Greek participle in *-ondas,* the Amharic "gerundives," the Turkish and cognate Altaic "gerunds" in *-ip* and *-erek*, the Japanese "gerund" in *-te*, the Korean "gerunds" in *-ŏ* and *-go,* the Hungarian adverbial participles in *-va* and *-van,* the Tibetan "gerund," the Persian *present* participle in *-aan,* the Rumanian, Italian, Spanish, and Portuguese *present* participles or "gerunds" in *-ind, -ende, -ando,* etc., the Latvian present participle in *-ot,* and the Burmese forms. Many of these languages have separate adjectival participle forms, sometimes derived from the adverbial forms (Dravidian), sometimes quite separate (Slavic). (The many forms in

Finnish confuse me, but apparently the form cognate with Hungarian *-va/ve,* namely *-va/vä* – if it is indeed cognate – can be used adjectivally in Finnish.)

The next division is according to the inherent "tense" of the participle. This may be determined by potential for perfect *vs.* continuous verb phrase formation in combination with auxiliaries and by contrast with other participles within the same system.

Bulgarian, Rumanian, Modern Greek, Latvian, English, French, and contemporary Hungarian as well as Japanese and Korean have only "present" participles (although English and French also have compound present *perfect* participles), but in several cases these function in both ways, that is, to indicate actions preceding as well as accompanying that of the main verb.

Russian and other Slavic languages other than Bulgarian and Macedonian, older Greek, Turkish, Persian, Italian and Spanish, Tibetan, Mongolian, and Burmese, Telugu, and most Indo-Aryan languages have both "present" and "past" adverbial participles used conjunctively – presumably contrastively, but the domains differ. Thus Romance and Slavic tend to use the "present" participle for prior as well as concurrent actions, while Indo-Aryan, Telugu, and Persian (I am not certain about Turkish, Mongolian, Tibetan, and Burmese) tend to use the "past" participle for manner-qualifications of the main verb as well as prior actions, reserving the "present" participle for stress on the occurrence of two *actions* together (usually renderable by *while* . . . , or *as (he) was . . . -ing*). English and French, insofar as they may be said to have a contrast between *-ing* and *-ant* on the one hand and *Having . . .-ed* and *ayant . . .-é* on the other, also fit into the former type in that they frequently employ the first alternative in place of the second. (French could also be held to belong to the second group on the grounds of the contrast between *disant* and *en disant,* but this may be regarded as a contrast at the phrase-level rather than at the word-level, developed on the basically "present" form *disant.* The basis of the present classification is quasi-etymological rather than functional, and necessarily also ignores combinations with particles, auxiliaries, adverbs, etc. The contrast in question can presumably be expressed in some manner by all languages. The question is, at what level – in the word itself, or with the aid of other devices? In this sense, English and French are securely in the first group with minor exceptions such as *Given this data. . . .*)

The South Dravidian languages have only "past" verbal participles (marked as such). Amharic and the Munda languages also seem to have only one form, essentially "past" (on the basis of function, not form, this time).

The next question concerns whether "past" participles (of transitive verbs) are, in the languages that have them, *active* or *passive*. (Present participles are all active, except in older Greek, where they may be either.) They are passive in (besides older Greek, where they may be either) only Spanish and Italian, where they are passive in terms of surface grammar, but often verge on having an active *function:*

Tomados los cinco panes. . . (lit.) 'Being-taken-up, the five loaves . . .' = 'He took up the five loaves and . . .';

E presa la fanciulla per la mano le disse . . . 'And being-taken, the girl by the hand, he said to her . . .' = 'And taking the girl by the hand, he said to her. . . .'

In all the other languages under discussion, including Persian, past verbal participles have an *active* sense, and this may be considered the norm, the Romance phenomena being somewhat marginal.

Frequency Sample of Conjunctive Participle Usage

Beyond the question of possession *vs.* nonpossession of conjunctive participial devices, and the question of what kind, there is another dimension worth investigating, namely, the predilection for their use. All of the languages concerned have alternative ways of connecting or at least of subordinating sentences, involving more specific conjunctions, adverbs of time, etc. The choice of one or the other mode of expression is in part stylistic – a question not only of individual preference, but also of genre and period. There is overriding this, however, something we might call the *general* stylistics of a language (if something so essentially a property of *parole* or "performance" can be regarded as belonging to a language) – habits of speech or writing not strictly speaking imposed by structure (although all sorts of questions arise here, including questions of relative ease or convenience of Path A *vs.* Path B that are difficult to measure), but somehow regularly or frequently chosen by speakers of language X to a degree different from speakers of language Y. Ultimately, of course, such predilections on the level of performance do affect structure significantly, through historical change.

It has been my hope that some hard evidence of these predilections, of which many of us may be already impressionistically aware, might emerge from frequency counts. My first attempt involved calculating the ratios of conjunctive participles vis-à-vis alternative modes of expression (both coordinative and subordinative) in texts. This turned out to involve too many decisions, and I abandoned it in favor of straight counting of the participles occurring in a given length of text. My plan next involved samplings of various texts in each language of around three thousand words each. This turned out to be too ambitious for present purposes, given the problem of trying to coordinate different authors' styles and different genres of writing. (For an indication of the range of frequencies in Hindi texts of various types see Dwarikesh, unpublished dissertation, [1971].)

To reduce some of these variables, and provide a rough-and-ready initial indication of these predilections, I have fallen back on that refuge for lazy linguists, Bible translations. There are some drawbacks to this, of course: archaic language, the influence of the original, the stylistic predilections of individual translators. The latter, however, are in no way comparable with the stylistic predilections of different authors writing different texts as far as skewing is concerned. Where the language is not merely archaic but drastically abnormal, for example, in the famed Bengali version of William Carey (probably the first modern translation in an Oriental language, eighteenth century), it cannot, of course, be used. (Fortunately, there is now a new Bengali version.) Other early Indian versions (Telugu, Malayalam) suffer from similar defects of concoctedness of language, but to a much lesser degree. (The language of the Telugu version is a curious mixture of classical and colloquial forms; a new version is in preparation for Telugu, but it hasn't been available to me.) The translators' problem in these cases was establishment of an appropriate prose standard at a period when there was no prose to speak of to use as a model. In spite of all this, I believe that the translations here chosen for comparison give a fairly good idea of the relative capacity of the languages involved for participial expression, whatever other problems they may present. The biblical passage is considerably richer in participial expressions than ordinary prose. I have good reason to think, however, on the basis of such other samplings as I did undertake, that if carefully chosen samples from different genres in each language were duly analyzed and added up and averaged out, the result, in terms of the *relative* standing of each language, would be much the same as that obtained by this disgraceful shortcut.

TABLE 9
Conjunctive Participles

Language	Markers		(Sample Test) Frequencies			
	Present	Past	Present	Perfect	Past	Total
Tamil	---	-ʉ				
		[-aamal, -aatʉ] [a]				
Malayalam	---	-ʉ[b]	---	---	432	446
		[-aate] [a]			[14]	
Kannada	-utta	-u				
		[-ade] [a]				
Telugu	-tu	-i	30	---	429	459
	*-ću	[-aka] [a]				
Sinhalese	-min	-laa				
Bengali	CB-te	CB-e				
	SB-ite	SB-iya	4	---	246	250
Assamese	-õte	-i				
Oriya	-u	-i				
Braj		-i(kãĩ)				
Hindi/Urdu	**(-te(hue)	-kar[c]	31		186	217
Nepali	-[n] da, -dai	-i, -era				
Panjabi	**(-daa?	-ike[d]				
Gujarati	**(-taa#	-ii(ne)				
Marathi	**(-taa(na)?	-uun				
Sindhi	-andō, -īndō	-ī, -ē, -yō				
Kashmiri	-aan	-ith				

TABLE 9 *Continued*

Language	Markers		(Sample Test) Frequencies			
	Present	Past	Present	Perfect	Past	Total
Balochi		-o				
Persian	-aan	-è	3	---	202	205
Uzbek		-ib				
Kirghiz	-e, -a	-ip[e]				
Turkish	-erek, -arak	-ip	28	---	153	181
	-e, -a					
Mongolian	-ss	-et, -at, -ot				
Korean	-go	-ŏ				
		[-ji] [a]				
Japanese		-(t)e				
Tibetan	-te[f]	-te				
Burmese	*-ywe'	-'pi(tɔ')				
Santali		-kate				
Sora		-le				
Hungarian	-va, -ve	*-ván, -vén				
Finnish		**(-ty*ään*#				
Russian	-i͡a, -a	-v (shi)	35	---	98	133
Ukrainian	-chi	-shi				
Polish	-ąc	*-wszy, -łszy				
Slovak	*-úc, -iac	*-vši, -ši				
Czech	*-a#, -e#	*-v#, -Ø#				
Serbo-Croat	-ći	-v(ši)				

Bulgarian	-eiki, -aiki	---				
Latvian	-ot	---				
Yiddish	-endik	---				
Modern Greek	-ondas	---	(5)			(5)
Rumanian	-ind, -ând, -înd	---	36	---	---	36
Italian	-endo, -ando	**(-to	87	15	48	150
Spanish	-iendo, -ando	**(-do	152	3	7	162
Portuguese	-endo, -ando					
French	-ant		45/12[g]	42	---	99
English	**(-ing	---	58	0	---	58
Amharic	---	-o#				

Notes and Symbols:

* = archaic or purely literary

** = non-unique form (adjectival or nominal form made to serve adverbial function).

= concordant endings: only masculine 3rd person singular given.

( ) = optional elements.

[a]Dravidian and Korean *negative* participles.

[b]Kannada *-u* = [u], Malayalam *-u* = [ə˞], Tamil *-u* = [ɯ]; some Tamil and Malayalam forms end in *-i*.

[c]Allomorphs *-ke, -karke, -Ø*.

[d]Allomorphs *-i, -ke, -kar, -karke, -ikar, -ikarke*.

[e]Uzbek allomorphs (Sjöberg) = *-ip, -b-, -p;* Kirghiz allomorphs (Hebert and Poppe) = *Cip, Vp;* Turkish allomorphs (Lewis) = *-ip, -üp, -up*.

[f]Same Tibetan suffix added to past and present *bases*.

[g]Total occurrences of the form *en V-ant*.

The passage chosen for comparison is the first nine chapters of the Gospel of Mark, amounting to around 7,500-8,000 words. All participial forms forming free adjuncts were counted as well as those forming manner-adverbials, but an effort was made to exclude predicative adjuncts (in retrospect, unnecessarily, I think, since preference for adverbial forms here would also have been indicative of the general tendency of the language – but the number of examples involved is negligible). A special problem arises in Indian languages, where certain conjunctive participle forms become so lexicalized as to be equivalent to mere postpositions or adverbs: where these seem sufficiently opaque (for example the Bengali present participle-SB – *hoite,* meaning "from") we have excluded them, but included them when a literal reading seems plausible, however un-English. I have included the Dravidian "quotatives," because their literal meaning ("saying") is near enough to the surface in speakers' consciousness to be translated literally into Hindi (*bolke*) in the Deccan. Excluded from the count are participles as the base of complex verb phrases, both perfect and continuous tense-aspect complexes and the so-called intensifier compounds so typical of India. The infinitive + *gaa* form has been excluded from the Telugu count.

The thought occurred in the middle of all this that, since we are dealing with a translation, it might be a good idea to look at the original too. This was no mean task, as N.T. Greek participles may not only be present, first and second aorist, active, middle, and passive, but masculine, feminine, or neuter, singular or plural, and nominative, dative, genitive, or accusative. For purposes of comparison, then, the first nine chapters of Mark have in the original a total of 226 participles of all kinds used "circumstantially" (= nonadjectivally, non-nominally). Of these 84 are presents, while 142 are aorists.

It might make for greater clarity if the total counts for each language were presented in terms of ranges:

0- 50: Modern Greek (5), Rumanian (36), German (zero)
50-100: English (58), French (99)
100-200: Russian (133), Italian (150), Spanish (162), Turkish (181)
200-300: Persian (205), Hindi (217), Bengali (250)
over-300: Malayalam (446), Telugu (459)

I have managed to count only a sampling of the languages, not all the languages. While it is not possible to count them all at this time, it would be desirable to add at least Marathi, Santali, Japanese, and

Amharic to the list. Looking at the present sample, the following points are worthy of comment:

The extremely high Dravidian counts are not due merely to the inclusion of the quotatives: they would be high without these. Yet it is obvious from the text that a conjunctive participle was *not* used wherever there was an opportnity to do so. Potential totals would be much higher.

The Balkan linguistic area begins to show clearly in the dramatic drop from N.T. to Modern Greek, and in the low Rumanian count. Actually none of the five Modern Greek items had our diagnostic free adjunct function, and only one of them was the modern active participle in *-ondas* (occurring as a manner-adverb in Mark 6:48: . . . *erchete pros aftus perpatondas epano is tin thalassan* '. . . he came toward them, walking on the sea'). It may be recalled that Rumanian had "gerunds" in all three of the predicative adjunct test slots, yet it uses the gerund comparatively infrequently in free adjunct formation. This shows, first, that these two functions are not very closely related, and second, that mere possession of a form gives no indication of its level of use.

No version slavishly followed the rather heavy pattern of participle use of the original, and even Dravidian translators balked at the magnificent succession of seven participles in Mark 5:25-27.

As a further illustration of the typological pattern observable in the counts above, we now present a mini-test showing the behavior of a single verse in a similar sample of languages. The verse (Matthew 15:29) has two circumstantial participles in the original: *Kai METABAS ekeithen ho Iēsous ēlthen para tēn thalassan tēs Galilaias. kai ANABAS eis to oros ekathēto ekei.*

1. The following use no participles at all:

(English: King James) "*And* Jesus departed from thence, *and* came nigh unto the sea of Galilee; *and* went up into a mountain, *and* sat down there."

(German: Luther) "*Und* Jesus ging von dannen fürbass *und* kam an das Galiläische Meer *und* ging auf einem Berg *und* setzte sich allda."

(Swedish) "Men Jesus gick därifrån vidare *och* kom till Galileiska sjön. *Och* han gick upp på berget *och* satte sig där."

(Arabic) "Thumma 'ntaqala iisuu^{c}u min hunaaka *wa*-jaa'a 'ilaa jaanibi baḥri-l-jaliili. *wa*-ṣa^{c}ida 'ila-l-jabali *wa*-jalasa hunaaka."

(Rumanian) "Isus a plecat din locurile acelea, *şi* a venit lîngă marea Galileii. S'a suit pe munte, *şi* a şezut jos acolo.

(Swahili) "Yesu a*ka*ondoka huko, a*ka*fika kando ya bahari ya Galilaya; a*ka*panda mlimani, a*ka*keti huko."

2. The following use two participles, like the original:

(Urdu) "Phir Īsuu vahãã se CALKAR Galiil kii jhiil ke nazdiik aayaa, aur pahaaṛ par CAṚHKAR vahĩĩ baiṭh gayaa."

(Marathi) "Nantar Yeshu tethuun NIGHUUN Gaaliil samudraajavaḷ aalaa, va ḍõgraavar CAḌHUUN tethẽ baslaa."

(Persian) " 'Isaa az aanjaa HARAKAT KARDE be-kenaare-ye-jaliil aamad va bar faraaz-e-kuuh BAR AAMADE aanjaa beneshast."

(Russian) "PERESHED ottuda, prishol Iisus k moriu Galileiskomu i, VZOIDIA na goru, sel tam."

(Czech) "A ODŠED odtud Ježíš, šel k moři galilejskému VSTOUPIV na horu, posadil se tam."

(Hungarian) "És onnét TÁVOZVA, méne Jézus a Galilea tengere mellé; és FELMENVÉN a hegyre, ott leűle."

(Japanese) "Iesu wa soko o SATTE, Garireya no umibe ni yuki, sorekara yama ni NOBOTTE soko ni suwarareta."

(Spanish) "Y PARTIDO Jesús de allí, vino junto al mar de Galilea; y SUBIENDO al monte, se sentó allí."

(Santali) "Ado Jisu oṇḍe khon UṬHAUKATE Gạlil disom reak' doreao aṛeteye hec'ena, ar burute DEC'KATE oṇḍeye duṛup'ena."

3. The following have three participles:

(Telugu) "Yeesu akkaḍanunḍi VEḶḶI, Galilaya samudra-tiiramunaku VACCI, konḍ' EKKI akkaḍa kuurcunḍagaa."

(Kannada) "Yeesu allinda HORAṬU Galilaaya samudrada baḷige BANDU beṭṭavannu HATTI alli kutukonḍanu."

(Japanese might belong in group 3, depending on the status of the form *yuki,* of which I am unable to locate readily a good account. It is not a "gerund" of the -TE type; it seems to be a stem: do such stems also have a linking function in some style of the language?)

4. Tamil has four participles:

"Iyeecu avviṭam VIṬṬU-p-PURAPPAṬṬU, kalileeyaa-k-kaṭalarukee VANTU, ori malaiyinmeel EERI, aṅkee uṭkaarntaar.

There is one more frequency-dimension we must look at. Some languages, it will be recalled, have both "past" and "present" adverbially used participles; some have "present perfect" as well as "present" participles.

In the sample biblical text, "present" participles dominate "past" or "perfect" participles in the following cases: English (58/0), French (57/42), Italian (87/63), Spanish (152/10).

"Past" participles dominate over "present" participles in the following cases: Russian (98/35), N.T. Greek (142/84), Turkish (153/28), Persian (202/3), Hindi (186/31), Telugu (429/30), Bengali (246/4).

Malayalam has no present participles in this function, and Rumanian no past participle. The French and Italian ratios are fairly close, it will be noted. The high number on the right in French comes entirely from perfects of the type *ayant/étant V-é*, which seems to be far more frequent than its English counterpart, *having V-ed* (which does not occur at all in the passage sampled, although it does elsewhere in the Bible). The Italian total, on the other hand, comes mostly from past participles used absolutely. This construction, sometimes called characteristically Spanish, seems to be far more typical of Italian (48 *vs.* 7). The theory of Arabic influence sometimes advanced to explain the Spanish construction seems absurd in this light (and in light of the fact that the construction does not occur in Arabic).

Areal Implications

That the facts cited in the preceding two sections have an areal dimension cannot but have already suggested itself to the reader. Participial syntax is characteristic of the "Indo-Altaic" area, including most of its border zone and outlying areas of Iran, Tibet, Burma, and Ethiopia, and also of parts of Europe; it is uncharacteristic of those areas that have also contrasted with Indo-Altaic in other respects: Southeast Asia, China, Africa, the Arabic speech-area.

As always, there are differences of detail on the boundaries, although the core of the area remains solidly that on all counts. A significant feature of the participle map is the irruption of an antiparticipial zone upward from Arabic to include (on grounds either of statistics or of structure) the Balkans and the Caucasus. Turkish interrupts this in turn, but Persian, despite its high frequency count, shows its influence also in the aberrant nominal potentiality of its participle. The absence of the participle from Pashto and Brahui can also be put down to this Balkan-Semitic areal pull. Persian again shows its transitional character in that, while its past participle has nominal uses like those of Mediterranean languages, it has an active rather than a passive sense, like those of Indian languages.

The zones of participle use to the west and to the east of this zone of interruption differ not only in importance (the eastern one is much larger and includes many more languages) and intensity (the eastern languages resort to the participle, on the average, at least twice as often as the western languages) but also in kind. In the eastern languages, it is a "past" participle that is specialized for this function and overwhelmingly dominates in use, with the "present" participle either lacking or dragged in and doctored-up to serve in an adverbial rather than its normal adjectival function (for example, by putting it into the oblique case in Hindi). In the western languages, it is a "present" participle that is specialized for the function and dominates in use, with the "past" participle either lacking (English, French, German, Rumanian) or dragged in and doctored-up to serve in this function – and in some ways remaining an adjective.

(The exception would be Japanese, but perhaps I have erred in calling the *-te* form "present" merely on the basis of its combinatorial properties with the auxiliary *iru*, giving "continuous" meanings. It may also combine with the auxiliary *aru*, giving "perfect" meanings, although this is restricted and less typical. More important is the fact that if we change the *-te* to *-ta*, we get the past tense, suggesting that what we really have before both vowels is the past stem – just as in Dravidian, that is, Malayalam. I have no doubt fallen victim myself to the aforementioned script-based tendency to segment Japanese according to CV syllables, ignoring other correlations. It is likely that Japanese fits the pattern also.)

In the north, there is no zone of interruption, but rather a gradual weakening of participial syntax toward the west. A dimension that has not been given proper weight is that of colloquial *vs.* literary language. Although Polish, Slovak, and Czech as well as Russian and Ukrainian have both present and past adverbial participles distinct from adjectival participles, in the West Slavic languages these are confined to a formal literary style and hardly ever used in conversation. With the decrease in participle use generally from east to west, there is also an increasing predominance of the present over the past participle. Although the past had it over the present in the Russian Bible passage, 98/35, the Russian version already used the present in many instances where, e.g., Hindi would have used the past. In a slightly longer passage from contemporary writing (Svetlana Aliluyeva's *Tol'ko odin god*), the proportion is reversed: *present* 55/*past* 18. Hungarian, which formerly had both a past and a present adverbial participle, is losing or has lost the former, while Latvian has only a present adverbial participle. This brings us to the situation in Germanic, where there are only present participles, used almost entirely adjectivally. That is, except in Yiddish, where the participle, although exclusively "present," has considerable use as an adverb; this can be put down to its eastern milieu and provides yet another confirmation of the areal picture.

To the south, the peculiar Amharic conjunctive participles with their personal endings may perhaps be regarded as a transition to such phenomena as the succession "tenses" of Swahili and other Bantu languages.

On the eastern border, as already noted, the forms of Burmese, Tibetan, and the Munda languages give the impression of being patched together in answer to the areal pull of "Indian" syntax, and thus provide an interesting example of convergence in action, worthy of more detailed attention than I am able to give it here.

General Typological Implications

It has been alleged that conjunctive participles are a property of "Type III" languages – languages characterized by SOV word-order, postpositions, and left-branching in general. While this correlation holds to a certain extent, it is overridden by areal and other factors. Russian is not a "Type III" language in any sense, but it is geographically near the Type III languages and is rich in conjunctive participles. Spanish and Italian are even less like Type III languages, but they also exhibit participial syntax to a degree, for reasons which are not clear. Areally, we have found the Mediterranean to be a zone of transition or mixture in other respects, however.

Similarly, although the Type III Dravidian languages show high conjunctive participle frequencies, the rate for equally Type III Turkish is only moderate, comparable to that for Russian or Italian. Moreover, if we compare the frequencies for Turkish with those for the Central Asian Turkic language Kirghiz, something very interesting comes to light. In samples of approximately 4,500 words (taken from modern secular literature[7] – no Kirghiz Bible was at hand), Kirghiz has more than twice as many (138) past (*-ip*) adverbial participles as Turkish has past and present (*-erek*) combined (61). In addition, as in Russian, the ratio of past to present participles in Turkish is reversed from Bible version to secular literature, present outnumbering past in the latter 43 to 18. This remarkable increase in the ratio of present participles, together with the rather sharp decrease in the absolute number of all participles, suggests that, compared with its Central Asian cousins, Anatolian Turkish has undergone more assimilation and "Balkanization" (or Westernization) than is commonly realized. Areal factors again apparently override general typological correlations, Anatolian Turkish having wandered "outside" the proper boundaries of Indo-Altaic and thereby exposed itself to more alien influences.

As has been shown by Dwarikesh (unpublished, 1971) for Hindi, there is another factor, besides the areal one, that can affect conjunctive participle frequencies and probably does so also in the Turkish case, namely, the stages in the development of a literary prose standard. In the early stages of the development of a prose style, the conjunctive participle device available in a language is freely used. As sophistication develops, there is apparently a search for more varied modes of expression to relieve this monotony. Modern Turkish is no doubt a more sophisticated and developed literary medium than is modern Kirghiz. In both the Turkish and the Hindi (as well as, for that matter, the Russian) cases, however, it may be difficult to keep this problem separate from that of what might be called "Westernization" – conscious or unconscious imitation of the prose style of English, French, or German.

There is another factor that probably accounts for some of the higher total in Kirghiz, but for that the reader will have to turn to the next chapter.

5

EXPLICATOR COMPOUND VERBS

DEFINITION: COMPOUND *VS.* OTHER PARTICIPLE + VERB SEQUENCES

The phenomenon to be discussed in this chapter is related to the topic of the last chapter, conjunctive participles. A conjunctive participle is followed immediately (or perhaps with an intervening emphatic particle) by a finite verb, the two forming a unit in which the main verb is the participle, the finite verb acting as a modifying auxiliary. This is just the opposite of an ordinary sequence of conjunctive participle + finite verb, where the finite verb is the main verb and the participle is a modifying or at any rate a secondary element.

Often the latter sequences, which we shall call *CP . . . V,* are distinguished from these compounds, which we shall call *Vv,* by the intervention of other material between the two verbs, but this is not always the case and cannot be relied upon to distinguish them. The critical difference between V_1V_2(= CP . . . V) and V_1V_2(= Vv) is rather the aforementioned shift in the semantic center of gravity from V_2 to V_1, with concomitant lexical emptying or grammaticalization of V_2.

In some cases, this lexical emptying is almost complete; in other cases enough of the literal meaning is retained to render a literal CP+V interpretation plausible; most are somewhere between, with the semantic contribution of the V_2 rather transparent but a literal translation not quite admissible: e.g.,

H. *kho baiṭhnaa* 'to lose' ("lose and sit" – ruefully?), *le jaanaa* 'to take away' ("take and go"), *likh deenaa* 'write down for somebody' ("write and give"), *gir paṛnaa* 'fall down' ("fall and lie there").

It would seem that such differences in degree of literalness, which have sometimes given rise to much discussion, are merely due to properties of the language of description or the amount of imagination at the disposal of the investigator and do not correspond to any real differences in the language concerned. In all the cases, the essential point is that the main action is represented by V_1.

In Hindi-Urdu, there has developed a strong tendency, perhaps a rule, to differentiate the two sequences formally also, by using the so-called long form of the conjunctive participle, in -KAR or -KE, for CP . . . V, and the short form, identical with the verb stem, for Vv.

V_2's in use as the auxiliary element in Vv compounds are generally described as belonging to limited sets. (Dwarikesh maintains, perhaps as a consequence of his position that CP . . . V in immediate sequence is *always* marked by *-kar/ke,* that one of the hallmarks of contemporary Hindi is the great expansion of this class to the point where it is practically an open one, "almost any verb" in the language being a candidate.[1] Others would not go so far.) Complicating this question is the fact that there is often a gradual progression from what might be called a "full" CP . . . V, where the construction merely indicates conjunction, through CP . . . V where the CP has become a manner adverbial but is always marked by *-kar* and thence to situations (in Hindi-Urdu) where *-kar* may be dropped or usually is dropped, to the point where the balance tips in favor of V_1 as main verb, and thence through progressively less transparent and more grammaticalized V_2's to ultimately the fully grammaticalized use of, e.g., Hindi-Urdu *rah-* or Tamil-Malayalam *kontu* to indicate the continuous aspect (which I would place outside the realm of this construction). Different investigators may choose to cut the progression at different points according to different criteria. In languages other than Hindi-Urdu, without the differentiation provided by *-kar vs. Ø,* the problem of judgment becomes even more difficult, with corresponding differences in proposed lists of auxiliaries.

These sets usually include such lexical items as *go, come, give, take, rise, fall, throw, put, sit.* It will be noted that these are all verbs of "motion" or "position," either in the primary sense (the intransitives) or in the extended sense of motion or position caused (the transitives: *throw, put, give, take*). When the lists are expanded by the discovery (whether by linguists or by speakers of the language is not clear) of more such auxiliaries, they generally turn out to be merely variations – somewhat more specific in semantic content – on the same theme: *emerge, move, run away, descend, arrive, lie, stand, send, release, lift up.*

Function

Exactly what sort of modifying function do these auxiliaries have? Sometimes Russian writers (e.g., Rastorgueva and Kerimova 1964:212) call it "aspectual" (*vidovoi*), but it is clearly not aspect in the usual sense of perfective *vs.* imperfective (although a number of these auxiliaries connote "completed action" among other things). The usual name for these compounds, "*intensives*," suggests a function proper to only a few of them. Moreover, for simple "intensification," as for example, in Arabic, *one* marker would be enough; there is no need for so many different ones.

From one perspective the function of V_2 is varied and manifold: it connotes completion, suddenness, directionality, benefaction, intensity, violence, stubbornness, reluctance, regret, forethought, thoroughness, etc., depending on the items involved and on the circumstances. As several writers (e.g., Hacker 1958, Katenina 1957) have pointed out, however, these can all be brought under one banner: greater specification (*utochnenie*) of features of the action already latent in the main verb itself or those that are compatible with it but have not yet been specified. It is for this reason that the combinations (unlike those, sometimes also called "compound verbs" in the literature, with present participles, infinitives, and the like, excluded from consideration here, which have modal and aspectual functions properly so-called) are *lexically selective;* a given V_2 combines only with such V_1 as are compatible with it, or to put it another way, as have the semantic potential for it. Many unspecified V_1 have the potential for combination with a number of V_2, of course: the selection of the particular one depends on the demands of the situation as the speaker sees it or chooses to characterize it.

This function of unfolding the latent semantics of V_1, of characterizing the manner and implications of its performance more precisely, has led K. C. Bahl (1967:329-30) to propose the name *explicator* for these V_2, which term we adopt here as at any rate more satisfactory than the other terms ("intensifier," "operator," etc.) in use.

It will be seen that there is a strong component of *directionality* to this lexical specification: away from the speaker (*go, run away, give, send, release*), toward the speaker (*come, take, arrive*), up (*rise, emerge*), down (*fall, throw, descend*), and perhaps motionlessness (*sit, stand, put*). Some items have other connotations in addition, such as suddenness (*fall*) or violence (*throw*). The connotation of "completion" probably emerges from the well-roundedness of the characterization of the action, a semantic completion, or "completeness" rather, which is not the same as the perfective aspect and indeed is compatible with the imperfective aspect.

Distribution Within India

Much can be and has been written on the subject of these explicator-compounds in Indian languages, which, straddling as it does the domains of lexicon and grammar, is both fascinating and intractable. It is not my intention here, however, either to recapitulate that discussion or to contribute anything new to it, but rather to investigate the distribution of the phenomenon – which the foregoing is meant merely to identify – and of possible analogies to it.

First, it is found in all the Indian languages, Indo-Aryan (including Sinhalese), Dravidian, Tibeto-Burman, and Munda. It is one of those features that is almost absent in Vedic, increases somewhat in Classical Sanskrit and Prakrit, and undergoes a great explosion in the Apabhraṁśa period and thereafter in the modern languages (Shivram Sharma 1967:95-96). This, plus the fact that it is found in Dravidian, has led Chatterji (1926) and others to attribute the presence of the feature in Indo-Aryan to the usual Dravidian substratum that is given credit for Indo-Aryan peculiarities. The trouble with this theory is that the feature seems to be more highly developed in modern Indo-Aryan (especially Hindi) than in Dravidian, at least in terms of the number of different "explicators" employed (perhaps as many as fifteen in Hindi – the usual number given is eight or nine. Kachru lists sixteen for Kashmiri, not all of which, however, would seem strictly to qualify).

It would perhaps be wrong to come to any conclusion on the basis of the available data, however. Many accounts are clearly fragmentary and incomplete. Existing grammars vary considerably in the attention they give to this subject, perhaps because it is sometimes regarded as more a part of lexicon than of grammar. Much more descriptive work needs to be done. For example, Arden lists only one explicator (*poo-* 'go') for Telugu (along with *kon-* 'take', which he treats separately because of special features in the formation of compounds with it); Krishnamurti doesn't mention the subject at all in his *Basic Course* (although he treats "compound verbs" of the *modal* type). Lisker (1963:139ff), however, adds *wees-* 'throw', as well as the somewhat aberrant *peṭṭ-* 'put' and *koṭṭ-* 'beat', while Shivram Sharma (1967:96-101) gives a list illustrating eleven different explicators (some of which seem to this writer to be instances of the CP . . . V construction, however, i.e., with V_2 still the main verb and V_1 a characterization of it, e.g.,

kaali caccu 'burn to death', *munigi caccu* 'die by drowning', *naligi caccu* 'be crushed to death').

Another dimension that needs to be considered is *frequency of occurrence.* Even if Dravidian turns out to be somewhat poorer in the number of different explicators in use (due perhaps to a very late elaboration of the category in Indo-Aryan) – and we do not know this for sure – those it has may be heavily used. This is certainly the case with Telugu *poo-*. The question is an open one.

I append to this chapter a list of explicators compared (Table 10), with the warning that it is based on insufficient data and therefore probably incomplete.

From it one thing can be seen, however: not only do the items largely correspond, but the correspondence within Indo-Aryan, for example, is *semantic* rather than etymological. It is the semantic category that is important, not the history of individual stems. As words change their meanings, it is the one with the proper current semantics that is plugged in as the auxiliary. Expansion likewise proceeds by the substitution of verbs with similar *meanings.*

There are a number of minor peculiarities in the construction among the various Indo-Aryan and Dravidian languages. Besides the Hindi-Urdu differentiation of V+$\emptyset$ *vs.* V+*kar*, there are such matters as the reversibility of the order of the constituents in Kashmiri (V_1-*ith* + V_2 ↔ V_2 + V_1-*ith* = Vv ↔ vV) in accordance with its peculiar order predilections; and the violation by Telugu of the CP-form for V_1 (some auxiliaries with the requisite semantic properties are attached to the "short infinitive" instead:

koṭṭ- 'strike' = "violence," *peṭṭ-* 'put,' *ett-* 'ascend,' e.g., *inṭloonunci veḷḷagoṭṭaemu* 'We threw (him) out of the house'

Koṭṭu also transitivizes. *Ettu* adds an inceptive meaning, while *peṭṭu* is also a verbalizer.(According to Arden [1937], the element *kon-* 'take,' which he calls "reflexive," is added to the *root* in -U. Sarma disputes

TABLE 10

CHIEF EXPLICATOR AUXILIARIES COMPARED. A. Indo-Aryan and Dravidian Languages

Basic Meaning as MV + Meaning as Vv	Hindi	Panjabi	Kashmiri	Gujarati	Marathi	Bengali	Telugu	Malayalam	Tamil	Sinhalese
GO 'completion'	jaa-	jaa-	gatsh-	jaa-	jaa-	ja-	poo-	poo-	poo-	--
COME 'completion with relevance to present time or place'	aa-	aa-	y-	--	ye-	ash-	vacc-	var-	var-	--
RISE 'suddenness; inception'	uṭh-	uṭh-	--	uṭh-	--	oṭh-	(Vn+)ett-	--		--
FALL 'suddenness; accident'	paṛ-	pai-	p'o-	paḍ-	paḍ-	paṛ-	paḍ	viiṇ		--
SIT 'regret; stubbornness, etc.	baiṭh-	bai	bih-	bes-	bas-	boṣh-	--	--		
MOVE 'departure'?	cal-				cal-			cenn-		
GIVE 'away from subject + "benefactive" '	de-	de-	d'-	de-	de-	de-	--	koṭutt-		denavaa
TAKE 'toward subject: "reflexive" '	le-	lai-	n'-	le-	ghe-	na-	kon-	koṇṭ-	koṇṭ-	gannavaa
PUT, KEEP 'forethought + "completion" '	rakh-	tshɨn	thav-		ṭhev-	rakh- tol-	unc-	vecc-	vai-	damanavaa
THROW 'completion + violence'	ḍaal-	saṭṭ-		naakh-	ṭaak-	phel-	vees-	kaḷay-		
LEAVE, RELEASE 'completion + ?'	choṛ-	chaḍḍ-	(traav-?)		tsoḍ-				viiṭ-	
(SEE attempt to, try)	dekh-		tshin-			daekh-		nookk-	paar-	

TABLE 10 *Continued.* B. Altaic and Other Languages

(Functions Similar to Part A)	Tajik	Uzbek	Kirghiz	(Turkish)	Mongolian	Korean	Japanese	Burmese	Santali
GO	raftan	bor- ket-	ket-	(gitmek)	yavax	ka-	iku	thwa:	
COME	omadan	kel-	kel-	(gelmek)	irex	o-	kuru	la.	
RISE	baromadan								
FALL									
SIT	nishastan	utir-	oltur-						
MOVE	gashtan	yur-	jür-						
(COME OUT)		(chiq-)							
(LIE)		(yot-)							
(STAND)	(istodan)	(tur-)	(tur-)	(durmak)					
(PASS)	(guzashtan)								
(REMAIN)	(mondan)	(ot-)	(kal-)	(kalmak)				nei	
GIVE	dodan	ber-	ber-	(vermek)	ögöx	ju- tɯl-	kureru (kudasaru) ageru (sashiageru) (yaru)	pei:	
TAKE	giriftan	ol-	(*Ve+al-* = "CAN")		avax		(morau)		(jom = "EAT")
PUT, KEEP		kφi-	koi-			tu- noh-	oku	hta:	
THROW	partoftan	tashla-							
LEAVE	sar dodan					pφr-			(goṭ = "PLUCK")
(BE USED UP)								koụn.	
(SEE)	didan	kφr-	kör	(görmek)	üzex	po/pwa-	miru	ci.	
(SHOW)								pya.	
(SEND)	firistodan	yubor-							
(WEAR)						ip-			
(WRITE)				(yazmak)					
(FINISH)			tügöt				shimau	pi:	

this, claiming that the -U here, which is in any case often a predictable element in Telugu, is due to assimilation under the pressure of vowel harmony and the form is really the CP.) Telugu appears to lack the "benefactive" use of *give.* Telugu *icc-* 'give' as an auxiliary (with the short infinitive, in -A) has the "permissive" meaning only.

Admitting our inability at present, therefore, to localize the center of gravity of the Vv phenomenon within India, let us turn to the question of its further extent.

European Analogies

Analogies to such verbal usages occasionally turn up in European languages. The one most often cited is perhaps Russian

vzi͡al 'took' + perf.V, denoting "suddenness or unexpectedness": *Poi͡ezd vzi͡al da ushol* 'The train suddenly left' (Unbegaun 1957:244).

It has been my feeling that such locutions (with vV order, of course, as appropriate in Russian) occur in substandard colloquial English as well: *He took and left.* See what you've *gone and done.* Lewy (1964:64n1) points out that the Russian usage is itself part of an areal phenomenon shared with Mordvin, Cheremiss, Lappish, Finnish, Swedish, and even Danish, however, and I am beginning to wonder if at least my first English example is not an example of Minnesota-English rather than normal English colloquial. (My uncertainty is a good example of the process by which such forms diffuse anywhere, of course, or at least of one end of it: in a region where a "native speaker" is used to hearing many bilinguals speak his language, he forgets where he has heard a particular expression and adopts it himself unconsciously.) J. A. B. van Buitenen informs me that such usages are quite common in colloquial Dutch, though not in German. Holland is, of course, not far from Denmark. (Kostas Kazazis adds that such constructions are also common in colloquial Modern Greek and other Balkan languages.) We face here a problem that arises in India itself: these usages are perhaps especially characteristic of colloquial language and have found their way into literary language (and thence to the notice of grammarians) very unevenly, though more in India than in Europe.

In any case, the Russian construction and its allies differ from the Indian in that they involve *two finite verbs* rather than a past verbal participle (available in Russian at least) + finite auxiliary. Moreover, "unexpectedness" is not the meaning of *take* in the Indian constructions, where it invariably means "for the benefit of the speaker."

Such verbal usages in Western languages seem to be sporadic and marginal. The traditional analogs cited in English for Indian explicator compounds have been the *verbal adverbs* – fall *down*, sit *up*, fly *away*, gobble *up*, run *off*, lie *down*, etc., and it is clear that, in spite of the fact that only a fraction of the Indian explicator compounds can be rendered in this way, this is more on the right track. These words correspond more than anything else in English to the "directional component" we noted as common to most of the Indian auxiliaries. They may correspond rather imperfectly, and the fact is that perhaps the majority of the explicators cannot be translated at all into normal English, even invoking the aid of lexical suppletion, full adverbial phrases, and other devices. They represent a category that English either regards as redundant or is unaware of, and does not consequently represent.

The English verbal adverbs are the broken fragments of a type of system found in better condition[2] further to the east, in the verbal *prefixes* of German, Hungarian, the Balto-Slavic languages, and Georgian (Vogt 1971:172-180). Here not only is the directional system intact and all-pervasive, but there is a tie-in with aspect and with other *Aktionsart.* In the Slavic languages this is quite explicit, of course. When Russian writers compare the explicator-compounds with their aspect-system, they have in mind not merely perfective *vs.* imperfective, but also the function of these prefixes, at once grammatical, perfective-forming, and lexically – *Aktionsart* (direction, manner, etc.) – specifying. In both cases, the fuller characterization of the action can also be retained with the imperfective aspect by the use of appropriate suffixes, although it is perhaps inherently more compatible with the perfective. There are interesting psychological parallels, e.g., between *vz-* 'upward', denoting commencement of an action, and the quasi-modal use of Dravidian *ettu* 'ascend' for the same purpose (cf. English *start up*). The German and Hungarian prefix-inventories also contain analogous quasi-aspectual elements alongside the purely directional ones: Hungarian *meg-* 'completion; inception'; German *ver-* 'completeness', *ent-* 'inception', *zer-* 'violence'. The German items belong to a different subcategory of prefixes (inseparable) from the directional prefixes.

Although the prefix-systems of central and eastern Europe and the Indian explicator-compounds bear some analogy to one another, they hardly can be termed parallel, however. One would be hard put to work out a system of item-for-item correspondences, however striking certain individual correspondences may be. There is simply too much position-awareness in the European systems, and not enough action.

Chinese and Southeast Asian Analogies

A much closer parallel to the Indian phenomenon – in that it involves *verbs* rather than purely relational elements – is found in a region hitherto largely excluded from our deliberations, namely China and its Indo-Chinese borderlands. I refer to what have been called in Chinese grammar *resultative compounds* (or by Chao 1968, *verb-complement compounds* – symbolized *V-R*). A main verb V_1 is followed by a "resultative verb" V_2 that "completes its sense" by indicating the state resulting from the action, or otherwise characterizing it.

There are several subclasses of these, according to adhesional and other formal criteria as well as semantic criteria. One of the largest subclasses consists of "stative verbs" (= adjectives), and these have no obvious analogy in Indian languages. E.g.,

byàn-cháng 'change (so as to) be long' = "lengthen," *nùng-hǎu* 'fix (so as to) be good' = "repair," etc.

Chao lists 155 such statives commonly used as V_2's in resultative compounds. From the examples just given it might be thought that

MAP 5. Distribution of Explicator-Compound Verbs and Analogous Phenomena

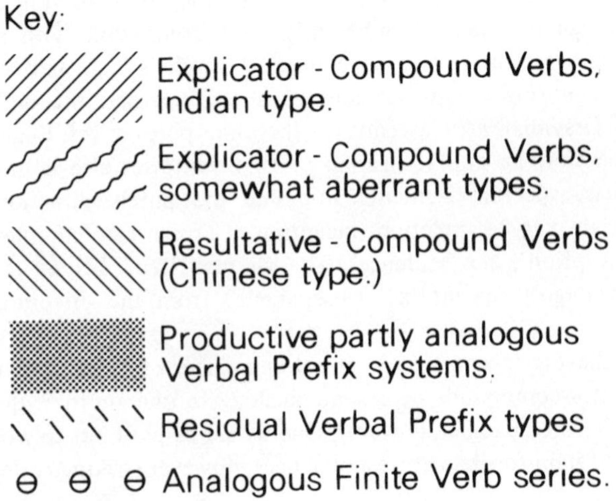
Key:
Explicator - Compound Verbs, Indian type.
Explicator - Compound Verbs, somewhat aberrant types.
Resultative - Compound Verbs (Chinese type.)
Productive partly analogous Verbal Prefix systems.
Residual Verbal Prefix types
Analogous Finite Verb series.

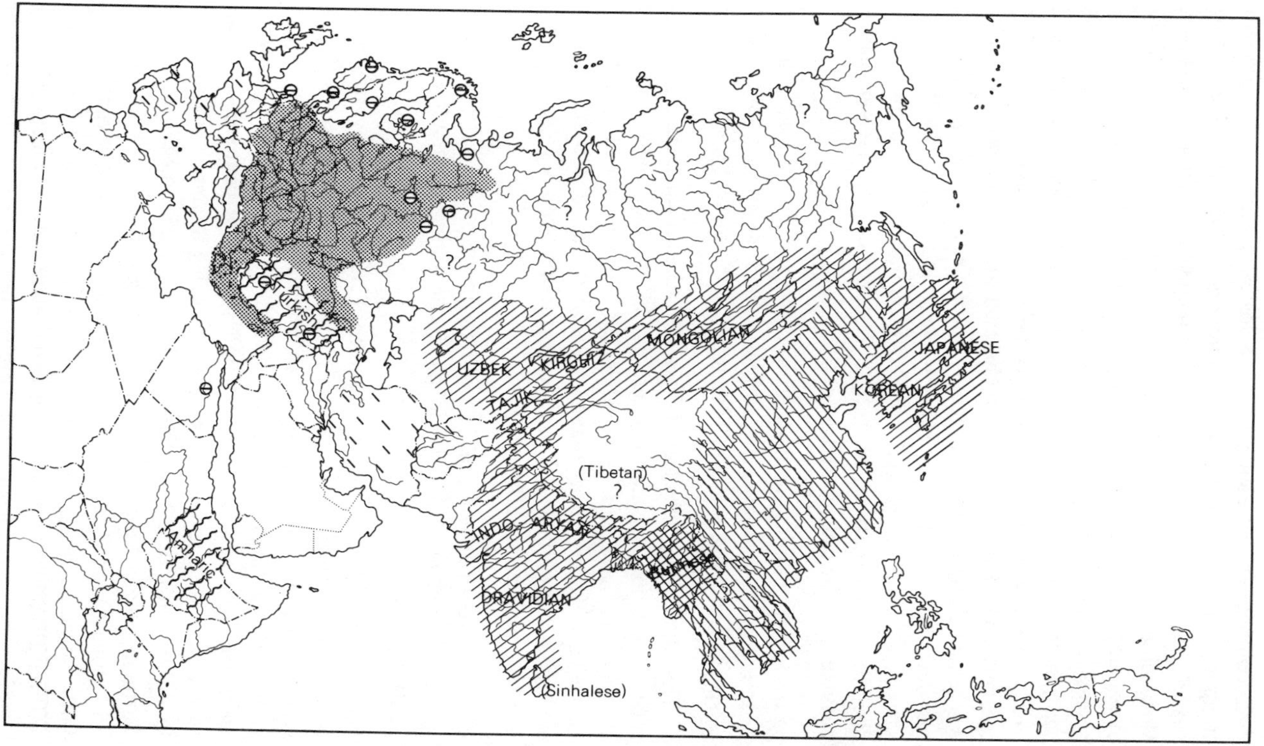

Turkish
Amharic
UZBEK
KIRGHIZ
TAJIK
MONGOLIAN
JAPANESE
KOREAN
(Tibetan)
INDO-ARYAN
DRAVIDIAN
(Sinhalese)

such compounds represent merely a logical joining of independent component ideas, generally with causative meaning, rather than a true *modification* of V_1 by V_2. It is more complicated than that, however. More idiomatic combinations, and items such as *-jyàn* (used with verbs of perception such as *kàn* 'see', *tīng* 'hear' to make explicit the idea of perception) grade into items such as *-wán* (*chī-wán* 'finish eating') and *-jáu* (*jǎu-jau* 'succeed in finding') with more aspect-like functions, and finally to the ubiquitous items *lái* 'come' (= action directed toward the speaker) and *chyù* 'go' (=action directed away from speaker) and a whole subclass of more specific "*directional* verbs" (*shàng* 'rise', *syà* 'descend', *jìn* 'enter', *chū* 'emerge', *gwò* 'pass', *hwéi* 'return', *kāi* 'open', *lǔng* 'tie, gather') that may combine with them to give directional specificity to an action to a degree even greater than is possible with the Indian explicators:

pá-shàngchyu 'climb up and away from speaker', *pá-shànglai* 'climb up and toward speaker', *pá-syàchyu* 'climb down and away from speaker', etc. (*pá* = 'climb, using both hands and feet').[3]

This directional subclass of V_2's is distinguished from the stative subclass not only semantically but also by the fact that the latter are stressed and have full tone, while the tone of the directionals is neutralized. This suggests that the case of the nondirectionals may be analogous to the Indian CP . . . V construction, with V_2 the main verb and V_1 a manner-modifier of it:

kàn-jyàn would thus mean 'perceive by means of (or as a result of) seeing', and *nùng-hǎu* 'be in good condition as a result of being fixed', etc.

On the side of this is the great number of stative V_2's – the subclass is practically an open one; against it, the fact that they do form, by certain structural criteria, *compounds,* not just a series of verbs.

Resultative compounds are also characteristic of Vietnamese. When we reach Thai and Burmese, we find systems of compound-forming verbal auxiliaries apparently greatly exceeding in complexity anything in either India or China (Stewart 1955 lists 25 "enclitic verbs" for Burmese,[4] while Noss 1964 lists 22 "completive verbs" and upwards of 35 "modals" for Thai). One reason for the elaboration is that verbs in both languages have the peculiarity of being basically *inchoative*: without the addition of one of these auxiliaries they are incomplete and signify action only begun or attempted, not completed. However, the lists referred to seem to contain items with aspectual and modal functions as well as the directional and resultative items analogous to Indian explicators and Chinese resultatives: there may of course be no structural reason for separating them. There seem not to be so many statives of the purely adjectival sort. The Thai set includes such items as *enter, emerge, rise, descend, see, hear, smell, taste, hit, meet, fall, catch, stick, come loose,* etc. Similarities and dissimilarities to the Indian inventory will be apparent to the reader. The Burmese set is yet closer to the Indian pattern by including *go, come, put, remain,* and *give,* in their usual senses.

It would seem that the directional resultative compounds, at least, of East and Southeast Asia form a very close analogy to Indian explicators. Even the order is the same (Vr = Vv) despite the fact that these are (except for Burmese) SVO rather than SOV languages. It must be remembered, however, that in Chinese and Vietnamese (I am not sure about Thai) the directional words in question can be adverbs – and nouns – as well as verbs; hence the analogy is as much with English as with Indian languages. Chao (1968:458) in fact finds the closest analogy in German separable prefixes, which can be made to line up with simple and complex Chinese V_2's one-to-one (*-shàng* = *auf-*, *-lái* = *her-*, *-shànglai* = *herauf*, *-shàngchyu* = *hinauf*, etc.).

This cannot really be done with Chinese and Indian items. The resultant compounds are not analogous in the majority of cases. The items *give* and *take*, so basic to the Indian, seem to be absent from the Chinese system. The Chinese verb *gěi* 'give', which is also the preposition *for; by* – see chapter 1 – is used in a different construction – more in its prepositional guise – in a vaguely analogous function:

Sùng-GEI tā ĭ-fèrh lĭ 'Send him a gift' (cf. *Wŏmen yĭ'rán bá'găudz GĔI yìnshwā 'jyú 'sùngchyule* "We've sent the manuscript off to the printers').

In the first example, *gěi* could be taken as an "enclitic verb," bound to *sùng* 'send', but in the second it seems to be acting – with the same verb – as a preposition "to the printers," and has been detached from *sùng* and moved to a position before the indirect object. Actually, Chao (1968:317-18) interprets it as *to* in both situations – or it could be taken as a verb in both situations. *Take* has no simple Chinese equivalent. One of its equivalents, *jiang,* is used in Literary Chinese and in modern Cantonese in a sense similar to Russian *vzi͡al.*

Even the order analogy breaks down with the insertability of objects between V_1 and V_2:

Chinese *hwéi GWÓ chyu* 'return-country-go' = "Go back to one's country"; Vietnamese *Tôi gio' TAY lên* 'I lift-hand-go up' = "I raise my hand."

There is of course no question of V_1 being in CP form.

Central Asian and Further-Altaic Parallels

A much more exact parallel with the Indian phenomenon is found in a region that by now should occasion no surprise (although I must confess I was surprised) – to the north, in central and northern Asia. In Uzbek, in Kirghiz, in Tajik, and to a lesser but still unmistakable extent in Mongolian, Korean, and Japanese, we have precisely the same construction: conjunctive participle of the main verb + auxiliaries chosen from approximately the Indian semantic set (*go, come, give, take, put, throw,* etc.) with more or less the same significance (see Table 13).

In Kirghiz, a few of the meanings seem to be somewhat aberrant and concerned more with aspectual-modal features (durative, habitual, perfective, potential, etc.), but others, particularly *go* and *come,* fall into line.

In Japanese and Korean, the verbs *go* and *come* appear mostly with verbs of motion, e.g.,

Japanese *dete iku,* Korean *na wa yo* 'exits and goes' = "goes out"; cf. Hindi-Urdu *nikal jaataa hai.*

They also occur in the combinations *bring* ("take and come") and *take away* ("take and go"), exactly parallel to the Indian idiom: Hindi *le aanaa, le jaanaa,* Japanese *motte kuru, motte iku.*

Japanese distinctions in the area of the verb *give* ("X gives to me," "I give to X," "someone honored gives," "someone honored is given," etc.) carry over into its use as an auxiliary:

jibiki wo kashite KUREMASHITA 'He lent me a dictionary'; *kutsu wo migaite AGEMASHŌ ka?* Shall I polish your shoes (for you)?' (Dunn and Yanada 1958:125).[5]

Note also the ubiquitous Japanese equivalent of "please," *V-te kudasai* (from *kudasaru* 'someone honored gives to me'). *Take* seems to be absent in Japanese and Korean, as in Chinese, and has an aberrant meaning ("possibility") in Kirghiz. Japanese uses *receive,* however, in the related sense of 'getting someone to do something for one':

tonari no hito ni pan wo katte MORAIMASHITA 'I got the neighbors to buy me some bread'.

There are in Japanese a number of additional compounds involving a partly different set of auxiliaries and the so-called (e.g. by Miller 1967:317) infinitive in -/i/:

toridasu 'take out' (*toru* 'take' + *dasu* 'cause to emerge'), *toriageru* 'pick up, adopt, take away' (*toru* + *ageru* 'lift up'), *kaerimiru* 'look back, reflect' (*kaeru* 'return' + *miru* 'see').

These *-I*-form compounds (i.e., rather than the *-te* "gerund"), like the *-I* conjunctives (see chapter 3), seem to be passed over in silence in most handbooks of the language.

The closest analogy of all with Indian usage, as well as the most elaborate development of the feature, seems to be in Uzbek and in Tajik. The latter is noteworthy in that the construction seems to be absent from Persian, at least from literary Persian, although possibly an investigation of colloquial dialects or a more thorough analysis of texts from this point of view might turn up some echo of it.

It is significant that it is also less typical of Anatolian Turkish. Of seven types of "compound verbs" given by Lewis (1967:191-192), one (*yazmak* 'write' = "narrowly escape") is obsolete and in any case *sui generis*; two (with 'go' *gitmek* and 'stand' *durmak*) tend to be replaced colloquially by a sequence of two *finite* verbs (reminding us of the Russian construction with 'take'); four ('come' *gelmek,* 'stand' *durmak,* 'be left' *kalmak,* and 'see' *görmek*) have quasi-aspectual meanings very similar to what Kellogg (1938:259-63) calls in Hindi the frequentative, continuative, and progressive forms, "be in the habit of," "keep on," "go on," etc. – rather than denoting *Aktionsart.* All of them (except optionally *durmak*) are, moreover, added to the *-A/E* gerund, analogous to the *present* participles used in the corresponding quasi-aspectual Indian constructions, rather than to the *-IP* gerund, analogous to Indian conjunctive or past-active participles, which *is* used in Uzbek and Kirghiz. There remains 'give' *vermek* with at least a function if not a form of the explicator type ("rapidity, ease, suddenness"). This is not, however, the "normal" function of *give* (= "benefactive") in either the languages of India or in Uzbek, Tajik, Mongolian, Korean, and Japanese. (The Kirghiz 'give', *ber-*, does have this meaning in part.)

It will be noted that one of the auxiliaries consistently listed for all these languages is the verb *see.* In conjunction with the CP it gives (in all the languages except Anatolian Turkish) the idea of *attempted* action, a meaning that is also widespread in India. Writers on Indian languages, however, have generally not listed it among the explicators (or intensifiers, as they are usually called), perhaps because its meaning is of a somewhat different sort, certainly not "intensifying," and the combination can be interpreted as indeed a stock but nevertheless transparent and logical phrase – "do something and see" = "*try*" – rather than appearing as a quasi-opaque "compound." Depending upon our imagination, this may be true in varying degrees of others as well, however. It hardly serves as a reliable criterion. "Opaqueness," then, is not a necessary qualification for a Vv auxiliary: it is too subjective to apply. There is, accordingly, no good reason from the standpoint of *form* and general (modifying) function not to include *see* on the Indian list as well – except for Hindi-Urdu, where it falls formally under the CP . . . V construction (*khaaKE dekho* 'try eating it') rather than under the Vv construction (*khaa lo* 'eat-it-up-for-your-own-benefit'). In Anatolian Turkish again CP + *see* does not have this common areal meaning of "try," but signifies instead "continued action": *söyliyegörmek* 'to *go on* speaking'.

Summary of Distribution of Analogies

There are thus basically three analogies to the Indian explicators – the verbal prefixes of eastern and central Europe, the resultative verbs of China and Indo-China, and the auxiliaries used with "gerunds" in certain Altaic and other languages, forming together one large more or less contiguous zone to the north, northwest, and east of the subcontinent. Beyond the limits of this zone, and toward its edges, such overt marking of the semantic categories in question weakens and disappears.

The system of directional prefixes weakens to the north, in English and Scandinavian, and seems to be absent in Finnish (although present to a considerable degree in Latvian).

To the south, only a faded and largely fossilized form of an already abbreviated Latin system exists in the Romance languages, which more typically resort to different lexical items (Sp. *entrar* 'go in', *salir* 'go out', *subir* 'go up', etc.), or what are now different lexical items. The surviving (in some cases still slightly productive) prefixes tend to have meanings (*to, into, onto, under, between, from, with*) that are hardly analogous to those of Indian explicators.

The Greek prefixes, on the other hand, seem somewhat more productive (Thumb 1964:99-100 lists seven that can be so labeled), and to produce somewhat more congenial effects:

ana- 'upward' + *stenázo* 'groan' = *anastenázo* 'sigh' (cf. Indian usage of *rise* with verbs of sound and light); *apo-* 'from' + *kimúme* 'sleep' = *apokimúme* 'fall asleep'; *kata-* 'direction toward' + *píno* 'drink' = *katapíno* 'swallow'.

Persian also has a small set of six or so fairly common (but unproductive?) "preverbs" (*gashtan* 'turn', *bar gashtan* 'return') that may be separated from the verb stem by the negative and aspect-mood prefixes (*bar namigasht* 'didn't use to return/wasn't returning').

South of the border zone formed by Romance, Greek, and Persian there is nothing left of the prefix system. Swahili, a language given to using prefixes where others use suffixes, not unexpectedly uses suffixes sometimes where others use prefixes; there is, accordingly, a fragmentary suffixal system of directional indicators (*enda/endea* 'go/go to', *fumba/fumbua* 'close/open'), in a kind of mirror image of parts of the Latin system (*ad-, re-, dis-*), but not really analogous to anything in India.

In Arabic and Amharic, however, there are the glimmerings of expression of this semantic area through auxiliary *verbs* rather than affixes.

According to Mitchell (1962:95-96), colloquial Egyptian Arabic employs sequences of *finite* verbs (cf. Russian, the Balkan languages, and Anatolian Turkish), one of which is typically a verb of motion (*go, come, stand up*) or *take*, in an essentially unitary function; the verb used expressively precedes what may be called the main verb:

XUD ishrab 'Take (and) drink' (cf. Hindi *pii LO* 'drink[ing] take')'

As many as four such quasi-auxiliaries may be piled up together.

In Amharic, there is a construction with explicator-like function that is formally somewhat closer to the Indian locution, namely what Leslau (1968:363) calls "composite verbs," which consist of a "fixed stem" + auxiliary. The parallelism does not go very far, however, for the "fixed stem" is not the conjunctive participle, and there is only one auxiliary, which is not one of the familiar set, but rather the verb 'say' *alä.*

On the eastern side, "resultative verbs" are not found south of Thailand, that is, do not occur in Indonesian languages. Other types of modification ("intensification" properly so-called, repetition, reciprocality, etc.) are effected by other types of devices (reduplication, suffixation, prefixation). The directional element is not present.

Of the three analogies, it is clear that the Central Asian and the Chinese-Thai have the greater bearing in that they at least involve *verbs.* The European (and Persian) prefixes are not only different in form but rather different semantically as well – in the particular *kinds* of directionality and other modifications they express (and do not express). Such dimensions as "for the benefit of the speaker," "for the benefit of the receiver" seem to be missing, in favor of a great elaboration of purely positional relations.

The Chinese resultatives also, as we have seen, are in many cases semantically nonparallel, while the Thai and particularly the Burmese type seem to be transitional. All three cases deserve a far more detailed study and comparison with the Indian phenomena than can be undertaken here. It would undoubtedly throw fresh light on the status of these constructions in these languages themselves to look at them from an Indian point of view (Chinese *gei*-constructions, for example), but the exchange could be mutually beneficial.

The absence of a marked CP *form* in these East Asian constructions need not detain us for long: we can hardly demand one in a language that does not possess one, especially when Hindi itself uses a form identical with the stem. The Munda languages may represent a type of verbal compounding closely allied to that of Chinese or Thai. There is some indication that verb stems may have a CP function in these languages to some extent.

There is thus a confused picture of gradual transition on the eastern frontier, which requires further study, a rather sharp break on the western frontier (there is no such construction even in Pashto [Lorimer 1915:225] and essentially none in Brahui),[6] and continuity, through a narrow isthmus, to the north. There the closest parallels are, significantly, with the languages closest to India, Tajik and Uzbek.

6

THE DATIVE CONSTRUCTION

Universal *vs.* Nonuniversal Categories: The Nature of the Dative Construction

Chapters 2 through 4 dealt with categories and functions (transitivity and action through a second agent, linking of clauses, linear positioning of syntactic elements) that have to be expressed or met, whatever the means or alternatives chosen. Our concern was accordingly with the areal patterning of particular expressional devices. In chapter 5, however, the category itself was of doubtful universality: we noted that explicator verbs perhaps in a majority of cases cannot be rendered into normal English at all. The aspect of a situation that finds expression through them either simply remains unexpressed in many languages or is expressed only occasionally and accidentally – not regularly, and not by any regular *device.* An attempt was made to track down possible analogs to this special semantic category, whatever their expression, as well as trace as usual the distribution of the specific complex of category + device characteristic of India.

The present chapter also deals with a category of probable nonuniversality – at any rate, nonuniversality of overt expression. (We must never underestimate the ingenuity of linguists in the discovery of covert categories, through transformational and other tests.) As is the case with a number of categories not represented or poorly represented in English – particularly the more abstract ones (e.g., "focus" in Philippine languages) – it is difficult to define, describe, or explain in English.

It is necessary to try, however. The essence of it is as follows. Predications involving experiences, particularly experiences of states or conditions, that can be definitively "known" (or somehow pertain) only or primarily to the subject undergoing them are treated differently in some languages from predications involving external acts, states, or conditions, while other languages make no distinction here. Such experiences, which we may call "subjective," typically include liking and disliking, states of health or sickness, happiness and unhappiness, dreaming, feeling, remembering, thinking, embarrassment, pity, doubt, pain, thirst, hunger, sleepiness, anger, urgency, and "knowing" itself.

This category of "subjective experience," as we might call it, is paradoxically marked, in the languages that distinguish it, by describing it from an *external* point of view – that is, by putting the experiencing subject in an *oblique case* (most commonly the dative), and either making the experience itself the grammatical subject or, less commonly, using an impersonal (and generally deleted) grammatical subject.

Put another way, in languages without this distinction – or viewpoint – the subject *does* or *is*, or, very typically, *has* these things, like everything else; in languages possessing it they *happen* or *come* or *exist* with reference to him (see Table 11).

The even-numbered statements in Table 11 are presumably objectively ascertainable; the odd-numbered ones, with MUJHE (= "to me") in Hindi, are not, according to that language. At least, not in the same ways: nowadays, of course, we have fever thermometers and brainwave-measuring electrodes and other fancy devices the inventors of this system could not have foreseen. Perhaps a better way of putting it would be *directly observable* vs. *not directly observable.* This would accommodate our modern inventions, as well as such problematic notions as *having* and *getting.* One may *deduce the existence* of certain situations indirectly, whether by noting the positions of needles on dials or deducing that you must be cold because you are shivering, or sleepy because your eyelids are drooping, or like turnips because your eyes light up when you see them. That is not the same thing as observing them directly, for the phenomena themselves cannot be observed directly by an outsider, being purely subjective sensations. It might even be said that I can interpret the secondary signs by comparing them with similar manifestations attending my own primary sensations.

There may be other ways of indicating such a distinction in the world's languages than by the use of oblique-case subjects, and there

TABLE 11
SUBJECTIVE VS. OBJECTIVE EXPERIENCE

English	*Hindi-Urdu*
1. I like it.	1. MUJHE pasand hai.
2. I'm going to buy it.	2. mãĩ usko khariidũũgaa.
3. I have a fever.	3. MUJHE buxaar hai.
4. I'm not a doctor.	4. mãĩ ḍaakṭar nahĩĩ hũũ.
5. I knew it.	5. MUJHE maaluum thaa.
6. I am finding out.	6. mãĩ maaluum kar rahaa hũũ.
7. I'm in a hurry.	7. MUJHE jaldii hai.
8. I'm hurrying.	8. mãĩ jaldii kar rahaa hũũ.
9. I sympathize with you.	9. MUJHE tumhaare saath hamdardii hai.
10. I will help you.	10. mãĩ aapkii madad dũũgaa.
11. I'm hungry.	11. MUJHE bhuukh lagii hai.
12. I'm eating.	12. mãĩ khaanaa khaa rahaa hũũ.
13. I envy you.	13. MUJHE tumse iirṣyaa hootii hai.
14. I'm going to kill you.	14. mãĩ tumko maar ḍaalũũgaa.
15. I'm feeling cold.	15. MUJHE ṭhaṇḍ lag rahii hai.
16. I'm going inside.	16. mãĩ andar jaanewaalaa hũũ.
17. I miss my village.	17. MUJHE apne gããw kii yaad aatii hai.
18. I work in an office.	18. mãĩ daftar mẽẽ kaam kartaa hũũ.

may be other distinctions somewhat related to it (that between hearsay and direct observation comes to mind as one), but we shall confine ourselves in this chapter to the particular complex of category and device discussed above.

"SUBJECT" AS A GRAMMATICAL CATEGORY

The construction brings up the problem of "subject" *vs.* "topic" and related matters. Is the oblique-case experiencer the "topic" but not the "subject"? Why can't the *experience* be the "topic" as well as the "subject"? Some would have it that way, and insist that the whole construction is *impersonal,* with the oblique personal reference to the experiencer a mere *adjunct* that can be dispensed with. Against this, it may be argued that:

a. the oblique-case experiencer normally occupies the subject *position* in the surface structure of the sentence;[1]
b. if it can indeed sometimes be deleted, so can other kinds of subjects – but deletion of an element whose presence is still implied is not

the same as absence of a truly adjunctual element that was never implied;

c. a number of hidden relations, involving reflexive-possessives, conjunctive participles, etc., indicate that the experiencer is still in some sense the "subject";

d. it is hard to see how an inherently personal experience can be "impersonal"

(This last rather weak – and nonlinguistic – argument may be refuted by such languages as Japanese and Korean, which have contrived ways of discussing these "personal" matters in a fully impersonal and noncommittal fashion. A comparison of this truly impersonal way of speaking with that under discussion here may be instructive, however. There is no personal reference at all, none that is merely deleted and may be readily restored. For *I'm hot, cold, in pain,* one says simply "It is hot, cold, painful"; for *I like it, dislike it,* one says "It is pleasing, distasteful" – not *"*to me*"; for *I'm hungry, thirsty,* one says "The stomach has become empty," "The throat has become dry"; for *I have to do it* [see below], one says "If it is not done, it will not do." If for some reason a personal reference is really necessary, which is usually not the case, it may be tacked on as a true adjunct. Generally the situation is relied upon to supply the implications needed.)

Calling the experiencer the "deep" subject (= "logical" subject?) of the construction but not the "surface" subject may be acceptable, if we keep in mind that, nevertheless, it occupies the positional slot of the surface subject. Perhaps we can give the name "topic slot" (rather than "subject slot") to that surface slot to accommodate these possibilities.

The unsatisfactory character of the grammatical notion of "subject," amalgamating as it does a number of different criteria that may conflict (e.g., agreement, government, position, hidden relations, "actor," "topic") is now widely recognized. It may be that case grammar holds the best solution to this situation by eliminating the troublesome notion of "subject" altogether. It would treat experience-word + predicator, where feasible, as a unitary "*stative verb*" with a valence of D, or perhaps (D). It is, after all, a matter of some interest that the so-called topic is marked as dative (or another oblique case), rather than merely as "topic" – as is possible in some languages (e.g., Japanese, Korean).

"Stative verb" is in some ways an unfortunate terminological choice, in view of the signification this expression has in the grammar of Chinese and similar languages, where it is practically equivalent to "adjective." In later versions of case grammar this seems indeed what is meant, rather than the more restricted meaning I have given it here, and "dative" has been replaced by a category called *"experiencer"; he is tall* is placed in the same category as *he is cold,* which may make sense in terms of English, but the dative-subject category of Indian languages is lost sight of (see Krishnamurti 1971). The earlier version of the theory was more promising for problems like the one under discussion here.

The transformational relations mentioned above still must be accounted for, however, along with agreement relations between the nominal (erstwhile "surface subject") and verbal parts, if such exist, of the "stative verb," so some loose ends remain. The concept of the "grammatical (or surface) subject" is temporarily suspended, but needs to be introduced later, even if under a different name, to account for any agreement relations. Perhaps this is a step forward.

In some languages (e.g., Malayalam), the verb with its dative NP can govern an object in the accusative, which again would seem to indicate some sort of "subject" status for the dative NP. These requirements can also probably be specified by case grammar with the minimum of fuss, however.

(Mal. *eniKKU raamanE ariññilla* 'to-me Raman-acc. knew-not' = "I didn't know Raman.")

The accusative NP in such sentences is certainly not even the "surface" subject (i.e., the sentence cited does *not* mean *'Raman was not known to me').

Fortunately, our concern is only with the distribution of the construction, not with its analysis. (For the present, I shall continue to use the ad hoc label, *dative-subject construction,* for want of a handier one.) In this connection, however, it should be noted that the presence *vs.* absence of the construction does not coincide with the formal separation *vs.* amalgamation of "topic" and (surface or grammatical) "subject." Although it is virtually absent from English and other Western languages, which have a strong tendency to *identify* the two, and its presence to any considerable degree itself constitutes separation of the two, it is also absent or weak in some languages, particularly in the Far East, that otherwise maintain such a separation.

The Domain of the Dative-subject

It is not simply a question of presence or absence, however. The domain of the construction varies from language to language. Indian languages happen to show a particularly strong development of it, or if you will, awareness of this psychological dimension in situations, which brings us back to our usual point of departure.

Certain other languages include varying smaller parts of this territory in the domain of the construction. The whole typological and areal picture here might lend itself to quantification were all the relevant data available in grammars and dictionaries. Unfortunately, much of it has to be laboriously gleaned from texts and/or informants. Complicating matters also is the existence of alternative constructions (regular and dative) for a number of situations, depending on the point of view the speaker wishes to adopt at the moment.

Such an undertaking has to be deferred to some later date, and only some general distributional indications can be given here.

It may well be that this is a criterion that sets off the "Indian area" more sharply than any other here examined. As already noted, a high development of this feature is characteristic of India – perhaps slightly more of Dravidian and slightly less of Bengali (and much less of the Munda languages), but nevertheless present in all the major languages to a degree that seems to be unparalleled elsewhere. On the other hand, the category is not only absent from Chinese, Thai, Indonesian, and Swahili, as we have learned to expect, but – significantly – is not, so far as I have been able to determine, characteristic of the Altaic languages, whether Turkic or Mongolic, nor of Korean or Japanese. It thus becomes the only Indic trait not shared with Altaic. It seems also not to be characteristic of Tibeto-Burman: in Burmese, at least, a type of impersonal verb with a topic occurs, but the topic is not put into any characteristically *oblique* relation, and many notions of this type are expressed, as so often in Altaic (and Greek), by directly constructed verbs: "I hunger," "I thirst," "I sorrow," etc. Conceivably the active/involuntary distinction in Tibetan (Goldstein 1973:35) may be a remotely related phenomenon, but the latter category is not consistently marked by any dative particle associated with a logical subject or topic. In a few cases, however (Goldstein p. 38), it does occur.

On the other hand, the dative construction does occur to some extent in European languages – to the greatest extent in Russian (and Finnish[2]), and diminishing steadily toward the west. It is also found in Arabic, but it is not characteristic of Greek or Persian. The latter language has a few expressions of puzzling structure involving adjectives + suffixed possessive pronouns + 3sg 'be': e.g., *gorosn-am-e* = 'hungry-my-is' = 'I'm hungry'. Significantly, however, the category is strongly present and elaborately developed in Georgian, which rivals Indo-Aryan and Dravidian in the broadness and consistency of the domain included (see Tschenkéli 1958: 1.446-490, Aronson 1970:293-297).

In Amharic, the "logical subject" of the possibly analogous construction is so clearly the grammatical object (suffixed object pronoun) that it is difficult to go on calling it the subject, dative or otherwise. The crucial attribute of subject *position* is no longer present. This might be counted as an example of the by now familiar peripheral attrition of characteristic trait-complexes. A rather similar case is provided by such German expressions as *es gefällt mir, es tut mir leid, es schmeckt mir, es kommt mir vor,* etc. (in contradistinction to *mir ist kalt, mir ist unmöglich, mir ist peinlich,* etc.): here the "experiencer" is present as a dative, but it does not occupy subject position, which is taken by the dummy subject *es.* This may be regarded as a half-way house between dative-subject constructions and full merger with nominative-subject constructions.

The Verb "Have"

This picture would not be complete, however, if we did not also examine a related category, that of the verb *have* and its equivalents. What does *have* "mean"? The first thing that comes to mind is probably "possession" – whatever that means – but a moment's reflection will bring to mind any number of examples – having a cold, a suspicion, a child, a grandmother, an opinion, an end, a lot of work to do, etc. – where this definition seems inadequate. According to Bendix (1966), if we boil all these down the only common meaning to all these A has B expressions is that *there is a relation* between A and B.

In any concrete situation, however, this "relation" has to be more specific: B is owned by A (*I have a set of the Great Books*), B is in A's hand or pocket or house (*I have your copy of Mr. Sammler's Planet*), B is in A's "mind" (*I have no opinion*), B is living kin to A (*I have four uncles*), B is part of A (*Our house has a summer kitchen*), B is an inherent quality of A (*I have a tendency to lose interest quickly*), B is a temporary condition of A (*I have the measles*), etc. Such underlying statements of the real relation are turned into *A has B* sentences by making A, which was in an oblique grammatical relation (but has the greater claim to "topic" status, as the more likely of the two to be a personal noun), the subject and B the object of the empty verb *have* and in the process suppressing (deleting) the remaining more specific information.

Not all languages have a "verb *have*," that is to say, a *have*-transformation: Indian languages do not. The presence or absence of one is one of the great typological watersheds. It will be noted that the underlying-sentence examples above include instances of the temporary location of an object, of invisible relations and inherent relations, as well as of conditions primarily known to the subject. In other words, we have something close to the difference between "observable" and "nonobservable" situations discussed earlier in this chapter.

Have-languages suppress these distinctions along with the other information in the underlying statements. It is not accidental that they happen to be largely the same languages which show weak or no development of the dative-subject category in connection with other verbs.

MAP 6. Distribution of "Dative-Subject" Construction versus the Verb *Have*

Key:

+ + + + +	major area of Dative (or Genitive) Subjects
– – – –	minor area of Dative (or Genitive) Subjects
XXXXX	Topics and Subjects contrastively marked
••••• ••••	other Oblique Case analogies
———	presence of an ordinary verb HAVE
o o o o o	use of verb HAVE in subjective - experience situations marked by use of Dative in Dative - Subject areas (hunger, cold, fear, etc.)

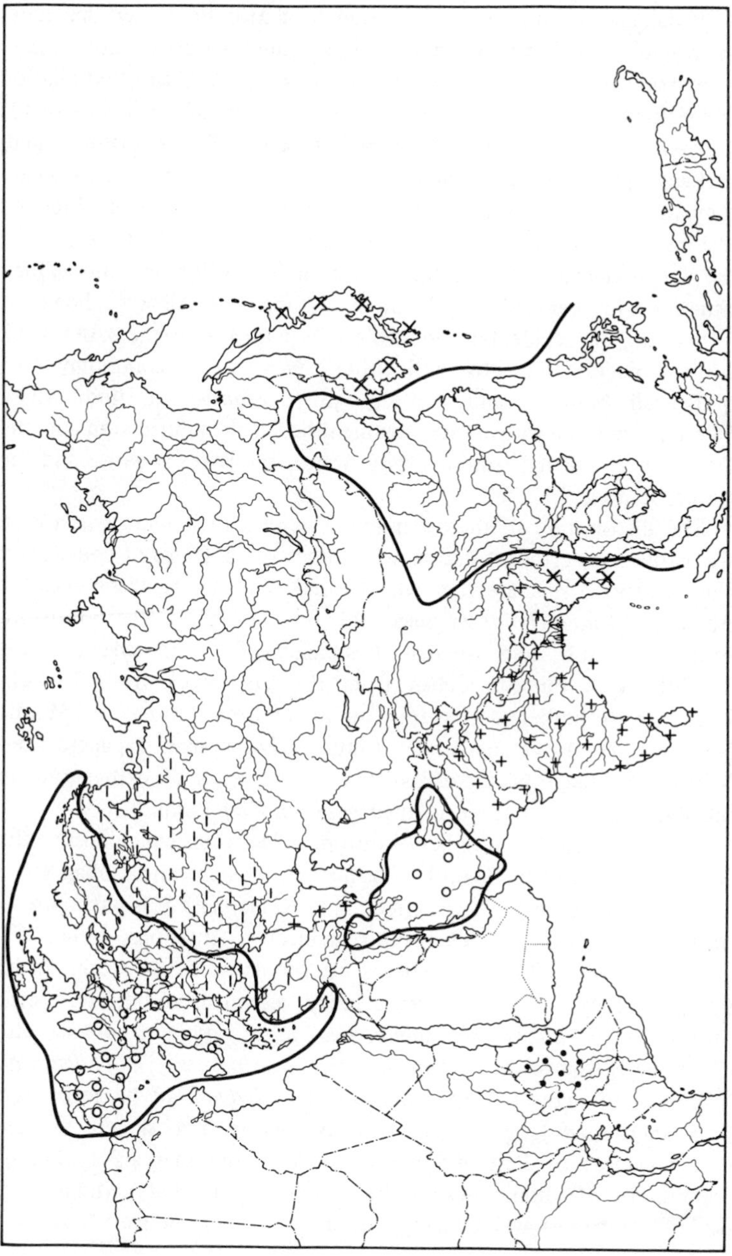

In languages without the *have*-transformation the underlying statement is more or less retained and these distinctions are not suppressed. Expression is always that B *exists* with relation to A, and that relation is specified – at least – as (1) temporary-accidental-*observable* or (2) *inherent/subjective;* sometimes these last two are further distinguished.

Languages – including Indian languages – differ on precisely where they draw the line between the two categories (or three, if three are distinguished). In Hindi, it is the "accidental" category that seems to be the *unmarked* one, which takes over in borderline and unspecified situations; in Dravidian it is the inherent/subjective. All agree, however, in marking the accidental/observable with a *locative* expression (of A), and the inherent/subjective with either a *dative,* or less commonly (e.g., in Bengali, Mundari, and Turkish) with a *genitive.* In Hindi, where inherent and subjective are distinguished (by intersection of the Dravidian and Bengali modes, as it were), the latter is dative and the former genitive.

The distribution of these *have*-equivalents cuts a wider swath than the dative-subject construction with other verbs. (It is, of course, not always easy to separate the two. See below.) That is, it includes the Altaic (and Finno-Ugric) languages this time as well as Tibeto-Burman, Ethiopic, Arabic, and Russian. Possession of a verb *have* cuts off Swedish from Finnish, Polish from Russian, Greek from Turkish, Persian from Hindi, and Thai and Cambodian from Burmese and Munda languages. It also characterizes Chinese, Indonesian, Japanese, and Korean (although in these last two both modes of expression are possible), and most European languages (including Basque).

That is not all. In a number of European languages which possess the verb *have,* especially Spanish, Portuguese, French, and Italian (to a lesser extent German, Czech, Greek, and Rumanian), it is put to use in many of the same so-called stative-subjective situations, earlier discussed, for which Indian languages use the dative construction: to be hungry, thirsty, sleepy, cold, in a hurry, ashamed, afraid, etc. = e.g., Spanish *tener hambre, sed, sueño, frío, prisa, vergüenza, miedo,* etc. The same is true of the Persian *have*-verb, *daashtan,* e.g., *meyl daashtan* 'like/want to enjoy' (cf. Sp. *tener ganas*), *xaab daashtan* 'be sleepy' (cf. Sp. *tener sueño*), etc. This is a peculiarity not shared by the *have*-languages of East and Southeast Asia, and suggests a kind of community of idiom between India and Europe that perhaps only becomes apparent when viewed from such a perspective. "Western" *have* becomes the "equivalent" of the dative construction within the same general semantic framework.

Not *all* languages that possess the verb *have* lack the dative construction, however. As we proceed eastward across Europe, languages that possess the verb *have* begin to use a dative construction rather than a *have* construction in these situations more and more – a little in German (*mir ist kalt, warm; es tut mir leid*), more in Czech (*je mi zima, teplo, dvacet let, líto, smutno*), to a dominant degree in Rumanian (*îmi e frig, cald, frică, foame, sete, dor, rău*, etc.).[3] Finally in Russian it prevails completely, despite the existence of a literary *have*-verb, *imet'*.

In the north, however, the *have* expressions begin to be replaced (in English, Scandinavian, partly in German, even occasionally in Russian – e.g., *i͡a goloden*) by a more alien device, the adjectival predication of the type in *I AM hungry, thirsty, afraid,* etc.

There is yet another category related to the dative construction that should be mentioned here. This is the category of compulsion (and/or moral duty) – for which English uses *have to* and Spanish *tener que* and Hindi, Bengali, and Russian, etc. the dative construction, with the infinitive of a verb playing the role of B this time. Unfortunately, this fine example of an invisible relation cannot be put down as a pan-Indian trait, as the Dravidian languages use nominative expressions here.

7

CONCLUSIONS

What do we conclude from all this?

First, on the most general level, we may conclude that a great many linguistic features *do* pattern areally – that is, they are meaningfully mappable across language boundaries and across genetic lines. *Area* is therefore an important dimension of linguistic features generally. It is an integral bit of information about them that should not be neglected, even though – and indeed partly because – its ultimate significance may not be fully understood. If there are features that, contrary to the general trend, do not so pattern, that too would be an important fact about them. (I have not turned up many here, but, to be sure, I have not been looking for them.)

It is also of interest whether they form isogloss patterns or merely cluster, although some of the mapping techniques resorted to here should not be construed as necessarily answering this question. At any rate, many traits do exhibit a "diffusionary" pattern somewhat analogous to those exhibited by a number of other cultural phenomena. The "trait core area" may or may not be clear, but there is typically a gradual attrition at the periphery of the distribution (the identifiability of which sometimes depends on the fineness of our measurement criteria). One classic example of this is the gradient from postpositions to prepositions (or vice versa) through a mixture of the two, ambipositions, and other peculiar transitional phenomena (found, e.g., between India and Iran, in Ethiopia, and in China). Another is the gradient between preposed and postposed attributive adjectives (found, e.g., in Europe and the Mediterranean, and again in Burma). A third involves the explicator-verb phenomenon, with both inventory of items and usage changing as we move through Tajik and Uzbek to languages more remote from India, or eastward into Burma. Several other examples could be cited, and many more are doubtless waiting to be discovered. The point is, we need to have the larger picture chalked in in order to see such phenomena for what they are.

The first two examples above may present imperfect analogies to culture-trait distributions in that involving the order of two necessary elements they necessarily imply a transition to the opposing case (at whichever end we start). Possibly excepting closed systems like kinship, diffused culture-traits will not involve, ordinarily, any opposite number or mirror image – but merely presence, attenuation, and absence. The third example above is of this latter type, however, and there are certainly many other linguistic examples of it: counter-words (noun-classifiers), gender, tone, retroflexion, palatalization, etc. The absence of these features does not imply the presence of something else.

It might be expedient to treat *all* linguistic traits, even the either/or variety, as instances of this type for certain typological and mechanical purposes; this could be done simply by assigning one alternative a plus (+) value and the other a minus (-) value. Which should be which may be determined by studying the distributions themselves. However, in order to accommodate the transitional phenomena just discussed, a representation slightly more complicated than a simple binary one is needed. Even when there seem to be only two alternatives, as we have just seen, languages find ways of mixing them – especially where such equivocation is areally appropriate.

Second, the areal distribution of a linguistic feature may or may not correlate with the distribution of other linguistic features. Which do and which do not, and why, is not in all cases within our present powers of explanation. For whatever reason, a number of such distributions do seem to correlate to the point where definite areal configurations of greater magnitude emerge. It is important to note that the distributions rarely completely coincide: even where a plausible relation has been suggested, as, for example, between conjunctive participles and SOV word order, it is hardly a matter of strict determinism and the two distributions do differ. Here, *correlation* will be defined as "enclosing (in terms of isoglosses) the same general area," i.e., rather than quite different ones. No structural relation is necessarily implied.

These areal correlations may range from very close (e.g. SOV and V + Aux) to quite loose (e.g. SOV and Adj + N), so long as the basic configurative condition is fulfilled. The implication, of course, is that in a certain area at the center of the distributions all such traits do coincide. The discrepancies between their outer ranges, on the other hand, serve to define areas of transition (in addition to those defined by the attenuation of a single trait).

Third, the implications of the foregoing for linguistic areas is obvious: they *can be more rigorously defined* than has generally been the case, if we bother to trace the geographic distribution of alleged characteristic traits. In addition to helping to ascertain boundaries and the true extent of these areas, such investigations serve also to confirm or deny the diagnostic status of the traits in question.

Linguistic areas are apparently phenomena of differing magnitudes, starting from the limiting case, the area defined by a single trait. A measure of such magnitude could be evolved, based on the number of traits that correlate to form a particular configuration (and perhaps their weightiness). This might be both useful and revealing.

Some Matters of General Linguistic Interest

In the course of the foregoing investigation a number of points arose of general theoretical, not merely areal-linguistic, interest. I might summarize them briefly here before proceeding to put things together specifically with regard to the ostensible problem of this exercise, the definability of an *Indian* linguistic area – although they do relate also to the adequacy of various typological indices.

With regard to word order, Greenberg's basic order typology forms a good basis on which to work and has brought order to a confused field. If possible without sacrificing this by the introduction of too many variables, it is desirable to introduce certain refinements, however, in order to deal with the transitional phenomena discussed above. Desirable, that is, from the standpoint of plotting the areal distributions of these things, where such phenomena are of great interest and in a sense even a confirmation of the validity of the distribution. Oversimplification, particularly at the cost of obscuring equivocations and forcing an artificial simple-binary choice, should be avoided.

It may be desirable to avoid it even for purposes of general typology. Our matrix needs to be refined to the point of providing for all the basic variants exemplified in natural languages. At the very least, we must record equivocations such as Pr/Po or NA/AN. Dezső, speaker of a language (Hungarian) where even the basic clause order type is very much in doubt, supports not only this expedient (Hungarian would be

SOV/SVO) but proposes an expansion of the basic order types themselves from three to four (SOV, SVO, VSO, and VOS) (Dezső 1968). Each would have "free" and "rigid" subtypes.

We have noted the difficulties encountered in finding criteria to establish the "basic" clause-element order in many languages. Transformational grammar offers no clear solution and we end up falling back on frequency. Even Greenberg's "rigid" Type III (SOV) appears to be misnamed: many of the languages included in it in fact exhibit extreme flexibility of word order, which would seem to be governed more by the presence or absence of morphological marking of clause function than by basic order type. In the circumstances, it might be a good thing at some stage to have a more elaborate typology taking into account the possible alternate and minor orders of a language, in order of precedence (based on frequency, any structural criteria, and such matters as degree of departure from normal intonation contours). This larger pattern also differs significantly from language to language, yet there seem to be general restrictions also, as Dezső 1968 has noted. Major alternate orders may also be of areal relevance, as I have suggested may be the case in Spanish and Greek. They may be relics of past or harbingers of future change. Establishing such a catalogue of alternative orders would involve difficulties, to be sure, at least equal to those involved in establishing the "basic" order itself. In a sense they are the other side of the same picture, however, and could be made to emerge from the same investigative process as a by-product if this were taken as part of the goal.

The following refinements in the matrix of order criteria also seem desirable for areal purposes: 1) inclusion of object pronoun position, which as we have seen in chapter 2 exhibits interesting reverse-shadow effects on both sides of the OV/VO line; 2) redefinition of AUX (Greenberg 1966: 84) to include languages without person and number inflection in the AUX; 3) inclusion of goals (G) of intransitive verbs: these generally follow the same order as direct object and transitive verb but in some cases do not.

A further refinement would be the investigation of adverbial adjuncts of time, manner, and place – a task made difficult, no doubt, by the variable position of these categories, but possibly quite rewarding. We know that slightly different normative positions for some of these categories are characteristic of different parts of SVO Europe, and we are familiar with how these patterns – precisely because of their nonessential character – are often carried over into non-native English. They are prime candidates for study of how linguistic patterns may spread. A related investigation would involve predicate adjuncts.

On the other hand, in compensation, some elements in the wider Greenberg-derived matrix can be dispensed with as less useful. "Less useful" for areal purposes means unpatterned and difficult to correlate with other patterns. This may indicate that the category includes more than one kind of thing. The main example of this is the category *numeral-noun,* which seems to behave in some languages analogously to other determiners and in others as a noun in apposition with another noun. Although the world norm according to Greenberg (1966:86) is Num + N, the appositional construction (N + Num) is often possible under special circumstances in such languages also (including English). Meanwhile it emerges as the norm in such otherwise staunchly left-branching languages as Japanese and Korean and is frequent in Dravidian also. (On the other hand, its presence in Tibeto-Burman merely compromises a situation that is already compromised by the position of other noun modifiers.) It is difficult to sort all of this out. Effort might better be expended on investigation of apposition and determination as such. Similar, though lesser, problems of definition attend the category *demonstrative-noun*, with respect to its demarcation from articles and other indicators of definiteness.

A similarly welcome order has been brought into the causative chaos by the Kholodovich typology – even though some of the symbols (e.g., V_i, V_j, V_e) are perhaps not the clearest, and though such terms as "lexical" and "morphological" are invested with meanings that some people seem to find confusing. At least the basic logic of stages of derivation is firmly established.

Emeneau's proposal for Dravidian emphasizes a dimension – semantics – that perhaps could be made more explicit in the basic Kholodovich notation (even though it may be implicit in it and is present in the discussion); it also gives us a convenient name, *mediative,* for a key aspect of this dimension. This function appears to correlate, as we have seen, with "morphological" rather than "lexical" causatives when both are present. The basic Kholodovich notation does not neatly provide for distinguishing these when they co-occur at the same derivational level. Much more work is needed on the precise semantics (and syntactic implications) of specific derivative verbs in all languages with complex causative morphologies.

In applying the "maximum-distinction" typology proposed here as a modification of the Emeneau typologies, there is a problem beyond that of merely getting the right information. What if the maximum distinction is exemplified by only one or two verbs? This may well be the case in Old Tamil and Malayalam (roots *naṭa* 'walk' and *uṇṇ-* 'eat' = +5). And what if some of their "terms" show definite indications of lexicalization? Should we apply the yardstick blindly, regardless (it would no doubt still indicate something)? Or perhaps set some arbitrary minimum – 5? 6? – of sets that would have to exemplify those distinctions?

I trust I have sufficiently belabored the point that not only is the transitivity or intransitivity of the base very relevant to causative formation and function but that *semitransitives constitute a distinct class in most languages* that is also relevant. These "ingestives," as I have half-seriously called them – verbs like *eat, drink, see, hear, learn,* etc. – show distinctive syntactic and morphological behavior that is closer to that of intransitives than to that of the transitives with which they are usually classed. Their first causatives are double transitives rather than mediatives, generally speaking; they accordingly may form first causatives when "other" transitives may not in a language, or may form second causatives when transitives may not. Their first causatives are generally equivalent to distinct lexical items in languages like English, something that is true of intransitives (when the distinction is not purely syntactic) but almost never of transitives. Their behavior should constitute a separate subtopic in the study of the causative system of a language and should never be taken as an indicator of the behavior of full transitives.

It was noted in passing in chapter 3 that the causative morpheme – the "morphological" causative, that is – is frequently also the denominative verbalizer in languages where it exists (though not in all, and to varying degrees of productivity). Semantically, this is logical enough, as is in fact noted in many grammars – *'to cause to be, or produce X'.* Syntactically, however, it often produces a surface anomaly that is not noted, in that the resulting verbs are sometimes intransitive, yet contain the causative morpheme, which may be restricted in its capacity to be repeated. Causativization of such verbs, if any, has to resort to other means in such circumstances. This suggests that the denominative mechanism (or mechanisms) should also be an adjunct to the causative "profile" of every language. It could further sharpen typological characterization.

The concept of *anticausative* is a particularly useful contribution of the Kholodovich typology. There is much to indicate, however, that it stands in need of more careful definition – and application. That is, it needs to be made clearer if and how it is to be distinguished from morphological passives and reflexives – a distinction members of the Kholodovich team themselves are not always careful to make. The problem is, of course, that prior to the introduction of the term *anticausative,* anticausatives were generally subsumed under those terms (also *middle, passive-neuter,* etc.). That does not mean that we should go to the opposite extreme; those terms may still have their valid areas of use, distinct from anticausative.

The most useful definition of anticausative would be a reverse marking of the transitive/intransitive distinction, with the intransitive term a morphological derivative of the transitive term. Presumably such a category would not co-occur with the category causative in the same verb stem (whereas there can be passives of causatives and causatives of passives). It is not necessarily excluded from co-occurring in the same language with a causative device, however: causative and anticausative devices may divide the work of maintaining the transitive-intransitive distinction between them – some verbs going one way, some the other.

In such a language (e.g., Arabic), moreover, a given device may be "anticausative" when it is performing this task, and otherwise reflexive, reciprocal, or passive – and as such *not* prohibited from co-occurring with causative stems, which complicates further the problems of definition. The function of the device may depend on other categories it contrasts with in the system of a language, or merely in the system of a particular verb. Suffice it to say that all this is as yet insufficiently sorted out, and the category as presently applied – by me or by certain members of the Kholodovich team – may well lump together a number of unlike things.

One of the more interesting things so lumped may be the area variously dubbed "reflexive," "middle," or (A. Zide 1972) "+ affectedness of subject" – an area overlapping with that considered under "dative-subject" in chapter 6 and overlapping in addition with one aspect of the material considered in chapter 5 – the "reflexive" auxiliary *take.* In Telugu, at least, that auxiliary serves not only its typical Indian function of "affectedness of (animate) subject"

(*nercuKONU* 'learn for one's own benefit', *wanṭa naayantaṭa neenee ceesuKONNAANU* 'I prepared the food *myself*'

[Dzenit 1972:735]) but also, as we have seen, to derive certain "anticausative" verbs (*teracuKONU* 'open of its own accord').

This element of reflexivity may not characterize all "anticausatives" – in Turkic and similar languages the two features would seem to contrast – but it is by no means confined to Munda and adjacent Dravidian languages. It is of the very essence of the European (and Arabic) expression of the anticausative. The anomalies of some West European (e.g., Spanish) usage are more readily derivable from "affectedness of subject" as the basic category than from "intransitivity."

In this connection it is interesting that in some languages (e.g., Indonesian) the category "causative" overlaps with "benefactive" in the same way that "anticausative" does with "reflexive". "Benefactive" (expressed by the verb *give*) is the paired antithesis of "reflexive" (expressed by the verb *take*) in the Indian system of explicator verbs. A morphological expression of these notions may therefore complement the expression through auxiliaries typical of India – but with a zone where the two overlap.

Simultaneous marking of both transitive and intransitive terms should probably be distinguished as a special type. This in fact seems to be Kholodovich's intention.

An especially intriguing aspect of the causative picture is the evident connection in a number of languages of anticausatives (or "passives") with the causative category itself. I am referring not merely to a syntactic and semantic connection, but to an overt morphological connection, often observed in these pages. That is, in some languages, the "causative" and "passive" markers are *one and the same morpheme* (e.g., Tuvinian, Manchu, Korean, certain Mon-Khmer tribal languages of Vietnam[1]): added to intransitive bases, it causativizes; added to transitive bases, it decausativizes. Many other languages contain anomalous fragments of this sort, e.g., Hindi *kahlAA-*, "causative" of *kah-* 'say', has a passive meaning 'be called or named.' Cf. also the Telugu suffix -CU in, e.g.,

kaaGU/kaaCU 'boil (intr/tr)' *vs.* *naḍuCU/naḍuPU* 'walk/drive'

(at least from a synchronic-descriptive point of view – whatever its origins); also the Georgian confixes A . . . EB "causative" and I . . . EB "passive", and Bilin *-S-* (allomorph of -IS) "causative" and -S- (allmorph of -əST) "passive."

It is even commoner for the causative device of one language to closely resemble the passive device of a related language, e.g.,

Hindi-Bengali causative -AA, Gujarati passive -AA; Mongolian causative -UUL, Turkish passive -UL; Turkish causative -T, Mongolian passive -T, Komi causative -ÖD, Hungarian passive -ŐD. Or the languages may be unrelated but contiguous: e.g., Baluchi causative -EN, Brahui anti-causative -ENG. What seems to be implied is a stage – protohistorical, deep-transformational, or even present-surface – where there is a category identified simply as *change of verbal valence,* for which the directionality of the change (addition *vs.* subtraction) is specified later.

It may be said that Soviet Turcologists, in whose domain this question is posed most sharply, are not unaware of it.

In summary, it may be said that while a good beginning has been made, by no means has the last word been said on causatives.

Although *langue* is not a statistical structure, *parole* may be treated this way for some purposes – and it is at the level of *parole,* we are reminded (Haugen 1950, Scotton and Okeju 1973), that borrowing and language change of all types, after all, are initiated, in which process frequency plays an important role.

In both general and areal typology frequency studies, therefore, have a legitimate place, sometimes an indispensable one. We saw how they may be in the end the only practical method for ascertaining certain word order norms. They are also particularly desirable for a finer characterization of transitional phenomena of all types.

Finally, it should again be noted that problems in the definition or identification of various categories are typically associated with the frontier of the areal distribution of those categories. In such cases, especially, to repeat, location and the typology of neighboring languages are very much part of the essential facts.

The Indian Linguistic Area

It remains to be seen how these several typological indices correlate with respect to the particular areal problem selected for this study. They turn out to correlate remarkably well when we overlap them, enclosing the Indian area in a series of concentric isoglosses of varying shapes and setting it off from Southeast Asia on the one side and the Middle East on the other. The sole exception among the criteria examined here was anticausatives, on which score the subcontinent, though partially involved, appears peripheral to the main centers of development (in the same way it does with respect to counter-words and to the ergative construction).

India appears to be a focal point of the distribution of such traits as second causatives, conjunctive participles, explicator compound verbs, dative-subjects, absence of a verb *have,* and the order features SOV, V + Aux, Po, Adj + N, Gen + N, Dem + N, Num + N, Qualif + Adj, and the SMA comparison formula. The core area, where all these traits are found together, seems to be southern, western, and northwestern India (roughly the same area, it should be noted, that Southworth [1974:211-4] and Ramanujan and Masica [1969] find to be the area of greatest development of retroflexion in phonology).

Around the periphery of this core, a complex series of transitional zones is defined as languages progressively lack, or equivocate on, more and more of these features. These transitions begin in northeastern India. Eastern Indo-Aryan lacks a double causative and has a genitive equivalent of the dative subject. The Austroasiatic languages are somewhat more deficient in Indian features than others, the extreme case being Khasi in Assam, which seems in fact to lack most of them; among the Munda languages Santali lacks a double causative, a "typical" set of Vv explicators, and hedges on Qualif+Adj; Sora has causative prefixes and infixes and hedges on OV; Burmese lacks Num+N and equivocates on Adj+N; Tibetan lacks both Adj+N and Dem+N. This is also the sector where retroflexes disappear (in Assamese) and where the Southeast-Asia-based counter-words intrude most strongly. By the time we get to Thai almost all the features are gone except for some resultative compound verbs of uncertain analogy to the Indian type. In Malay even this is gone.

On the south, Tamil shows a weakened second causative; Sinhalese lacks a second causative as well as Num+N, and weakens on OV. On the west, Brahui, Baluchi, and Pashto lack a pure Po and Vv explicator compounds, the latter two a pure V+Aux and the SMA comparison, and Pashto a second causative; Persian lacks in addition Adj+N and Gen+N and possesses a verb *have.* (Kashmiri lacks SOV and V+Aux but otherwise is quite "Indian" – except in phonology.)

All this is normal enough. What is most peculiar is that there is an almost identical and much larger core to the north, in Central and Northern Asia. This phenomenon, which was first noted in connection with word order features (chapter 2), repeats itself with all the others except, apparently, dative-subject. (This *may* have been merely hard to identify. Absence of a verb *have* in, e.g., Altaic, may signal the presence of such a category, but not necessarily). There is analogous attenuation of features along the periphery of this northern area, reaching into Russian and Chinese.

The two areas are connected through a narrow stem in the Hindu Kush and Pamirs and through a wider belt of transitional zones in Tibet and Iran, which are really common to both. In the larger context, the Indian area appears as a southward extension of the Northern Eurasian area.

There is a third center of these traits, smaller and weaker, centering on Ethiopia. It too can be connected with the Indian area, in the sense that no barrier intervenes between them other than the sea.

EXPLANATIONS

What possible explanation can lie behind this strange but apparently quite definite configuration? Admittedly, this question is hard to discuss intelligently without reference to data concerning the history of the configuration, especially clues to the directions of its expansions or contractions, if any, and that inquiry has been deliberately postponed. All that can be done here is to list – and criticize – a few possibilities. (The "Northern Eurasian linguistic area," like a number of others, was first set up on a phonological basis [Jakobson 1931]. It should be pointed out that in this respect it does not form a common unit with the Indian area, its characteristic marks intruding only as far as Kashmiri. The larger configuration is based rather on syntax, morphology, and semantics.)

First, there is the genetic explanation: certain languages resemble each other because they are in fact related. Since the time of Caldwell

---

MAP 7. Selected Distributions Superimposed

Key:

-•-•-•-•- domain of second causatives

• • • • • (first causatives only)

- - - - - - Adjective + Noun order

□ □ □ □ Past Gerunds

////////// Explicator - Compound Verbs

+ + + + Dative - Subject construction

(stippled) OV word order

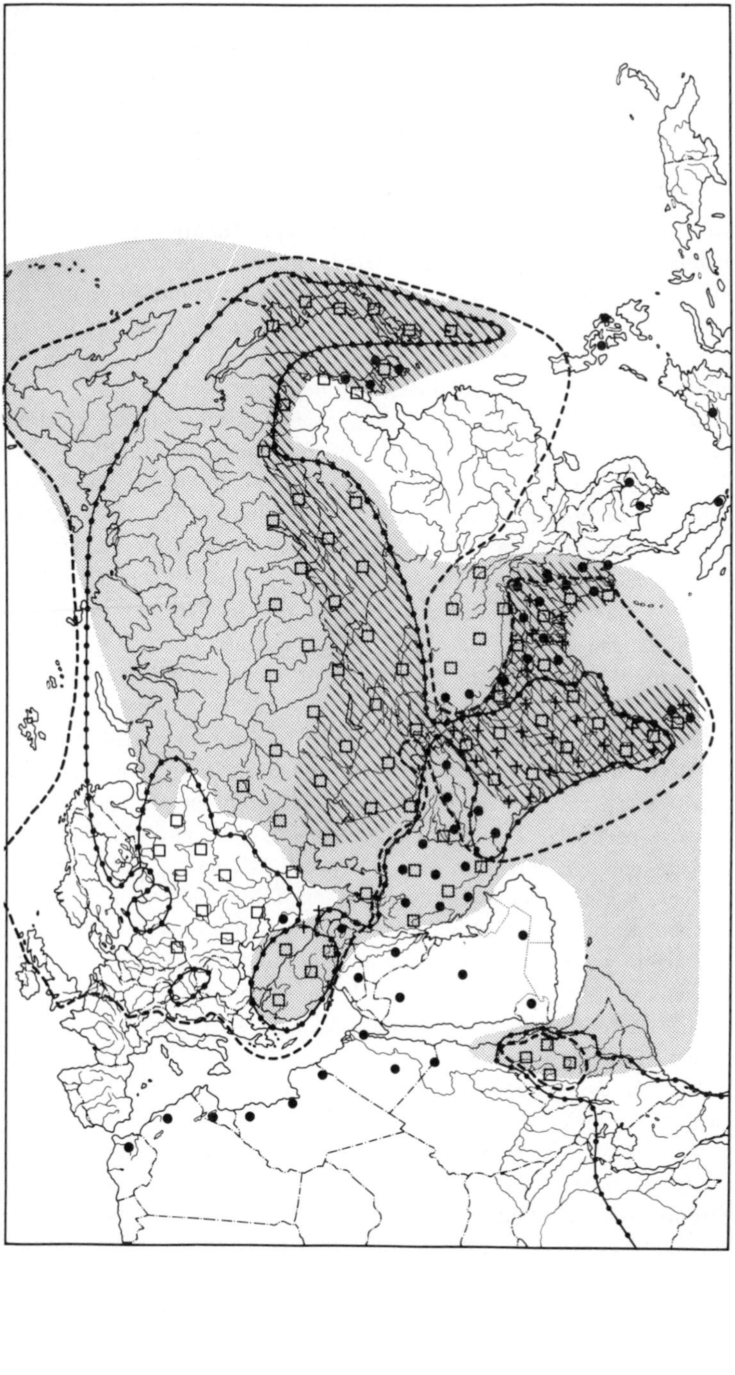

(1856), the possibility of a genetic relation between Dravidian and Altaic has been suggested. More recently (Tyler: 1968, et al), substantial arguments in support rather of a Uralic-Dravidian connection have been advanced. Even at their broadest, however (e.g., Swadesh's "Basque-Dennean"), phylogenetic theories still leave us with the fact of linguistic convergence – of intrusive Indo-European and Munda adapting themselves to some degree to these conditions. They also do not account for the Ethiopian case. (Theories of a universal *Ursprache* or of a "Nostratic" family including Semitic and Indo-European as well as Altaic and Dravidian cannot account, of course, for subsequent typological divergences, e.g., between Ethiopic and the rest of Semitic or between Indo-Aryan and the rest of Indo-European, by reference to such a postulated genetic inheritance.)

There is something also mildly inconsistent about positing immutability of genetic inheritance as an explanation for the resemblances between Altaic and Dravidian and accepting radical changeability of genetic inheritance as an explanation for the resemblances between Indo-Aryan or Munda and Dravidian (because the known facts will not permit the former hypothesis). Nor is it merely a matter of the supposed stability (and therefore perhaps also gravitational pull) of a certain language type, i.e. SOV, or of migratory vs. stay-at-home languages. It can be shown that Dravidian, Uralic, and Altaic have also not been immune to forces of areal convergence, even in word order (as is shown by Finnish and Hungarian). To take another small example, the Dravidian languages by no means constitute a uniform bloc with regard to causative categories or formations. A number of convergences between particular Dravidian languages and adjacent non-Dravidian languages present themselves, e.g., between Malayalam and Sinhalese, between Kannada and Marathi, between Telugu and South Munda, between Kurukh and Oriya or Hindi. Brahui shows a number of adaptations to its Iranian environment. Still, it may be conceded that the relative number and degree of such changes is in favor of a hypothesis of a fairly stable typological area where the brunt of the burden of adaptation is borne by intrusive rather than local languages.

Another explanation might be general-typological: the features in question are all somehow related to SOV or "left-branching" syntax. In most cases, there is no reason why this should be so, and sometimes clearly contrary evidence. Causative suffixes are also found in the extreme right-branching Bantu languages, for example. Verbal compounding somewhat analogous to the Indian type is found in Chinese,

Thai, and Vietnamese. While most of the SOV languages of the Old World lie within the configuration, a few do not, e.g., Basque, and Kanuri in mid-Saharan Africa. These tend toward right-branching in the noun phrase. Basque, moreover, has inflectional *pre*fixes, a verb *have*, a suffixed article, incorporated objects, no conjunctive participle, no causative, no dative subjects – it is not at all like Indian or Altaic languages. It even has a good deal in common with the fringe West European type exemplified by VSO Celtic. All these features would seem to be more or less independent variables, therefore: SOV is not the determining factor.

Correlations are primarily on an areal rather than – or at least in addition to – a typological principle. Proximity to a core-feature zone is the main factor in whether, e.g., an SVO language like Russian has conjunctive participles and many dative-subject constructions while SVO languages farther away such as English, German, and French do not.

We still have to account, in any case, for the concentration of SOV languages in this one area.

The usual explanation advanced for linguistic convergence areas is extensive cultural intercourse and/or domination by a particular higher culture. Thus Sandfeld (1930) attributes the formation of the *Balkan* linguistic area primarily to Greek (Byzantine) cultural domination.

This fits the situation in the Indian subcontinent itself well enough (in which connection the concentration in the south, west, and northwest *vs.* the incomplete assimilation of the northeastern tribal hinterland is an interesting detail). Three aspects of the wider areal picture, however, raise important questions concerning both this theory and the general history (or prehistory) of this part of the world. They are: 1) the strong, unexplained affinity between India and Northern Eurasia; 2) the profound hiatus between India and Southeast Asia beyond Burma; 3) the affinity of India and Ethiopia (but excluding the rest of Africa).

India exerted prolonged and intense cultural influence on Southeast Asia, but this seems to have had little or no effect on the typology of Southeast Asian languages. "Linguistic" influence was supposedly prominent among these cultural influences – involving much lexical borrowing, adoption of scripts (Mon, Cambodian, Thai, Lao, originally Javanese, and possibly some Philippine languages are among those that took their scripts from India, as well as, of course, Burmese), and local cultivation of Sanskrit or Pali for partly administrative as well as esthetic purposes. Mighty as these influences have been, they apparently were not the kind that bring about typological changes. Southeast Asian languages stand among those furthest from Indian languages typologically.

An analogous relationship holds between China on the one hand and Japan and Korea on the other. The evidence of these Chinese and Indian cultural colonies may be submitted as conclusive: domination by a ruling culture, even for prolonged periods, is insufficient to produce convergences of the sort under discussion here. Direct participation may be confined to an elite, in which case borrowing may be selective and predominantly lexical. A more intimate, less structured, intercourse seems to be required. Such a situation probably prevailed in the Balkans in addition to the cultural domination by Byzantium. (The Balkan case seems to be a matter of continued evolution on the basis of an already common substratum, with which subsequent influences – except the Turkish – were essentially in harmony. Since some of the known historical accommodations – such as loss of the infinitive – involved Greek also, that language emerges as much a victim as a cause. The failure of Turkish to make more than a lexical imprint on the Balkan languages despite centuries of political dominance is another case in point.) It also seems to have prevailed in the subcontinent.

Contacts between India and Ethiopia, particularly in early (and more formative?) times, may have been more important than is generally realized. In later times they do not seem to have been as spectacular as those between India and Southeast Asia, however. The evolution of the Ethiopian area appears to have been a continuous process extending into recent times, on the basis of a momentum already present – the affinity of which for India is unexplained.

Contacts between India and Central Asia, particularly in the sense of migrations, have been important since very early times. Migrations can involve the kind of intimate mingling of people that seems to be required. It is conceivable that the six-hundred years of Turkish rule in India also had more profound effects than Turkish rule in the Balkans, involving a moving in and settling down of larger numbers of people. Turkish rule was over the North, however, and the greatest affinity is between Altaic and the languages of the South.[2] This clearly must go back to a period long before the Muslim invasion of India. (For whatever reason or combination of reasons, it is worth noting that the hiatus between India and the Perso-Turkish Middle East – as distinct from the Semitic Middle East – is much less profound than that between India and Southeast Asia. In fact, there is no hiatus, but rather an allied border zone, with gradual transitions.)

There is no reason, of course, why we must seek a single explanation for the "Indo-Altaic" configuration. A succession of factors may account for its present shape. As noncorrelating distributions (counter-words, ergatives, phonology) show, a given cultural area is not, perhaps fortunately, a rigidly self-contained entity, open to influences from only one direction. The configuration is the result only of a tendency for certain influences to be more important than others. All the features considered here do not necessarily go back to the same period. Some no doubt developed and spread in subsequent periods, in different directions from others. It is quite possible, for example, that explicator compound verbs are a speech fashion that spread at a time when northern India was in close contact with Central Asia, perhaps from the former to the latter.

Suggestions for Further Work

Let us leave these questions unanswered for the time being and conclude by listing a few directions in which research might most usefully proceed in the immediate future.

1. Additional potential all-India criteria should be explored, I do not pretend to have exhausted them here. Mapping out of *non*correlating distributions is also important.

2. Attempts should be made to find criteria that define other assumed linguistic areas. Ultimately a scale of magnitude for linguistic areas may be drawn up by comparing these criteria.

3. Criteria can be found that begin to define subregions within India (or within Indo-Altaic). The transitional phenomena noted here already begin to define certain regions, e.g., northeastern India. These may be supplemented by positive criteria.[3]

(In all three cases above, the essential methodological principle should be observed of following out the distribution to its end – to the points of its exhaustion or confrontation with an opposing phenomenon.)

4. Refinements may be introduced into the study of the distribution of features taken up here – particularly statistical refinements. One possibility would be to draw up standard Swadesh-type lists of, e.g., verbs typically occurring in transitive/intransitive pairs, and of typical dative-subject "stative verbs," against which to test the behavior

of each language with regard to devices employed and come up with a statistical measure.

5. The process of development of "Indo-Altaic" should be studied, particularly through systematic use of written materials from earlier periods, correlated geographically and chronologically. Methods for a "historical linguistic geography" should be evolved.

6. An area should be explored for its relevance to "Indo-Altaic" that has been unfairly neglected here: Australia. If the affinities, which seem promising, are confirmed, important new questions would be raised, not covered by the speculations in this chapter.

APPENDIX A.

INVENTORY OF PROPOSED INDIAN AREAL FEATURES

It has been thought useful, both to put the foregoing chapters into perspective and to serve as a basis for further work, to append here a list of convergence features in the Indian area pointed to over the years by various writers, together with a rough evalution in terms of area-*defining* utility. It is quite possible that it is not a complete list of such proposed features, but it may serve as a starting point.

Feature	*Source(s)*	*Indian Area-Defining?**	*Distribution*
A. phonological			
1. retroflex consonants, esp. stops	Caldwell 1875 Grierson 1927 Emeneau 1956, 1972 Kuiper 1967 Ramanujan & Masica 1969 Bhat 1973 Southworth 1974	yes	Dravidian, Indo-Aryan (except Assamese), Tibetan, Pashto, Burushaski, Munda (except Korku, Sora) (retroflex sibilants & affricates char. of *Chinese*)
2. aspirated consonants	Ramanujan & Masica 1969	no	Indo-Aryan + Tibeto-Burman, Burushaski, Khasi,

*Parentheses ( ) indicate distribution goes significantly beyond "Indian." Chapters refer to chapters in this book.

APPENDIX A

Feature	Source(s)	Indian Area-Defining?*	Distribution
			Palaung, some Munda (also Chinese – but *not Dravidian*)
3. nasalized vowels	Ramanujan & Masica 1969	no	Indo-Aryan (except Marathi), Tibetan-Burmese-Newari, some Munda, Nicobarese (but *not Dravidian,* except Kurukh)
4. affricate opposition ts/tš (dz/dž)	Bloch 1934 Emeneau 1956 Ramanujan & Masica 1969	no	regional: 1) Marathi-Telugu, s. Oriya, n. Kannada, Gadba-Ollari; 2) Burushaski, Kashmiri, Pashto, Kafiri, Khowar, Bhalese, Ishkashimi, Tibetan (also Chinese, Slavic, etc.)
5. syllabic structure and phoneme distributions?	Emeneau 1971	?	?
6. tendency to initial stress?	Beames 1872	?	?
B. morphological			
1. absence of prefixes	Bloch 1934 Emeneau 1956	(yes)	Dravidian and Indo-Aryan (excluding borrowed Skt. & Pers. words); also Altaic, etc. (*but not* Munda, Tibeto-Burman, Burushaski, Eastern Iranian)
2. verbal prefixes	Emeneau *et al.* 1971	no	Iranian + Brahui
3. two stems in personal pronouns	Bloch 1934 Emeneau 1956	(yes)	Dravidian and Indo-Aryan (but also Indo-European generally; *not Munda*)
4. same case morphemes added to singular and plural stems	Grierson 1927 Bloomfield 1933 Emeneau 1956, 1971	(yes)	Dravidian, Indo-Aryan; but also Altaic, Uralic

INVENTORY OF PROPOSED INDIAN AREAL FEATURES

Feature	Source(s)	*Indian Area-Defining?**	Distribution
5. dative in *k-/g-*	Grierson 1927	no	Dravidian + Oriya, Assamese, Bengali, Hindi, Sindhi (*but not* Marathi, Gujarati, Rajasthani, Nepali, Panjabi, Sinhalese, Tibetan)
6. morphological causatives	Emeneau 1971 (chapter 3)	(yes)	Dravidian, Indo-Aryan (also Iranian, Altaic, Uralic, etc.)
7. anticausatives	(chapter 3)	no	NW Indo-Aryan; Munda (more char. of Altaic, Uralic, W. Indo-European)
8. negative conjugation	Emeneau 1971	no	Dravidian + Marathi, Nepali; also Altaic
9. phonaesthetic forms a) reduplicated b) in *-k*	Bloch 1934 Kuiper 1967 Emeneau 1969, 1971	(yes)	Dravidian, Indo-Aryan (characteristic of Austroasiatic)
10. echo-words	Bloch 1934 Emeneau 1938, 1971	yes	Dravidian, Indo-Aryan, Munda
C. syntactic			
1. conjunctive participle	Bloch 1934 Emeneau 1956, 1971 Kuiper 1967 (chapter 4)	(yes)	Dravidian, Munda, Tibeto-Burman, Indo-Aryan (but also Altaic, Uralic, Russian, Japanese-Korean)
2. quotative c.p. "having said" a) w. phonaesthemes	Bloch 1934 Kuiper 1967 Emeneau 1971	?	Dravidian (*not* Central & Northern) + Marathi, Dakkhini, Nepali, some Munda
3. agentive (quasi-ergative) construction, esp. "impersonal" type	Grierson 1927	no	Indo-Aryan (*not* in mod. Bengali), Tibeto-Burman, Baluchi, Pashto (*but not* Dravidian or Munda); also Georgian, etc.
4. numeral classifiers	Emeneau 1956 Southworth 1974	no	mainly *eastern* Indo-Aryan and *NE* Dravidian

Feature	Source(s)	Indian Area-Defining?*	Distribution
			+ some Munda (Korwa, Santali); main center Southeast Asia
5. enclitic particle *-api/-um:* 'even/also/ indefinite/and'	Emeneau 1972	yes	Indo-Aryan, Dravidian
6. dative-subject construction	(chapter 6)	yes	Dravidian, Indo-Aryan; also Georgian; partly eastern Europe
7. absence of verb *have*	(chapter 6)	(yes)	Dravidian, Indo-Aryan, Munda, Tibeto-Burman, eastern Iranian (but also Altaic, Uralic, Russian, Arabic, Ethiopic)
8. word order features SOV, AN, GN, demN, Po, SMAdj, etc.	Masica 1974 (chapter 2)	(yes)	Dravidian, Indo-Aryan, Munda (+ Altaic, + *partly* Tibeto-Burman, Iranian, Uralic, Ethiopic, Cushitic, etc.)
9. explicator compound verbs	(chapter 5)	(yes)	Indo-Aryan, Dravidian + Altaic & Iranian of esp. Central Asia; partly Japanese-Korean, Chinese Burmese, etc.
10. recapitulation of final finite V by initial conjunctive ppl. in following sentence	Bloch 1930 Emeneau 1971	?	Dravidian + Pali + ?
11. relative participle	Bloch 1934 Emeneau 1956 Masica 1972	?	Dravidian + Marathi, Oriya, Sinhalese, Bengali, Munda; Tibeto-Burman

APPENDIX B.

A DEVICE FOR GENERALIZING TYPOLOGICAL DISTANCE

The plotting of isoglosses is important, but they present an exceedingly complex and therefore potentially confusing picture when superimposed. (See map 7, where only selected features – not all those discussed in this book, let alone all those that could be discussed – are superimposed.) It would be desirable also to have a simple measure abstracted from all this. This is quite possible, at least for areal typology, through the device outlined below.

Taking the Indian trait-complex (or whichever areal complex is the focus of interest) as a point of departure, we can assign a numerical value to each trait that has been identified as part of the complex. Depending on the presence or absence of each of these traits, any language will then yield a total (the sum of the numerical values of the traits of the complex it does possess) expressive of its nearness to or distance from this characteristic norm. That is, languages with the highest totals will be the most "Indian" (or "Balkan" or "West European" or whatever it is we are testing); those with the lowest totals the least. Naturally, it would be of greatest interest to apply this measure to languages in and around an identified convergence area and progressively further away, correlating it with the search for more precise areal-typological boundaries, but it could also be applied to languages in general, without regard to this (for such purposes, conceivably, as input into a prediction of the relative difficulty of various foreign languages for speakers of a given language – assuming, perhaps without proper proof, that typological distance is at least one component of such difficulty).

APPENDIX B

The simplification of perspective that a device such as the one proposed would effect is best illustrated by languages intermediate in distance from a trait-complex core. Such languages vary in the traits of the complex they exhibit: one may have trait A but lack trait B, while a second may have trait B but lack trait A, and so on. Such differences will show up on an isogloss map as isoglosses with different parameters. We shall certainly want both to work out such details and to superimpose and compare them for certain purposes. For other purposes, however, it becomes, as noted above, progressively more and more difficult to read if more than a few are superimposed at once. The proposed device makes it possible to merge such differences into one generalized measure of typological distance.

It might seem desirable to weight certain traits more heavily than others. However, it is also desirable that the numerical value assigned to every trait be +1, making the entire measure uniformly a matter of binary, yes/no choices. These two desiderata to a large extent can be reconciled by the fact that some core-area traits turn out on closer examination (which is to say, examination of border-zone cases) to be trait-complexes within which different components may exhibit different areally-correlated behavior. If such trait complexes are broken down into as many simple components as necessary, to be checked off separately even for the core area, they in effect gain a weighting that is both probably close to the one desired and nonarbitrarily motivated.

The trouble is, we do not know either how many components are necessary, or even that an apparently monolithic core-area trait is "complex" (exclusively in the sense that it involves components that vary elsewhere in their areal patterning) until we have examined mixed languages *on the border of or outside* the core area itself. In other words, studies such as that to which this book is devoted are necessary preliminaries to setting up such a measuring device for a given areal complex.

In addition to breaking down traits that turn out to be complex into their component variables, it is also necessary to develop a method of dealing in binary terms with simple mixture of traits, conditioned or otherwise, for example SOV/SVO (as in Hungarian), or Po/Pr (as in Pashto). This may be done by dealing with such traits as *SOV* and *Po* in two steps: 1) trait *x* is a dominant order, or the dominant order; 2) trait *x* is the dominant order. Affirmation of *1*) by itself neither implies nor denies a sharing of dominance with another order, hence is possible for both *x* and *x*/*y* languages. It only excludes *y* languages. In the event of a negative response to *2*), however, affirmation of *1*) will imply the mixed dominance *x/y*. Unmixed languages *x* will thus accrue two points (++) in these two steps, while mixed languages *x/y* will accrue only one (+). (It may be asked, why not work with the simpler feature of presence/absence in the first step? The answer is that mere presence, perhaps as an isolated, exceptional item, is not the same thing as possible dominance, that is to say, importance for questions as to basic *type*, and our concern is with the typical, not the exceptional. Admittedly, however, mere presence can be construed as the first step along the way, and a more detailed measure might reasonably provide for it also.)

Such a measuring device for the *Indian* trait-complex might look something like this:

1. (OV) – nominal object before verb a dominant or the dominant order in main clauses;
2. OV – nominal object before verb the dominant order in main clauses;
3. oV – pronoun object generally before finite verb;
4. [OV] – nominal object before verb in subordinate clauses;
5. GV – goal precedes verb of motion;
6. (Po) – the language has both postpositions and prepositions, or only postpositions (x/y, xy, x);
7. Po – the language has exclusively or almost exclusively postpositions (x);
8. (V+aux) – auxiliary follows main verb, either some of the time or all of the time (x/y, x);
9. V+aux – auxiliary generally follows main verb (x);
10. (Adj+N) – some or all adjectivals precede their head noun (x/y, x);
11. Adj+N – almost all adjectivals precede their head noun (x);
12. (Gen+N) – modifying genitives either both precede and follow their noun, or exclusively precede (x/y, xy, x);
13. Gen+N – modifying genitives almost exclusively precede their noun (x);
14. (Dem+N) – demonstratives either both precede and follow the noun, or exclusively precede (x/y, xy, x);
15. Dem+N) demonstratives exclusively precede the noun (x);
16. (qualif+Adj) – some or all qualifiers precede adjectivals (x/y, x);
17. qualif+Adj – all qualifiers precede adjectivals (x);
18. S, M (= MS/SM) +Adj – standard and marker both precede adjectival in comparisons;
19. S+M+Adj – standard precedes marker precedes adjectival in comparisons;

20. $V^{in} \neq V^{tr}$ – transitive/intransitive distinction formally marked in verb (either $V^{tr} = V^{in} + k$, or $V^{in} = V^{tr} + ak$);
21. $V^{in} + k = V^{k,\ tr}$ – some transitives as causative derivatives from intransitive bases;
22. $V^{tr} + k = V^{k,\ med}$ – some causative derivatives from transitive bases;
23. $V^{k} + k = V^{kk,\ med}$ – some second causative derivatives from causative bases;
24. (CP) – participles used to join clauses;
25. CP – 'past adverbial' or 'conjunctive' participles used to join clauses;
26. (Vv) – verbal auxiliaries used to express Aktionsart or directionality (explicators, resultatives, completives);
27. Vv – explicator auxiliaries including several of the set *come, go, give, take, put, throw, fall, rise, remain;*
28. (Dat) – a set of "dative-subject" constructions present;
29. Dat – "dative-subject" category highly developed;
30. ~~HAVE~~ – absence of a verb *have* for most purposes, with resultant retention of distinction between accidental and inherent/subjective "having."

It does not seem possible to avoid an element of subjective judgment or arbitrariness at this stage, particularly pending frequency counts or preferably theoretical refinements in such areas as dative subjects. A measuring device such as the one just outlined can obviously be both expanded (e.g., by the addition of a phonological component – but let us confine ourselves for the present to the subjects covered in this book) and refined. Readers more familiar with such matters than the writer are encouraged to try their hand at it. Let us proceed, however, to apply the present crude instrument to a number of the languages that have been dealt with here, to demonstrate how it works and the kind of results obtained (see Table 12).

The generalized measures of conformity to a given norm thus obtained (the "scores" in the far right column of the table) tend naturally to break into ranges, as indicated. This becomes more obvious as more languages are dealt with. Such categories may be readily mapped, and constitute another approach to defining a linguistic area, useful when used in conjunction with other methods.

TABLE 12

MEASURING CONFORMITY TO THE INDIAN NORM

Trait No.	1	2	3	4	5	6	7	8	9	10	11	12	13	14	15	16	17	18	19	20	21	22	23	24	25	26	27	28	29	30	SCORE
Hindi	+	+	+	+	+	+	+	+	+	+	+	+	+	+	+	+	+	+	+	+	+	+	+	+	+	+	+	+	+	+	30
Telugu	+	+	+	+	+	+	+	+	+	+	+	+	+	+	+	+	+	+	+	+	+	+	+	+	+	+	+	+	+	+	30
Bengali	+	+	+	+	+	+	+	+	+	+	+	+	+	+	+	+	+	+	+	+	+	+	–	+	+	+	+	+	+	+	29
Sinhalese	+	–	+	+	+	+	+	+	+	+	+	+	+	+	+	+	+	+	+	+	+	+	–	+	+	+	+	+	+	+	28
Japanese	+	+	+	+	+	+	+	+	+	+	+	+	+	+	+	+	+	+	+	+	+	+	+	+	+	+	+	–	–	–	27
Burmese	+	+	+	+	+	+	+	+	+	+	–	+	+	+	+	+	+	+	+	+	+	–	–	+	+	+	+	–	–	+	25
Amharic	+	+	–	+	+	+	–	+	+	+	+	+	+	+	+	+	+	+	–	+	+	+	+	+	+	+	–	+	–	+	25
Turkish	+	+	+	+	–	+	+	+	+	+	+	+	–	+	+	+	+	+	+	+	+	+	+	+	+	–	–	–	–	+	24
Tibetan	+	+	+	+	+	+	+	+	+	–	–	+	+	–	–	+	+	+	+	–	–	–	–	+	+	–	–	–	–	+	18
Chinese	+	–	–	–	–	+	–	+	–	+	+	+	+	+	+	+	+	+	–	–	–	–	–	–	–	+	–	–	–	–	13
Persian	+	+	–	+	–	–	–	+	–	–	–	–	–	+	+	+	+	+	–	+	+	–	–	+	–	–	–	–	–	–	12
Russian	–	–	–	–	–	–	–	–	–	+	+	–	–	+	+	+	+	–	–	+	–	–	–	+	+	–	–	+	–	+	11
German	–	–	–	+	–	+	–	+	–	+	+	–	–	+	+	+	+	–	–	+	–	–	–	–	–	–	–	+	–	–	11
Spanish	–	–	+	–	–	–	–	–	–	+	–	–	–	+	+	+	+	–	–	+	–	–	–	+	–	–	–	+	–	–	9
English	–	–	–	–	–	–	–	–	–	+	+	+	–	+	+	+	+	–	–	–	–	–	–	+	–	–	–	–	–	–	8
Swahili	–	–	+	–	–	–	–	–	–	–	–	–	–	–	–	–	–	–	–	+	+	+	+	–	–	–	–	–	–	–	5
Arabic	–	–	–	–	–	–	–	–	–	–	–	–	–	+	–	–	–	–	–	+	+	–	–	–	–	–	–	+	–	–	4
Thai	–	–	–	–	–	–	–	–	–	–	–	–	–	–	–	–	–	–	–	–	–	–	–	–	–	+	–	–	–	–	1

NOTES TO THE TEXT

NOTES TO CHAPTER 1

1. It might be helpful to note Jakobson's terms for these movements, which are *differentiation* vs. *integration* (Jakobson 1944: 193).

2. The latter was specifically identified by Emeneau.

3. For a cogent summary of the controversy see Kuiper 1967.

4. Lackner and Rowe 1955: 127. Sapir's 1929 division of Amerindian languages into "macrophyla" was based on such criteria, it is commonly held. The attractiveness of such a shortcut in making sense out of a vast area of unclassified tribal languages is no doubt great. It is also commonly held that this viewpoint was carried furthest by Sapir's pupil Swadesh. In a posthumous work (Swadesh 1971), *The origin and diversification of language,* Swadesh emphatically denies this, however, claiming that both his and Sapir's classifications rest ultimately on the orthodox criterion of etymologies, with morphological resemblance only pointing the way.

5. Eugenie J. A. Henderson has provided some excellent maps with her article (1965) on areal traits of Southeast Asian languages.

6. Voegelin 1945, referring to remarks of his on p. 30 of Leslie Spier *et al.* (eds.), *Language, culture, and personality,* Menasha, Wis. 1941.

7. Jakobson 1944: 193: "The areas of single grammatical or phonemic features do not coincide, so that one and the same language happens to be linked by different features with quite different languages."

8. It is being accumulated in particularly convenient form by Greenberg's Language Universals Project at Stanford, the results of which are available in a series of working papers edited by Edith A. Moravcsik. Geographical correlations, it should be noted, are deliberate-

ly avoided in this research. It is sought to compare only languages that are "areally distinct", lest areal correlations be mistaken for universal correlations.

9. A phonemic atlas of the world, Jakobson implies in recalling it in 1961. In an article soon after the event, however, he says "of Europe." Cf. Sur la théorie des affinités phonologiques entre les langues, *Actes du IV*[e] *Congrès international de linguistes,* 1936, Copenhagen: Munksgaard, 1938, reprinted as Appendix IV to Trubetzkoy 1931 (1957): p. 364n.

10. Grierson 1927 (esp. 1.1:130-133).

11. Bloch 1934. See also his *Formation de la langue marathe* and various articles.

12. See Henderson 1965 and Ramanujan and Masica 1969, as well as discussion of the retroflexion problem in Bloch 1934, Emeneau 1956, Kuiper 1967 and elsewhere.

Notes To Chapter 2

1. Some of these he would perhaps not defend today, e.g., "The order of elements in language parallels that in physical experience or in the order of knowledge" (p. 103).

2. The relevance of Greenberg's notions of dominance and harmony to questions of change of type may be particularly worth examining.

3. In commenting on the Ross paper at Bucharest, Moulton points out that there is very much a question whether linear order can be said to exist at all in deep structure.

4. In the published version of his paper Ross briefly proposes a "deep" SVO structure for Turkish also, however. For more on deep order see McCawley (1970).

5. In this connection see Southworth (1971a).

6. For a discussion of stylistic order status, see Jakobson (1963:268-69).

7. Ross (1970:841) confirms my assessment here: "[Greenberg] does not explain which phenomena he takes as critical in deciding which of the many orders of S, V, and O that can be observed in a language is basic. . . ."

8. Dezső (1968:136): "Die Wortfolgetransformationen bietet nur eine Möglichkeit zur Anwendung der Betonungsregeln."

9. Conscious of its inadequacy, I might nevertheless give the results here of a spot check involving short stories and other fictional passages by Hindi and Telugu writers: 95 percent of the Telugu and 72 percent of the Hindi constructions had the object before the verb. Of the contrary cases, most involved clausal objects, especially quotations ("He said that . . . ," "He thought that . . . ," or even "He said, '. . .' " – the last doubtless in imitation of written English and preferably excluded from the statistics altogether, thus removing most of the Telugu examples). Only one Telugu example involved a true NP object:

testaaḍu ḍabbu 'He'll bring the money'. In the Hindi sample there were six of these. These were augmented by the postverbal clausal objects with *ki* 'that' – something that is normative in Hindi but quite foreign to Telugu (Dravidian) structure. The subject where it was mentioned, incidentally *followed the object* (OSV, OVS) in 53 percent of the Telugu but only 17 percent of the Hindi cases. This may merely reflect the stylistic predilections of the authors (Sonthi Krishnamurti and Kommuri Venugopala Rao *vs.* Premchand and Mohan Rakesh), but I suspect a real stylistic difference between the two languages. An additional count of a somewhat different sort, involving thirty-two pages of the screenplay of the Hindi film *Anand* (dialogue by Gulzar, pub. Hind Pocket Books Pvt, Ltd, Delhi, n.d.) showed 368 sentences ending in a verb, 19 in a negative equivalent to a verb, 24 in various emphatic particles (allowed by Greenberg), 13 in various kinds of subject, 12 in locative adverbials, 3 in time adverbials, 10 in the kind of postposed genitive described above, and only 4 in objects.

10. E.g., Chinese is listed as Pr on p. 90 and as Po on p. 109; Greek is listed as AdjN on p. 107 and as NAdj on p. 109.

11. "Adjectives" as a special word class are absent from many languages. In seeking a more universal category for the comparative syntax of the noun phrase, it will be necessary to fall back on something like "adjectival," defined in terms of derivation by transformation from a certain subtype of predicate.

12. For more on this subject, and further references, see Y. Kachru 1973, also Masica 1972.

13. That is, according to Tschenkeli 1958. According to Howard Aronson, borderline Georgian is essentially an OV language. Hans Vogt 1971 agrees with him.

14. According to Dezső 1968, this represents an assimilation under Germanic influence, still in progress in older Finnish literature, where OV appears as a common alternant. The assimilation of Hungarian is less complete. It is a rare example of a language with two basic orders (plus every possible alternant) – SVO with definite objects and SOV with indefinite objects.

15. Fairbanks, Gair and De Silva (1968): 7, 43, etc. A. K. Ramanujan points out that the pronominalized verb in South Dravidian has a like effect.

16. It is significant that in both Persian and Amharic the "accusative" is expressed by suffixed elements (*-raa* and *-n/-in* respectively) although they are prepositional or modified prepositional languages.

17. Stevenson 1970:111-13. According to Dezső (1970:554), *Albanian* is also a VSO language.

Notes To Chapter 3

1. Bruce Pray (1970:92-114) outlines a much more sophisticated derivation than the one given here in terms of generative phonology,

based on the hypothetical underlying form *-AAV, which undergoes various phonetic modifications and truncations in combination with verb stems, with itself, and with elements that follow. See Y. Kachru (1966:71-81) for an extensive list of the stems involved in these derivations.

2. The vowels /e,o/ have the structural status of "long vowels" in Hindi, although (in contradistinction to Dravidian) there are no short counterparts with which they contrast. Because their "long" status is cogent to the discussion here, they will be transcribed *ee,oo* in this chapter only, but with *e,o* normally in the rest of the book.

3. Turner (1966): entries No. 7478 and 7484.

4. Bahl (1969:168ff.) and Shackle (1972:107-9) give the Punjabi suffixes as *-ā/,vā,* but a number of older works (Beames 1872-79:v.3:82, Grierson 1928:v.9.1:632, and the *Panjabi Manual and Grammar,* no author, reprinted officially by the Language Department, Government of Punjabi 1961:212ff.) all agree in giving it as *āu/vāu*. Is it a question of the period or variety of Punjabi, or of a segmentation decision? When /-v-/ occurs in Shackle's forms, which is only between (most often identical) vowels, he takes it to be a predictable euphonic device.

5. I have taken the liberty of phonemicizing Lorimer's narrow phonetic data in accordance with the suggestions of his editor.

6. Some refinements of this are possible, generally in the semantic area of "help to" *vs.* "cause, order, get to," as we have seen in Hindi. This seems to affect syntactic relations – cases – and not morphology and will not concern us here.

7. For example, in the area of the labial stop, classical Tamil -PPI (allomorph of -VI) is a sign of the mediative-causative, -PP- (allomorph of -V-) is a sign of the future, -PPU (allomorph of -TTU) is a sign of the contactive-causative, and -PPU (allomorph of -PU) is a marker of abstract deverbal nouns.

8. I was much confused by this in the first version of this study, copies of which may unfortunately still be circulating.

9. This was first pointed out to me by A. K. Ramanujan. William Bright makes the same point in his *Discussion* of Emeneau 1971 (p. 70 in the same volume). It should be noted that some other Kannada speakers persist in rejecting this, however, claiming never to have heard a form like *maaḍisisu.* Are subvarieties of Kannada possibly involved? Or is the authority of grammar too strong?

10. My horizons on Baluchi were greatly enlarged by M. A. R. Barker's excellent textbook (1969) from which most of these examples are taken. My apologies, however, for transmuting his modified-Firthian transcription into one that will facilitate comparison with those used for Indic languages in this chapter.

11. My thanks to Gerald Lind for interviewing informants in Sweden for me.

12. The most ambitious attempt I have seen to sort out the allomorphs is that in Lukoff 1945 (v.2:704-8). I have not seen Martin's

long-anticipated reference grammar. When it is available, it may well throw further light on some of these questions.

13. It appears that I have here mixed up spoken with literary Arabic. Form IV is essentially a Classical form, and – at least according to some sources (e.g., Drive 1925) – has been largely replaced in the colloquial by Form II. Arabic has thus shifted from an at least partly prefixal to a "strengthened root" mode of causative expression.

Notes To Chapter 4

1. For example, in Jacobs and Rosenbaum (1968, chap. 29).

2. Some would restrict the application of the term "participle" to verbal *adjectives.* I am accepting a broader (even though perhaps looser and "incorrect") usage of the term here, after the grammarians of Indian, Altaic, Uralic, Slavonic, and other languages.

3. The authors of this work claim (p. 4) to be following the official terminology of the Ministère français, as issued in 1961.

4. Edward Stankiewicz supplies me with the term *taxis* for this relation.

5. These authors also note (p. 131) a disagreement regarding the precise status (adjective *vs.* noun) of the *-ing* form in another context between grammarians of the stature of Henry Sweet and Otto Jespersen.

6. Such an assumption is not always borne out, however. For example, in Cardona's otherwise excellent reference grammar of Gujarati (1965), one is certainly hard put to find an account or even a mention of the conjunctive participle that we know exists in that language. I finally tracked it down, listed without a name under "Nominal Forms [!] of the Verb", by looking under the suffix involved (*-iine*) in the index. If one did not know the suffix in advance, however, and wanted only to learn something about Gujarati, it would be difficult, as none of the usual terminological signposts – manifold and confusing though they may be – are there to help. I have been less successful in Kachru (1969) on Kashmiri, although Kachru's own examples contain this form (in *-ith*). This was meant to be a preliminary draft, however, "not for quotation," so perhaps I should not complain. Suffice it to say that the conjunctive participle does not always get the attention it deserves commensurate with the importance of its function in a language.

7. Kirghiz sample: first pages of each of the ten reading selections (pp. 71-91) in the back of Hebert and Poppe (1963). Turkish sample: every other page (pp. 11-39) in Spies (1968).

Notes To Chapter 5

1. Private conversation. See also his "Historical syntax of the conjunctive participle phrase in the New Indo-Aryan dialects of the

Madhyadesa ('Midland') of Northern India" (unpublished dissertation, University of Chicago, April 1971).

2. I have noted a tendency, however, which I cannot at present properly document, for these verbal adverbs to be used more widely and more consistently in British than in American English.

3. Examples are taken from Chao 1968 but rendered into "Yale" romanization from his GR.

4. The more complete and systematizing analysis of Allott 1965, however, reduces the number of really relevant items to about nine, much more parallel with the Indian inventories.

5. It is noteworthy that no attention is paid to this subject in Miller 1967, Henderson 1945, or Vaccari 1954.

6. The only analogous Brahui locution – with 'go' – involves two *finite* verbs, as in Arabic, etc. (Bray 1909:183).

Notes To Chapter 6

1. Lewis (1967) says with regard to Turkish (p. 250): "Although as a rule the subject comes first in the sentence, we not infrequently find a sentence beginning with a word or phrase in the genitive case. The reason is that if the logical subject, the topic-word of the sentence, does not coincide with the grammatical subject, it is the logical subject which comes at the beginning." The same statement holds good for Indian languages – both Aryan and Dravidian – except that the case is usually dative rather than genitive.

2. The Finnish construction (*minun on jano, nälkä, kylmä, ikävä, etc.* = 'I am thirsty, hungry, cold, lonely, etc.') is actually genitive in terms of the present grammar, but there is evidence that this preserves an old dative (Eliot 1890:138).

3. My thanks to Bill Darden for calling my attention to the fact that the construction exists also in Lithuanian, and with the verb *need*, at least, involves an oblique-case (genitive) object along with its personal dative (cf. Malayalam). My thanks to Ruta Pempe for pointing out further that Lithuanian uses "northern" *adjectival* expressions to express hunger and thirst, along with the dative constructions for sensations of cold, heat, sleepiness, and the like.

Notes To Chapter 7

1. I owe this information to Gérard Diffloth.

2. I am aware that Persian was the cultural language of the Muslim invaders of India for several centuries. It is difficult to ascertain to what extent and how long Turki may have been the spoken language, but that is more important for this discussion.

3. Some interesting steps in this direction – with maps! – have been taken in Southworth 1974.

BIBLIOGRAPHY

ABBREVIATIONS

ACLS	American Council of Learned Societies
AO	Acta Orientalia
BSOAS	Bulletin of the School of Oriental and African Studies, London University
IJAL	International Journal of American Linguistics (Indiana)
IJDL	International Journal of Dravidian Linguistics (Trivandrum, Kerala, India)
IL	Indian Linguistics
JAOS	Journal of the American Oriental Society
JOIB	Journal of the Oriental Institute of Baroda
Lg	Language
LSI	Linguistic Survey of India (1903-1928, George Grierson, ed.)
MIT	Massachusetts Institute of Technology
TCLP	Travaux du Cercle Linguistique de Prague
USAFI	United States Armed Forces Institute

1. Aaltio, Maija-Hellikki. 1967. Finnish for foreigners. 3d ed. Helsinki: Otava.
2. Agard, Frederick B., R. W. Willis, Jr., and Helio Lobo. 1944. Brazilian Portuguese from thought to word. Princeton: Princeton University Press.
3. Agard, Frederick B., and Robert J. Di Pietro. 1965. The grammatical structures of English and Italian (Contrastive Structure Series). Chicago: University of Chicago Press.

4. Akedemiia͡ Nauk SSSR, Institut Narodov Azii. 1961. Koreiskii ia͡zyk: sbornik statei. Moscow: Vostochnoi Literatury.
5. Alexander, H. 1940. Linguistic geography. Queen's Quarterly, 47.1: 38-47.
6. Allott, A. J. 1965. Categories for the description of the verbal syntagma in Burmese. Indo-Pacific studies, G. B. Milner and Eugenie J. A. Henderson, eds., vol. 2 (Lingua 15): 283-309. Amsterdam: North-Holland Publishing Co.
7. Alone, J. P. H. M. 1962. Short manual of the Amharic language. Revised by D. E. Stokes. 5th rev. ed. Madras: Macmillan.
8. Andersen, Henning. 1970. The dative of subordination in Baltic and Slavic. Baltic Linguistics, Thomas F. Magner and William R. Schmalstieg, eds., University Park: Pennsylvania State University Press. Pp. 1-10.
9. Anderson, J. D. 1920. A manual of the Bengali language. Cambridge: Cambridge University Press.
10. Anderson, Stephen, and Avery Andrews. 1972. Syntactic typology and contrastive studies: research on syntactic typology, vol. 1. Cambridge, Mass.: Language Research Foundation.
11. Andrewskutty, A. P. 1972. Intransitive and transitive verbs in Malayalam. IL 33.2:135-42.
12. Andronov, M. S. 1962. I͡Azyk kannada. Moscow: Vostochnoi Literatury.
13. ——. 1966. Grammatika tamil'skogo ia͡zyka. Moscow: Nauka.
14. Angere, Johannes. 1956. Die uralo-jukagirische Frage: ein Beitrag zum Problem der sprachlichen Urverwandtschaft. Uppsala: Almqvist & Wiksell.
15. Apresian, I͡U. D. 1967. Eksperimental'noe issledovanie semantiki russkogo glagola. Moscow: Nauka.
16. Arakin, V. D. 1963. Mal'gashskii ia͡zyk. Moscow: Vostochnoi Literatury.
17. ——. 1965. Indoneziiskie ia͡zyki. Moscow: Nauka.
18. Arden, A. H. 1937. A progressive grammar of the Telugu language. 4th ed. rev. by F. L. Marler. Madras: Christian Literature Society.
19. ——. 1942. A progressive grammar of common Tamil. 5th ed. rev. by A. C. Clayton (Tamil Study Series, No. 2). Madras: Christian Literature Society.
20. Aronson, Howard I. 1969. Towards a formal analysis of the Georgian declension. General Linguistics 9:173-84.
21. ——. 1970. Towards a semantic analysis of case and subject in Georgian. Lingua 25: 291-301.
22. Arotçarena, Abbé. n.d. Grammaire basque: dialectes navarro-labourdins. Tours: Maison Mame.
23. Asher, R. E. 1966. The verb in spoken Tamil. In memory of J. K. Firth, ed. by C. E. Bazell *et al.* London: Longmans.
24. ——. 1968. Existential, possessive, locative, and copulative sentences in Malayalam. The verb *be* and its synonyms (Foundations

of Language Supplementary Series, vol. 2). Dordrecht, Holland: D. Reidel.
25. Ashton, E. O., *et al.* 1954. A Luganda grammar. London: Longmans.
26. Attaoullah, Fuad A. 1946. Turkish grammar self-taught. London: Marlborough.
27. Bach, Emmon. 1967. *Have* and *be* in English syntax. Lg. 43.2.1: 462-85.
28. ——. 1970. Is Amharic an SOV language? Journal of Ethiopian Studies 8: 9-20.
29. Badi, Sh., *et al.* 1959. Karmannii russko-persidskii slovar'. Moscow: Gosudarstvennoe Izdatel'stvo Inostrannykh i Natsional'nykh Slovarei.
30. Bahl, Kali Charan. 1967a. The causal verbs in Hindi. Language and areas: studies presented to George V. Bobrinskoy. Chicago: University of Chicago Press. Pp. 17-23.
31. ——. 1967b. A reference grammar of Hindi. Chicago: University of Chicago, South Asia Center (mimeographed).
32. Bailey, T. Grahame. 1924. Grammar of the Shina (Ṣīṇā) language (Prize Publication Fund, vol. 8). London: Royal Asiatic Society.
33. ——. 1937. The pronunciation of Kashmiri (James G. Furlong Fund, 16). London: Royal Asiatic Society.
34. ——. 1938. Studies in North Indian languages. London: Lund, Humphries & Co.
35. ——. 1950. Teach yourself Hindustani. London: English Universities Press.
36. Bánhidi, Z., *et al.* 1965. A textbook of the Hungarian language. London: Collet's.
37. Barker, Muhammad Abd-al-Rahman, and Aqil Khan Mengal. 1969. A course in Baluchi. 2 vols. Montreal: Institute of Islamic Studies, McGill University.
38. Barua, Hem Chandra. 1965. Hem-Kosha, the Assamese-English dictionary. Ed. by Debananda Barua. 4th ed. Sibsagar, Assam.
39. Beames, John. 1872-79. Comparative grammar of the modern Indo-Aryan languages of India. 3 vols. Reprinted Delhi: Munshiram Manoharlal, 1966.
40. Beeston, A. F. L. 1968. Written Arabic: an approach to the basic structures. Cambridge: Cambridge University Press.
41. Beite, Ann-Mari, *et al.* 1966. Basic Swedish grammar. 3d ed. Stockholm: Almqvist & Wiksell.
42. Bell, C. A. 1939. Grammar of colloquial Tibetan. 3d ed. Alipore, Bengal: Bengal Government Press.
43. Bell, C. R. V. 1953. The Somali language. London: Longmans, Green.
44. Bender, Ernest. 1967. Hindi grammar and reader. Philadelphia: University of Pennsylvania Press.
45. Bendix, Edward Herman. 1966. Componential analysis of general vocabulary: the semantic structure of a set of verbs in English,

Hindi, and Japanese. IJAL 42, Pt. 2. (Bloomington: Indiana University.)

46. ——. 1974. Indo-Aryan and Tibeto-Burman contact as seen through Nepali and Newari verb tenses. IJDL 3.1: 42-59.

47. Benzing, Johannes. 1955. Lamutische Grammatik. Wiesbaden: Franz Steiner.

48. Bergethon, K. Roald. 1950. Grammar for reading German. Boston: Houghton Mifflin Co.

49. Beschi, Constantino Giuseppe. 1843. Grammatica latino-tamulica. Pudicherri: Typographio missionariorum.

50. Bese, L., L. Dezső, and J. Gulya. 1970. On the syntactic typology of the Uralic and Altaic languages, in Theoretical problems of typology and the Northern Eurasian languages, L. Dezső and P. Hajdú, eds. Amsterdam: B. R. Grüner. Pp. 113-28.

51. Bezikovich, E. I., and T. P. Gordova-Rybal'chenko. 1957. Bolgarskiĭ i͡azyk: uchebnik dli͡a vuzov. Leningrad: Leningrad University.

52. Bhat, D. N. S. 1973. Retroflexion: an areal feature. Working papers on language universals, No. 13 Language Universals Project, Stanford University. Pp. 27-68.

53. Bhattacharji, Somdev. 1961. Introductory Bengali reader. University of Chicago: South Asia Center (mimeographed).

54. Biligiri, Hemmige Shriniwasarangachar. 1965a. Kharia (Deccan College Building Centenary and Silver Jubilee Series, 3). Poona: Deccan College.

55. ——. 1965b. The Sora verb: a restricted study. Lingua 15:231-50.

56. Bittle, W. E. 1953. Language and culture areas: a note on method. Philosophy of Science 20: 247-56.

57. Björkhagen, Im. 1956. Modern Swedish grammar. 8th ed. Stockholm: Svenska Bokförlaget.

58. Bloch, Jules. 1934. L'indo-aryen du Veda aux temps modernes. Paris: Adrien-Maisonneuve.

59. Bloomfield, Leonard. 1944-45. Spoken Dutch. New York: American Council of Learned Societies and Linguistic Society of America.

60. Bodding, P. O. (ed.) 1925. Santal folk tales, 1. Oslo: Instituttet for Sammenlignende Kulturforskning.

61. ——. 1930. Materials for a Santali grammar. 2d ed. Dumka (India): Santal Mission of the Northern Churches.

62. Bolufer, Jose Alemany. 1941. Gramática de la lengua griega. 2d ed., rev. by Bernardo Alemany Selfa. Madrid: Editorial Aldecoa.

63. Bonfante, G., and T. A. Sebeok. 1944. Linguistics and the age and area hypothesis. American Anthropologist 46: 382-386.

64. Bonfante, Giuliano. 1947. The Neolinguistic position. Lg.23.4:344-75.

65. Borras, F. M., and R. F. Christian. 1959. Russian syntax. Oxford: Oxford University Press.

66. Bottiglioni, Gino. 1954. Linguistic geography: achievements, methods, and orientations. Word 10:375-87.
67. Boyle, John Andrew. 1966. Grammar of modern Persian. Wiesbaden: Otto Harrassowitz.
68. Bray, Denys de S. 1909. The Brahui language. Part 1: Introduction and grammar. Calcutta: Government Superintendent of Printing.
69. Buenaventura, Amparo S. 1967. A syntactic analysis of basic sentence types in Tagalog (San Carlos Publications, Series A: Humanities. No. 6). Cebu City, Philippines.
70. Burling, Robbins. 1961. A Garo grammar (Indian Linguistic Monograph No. 12). Poona: Deccan College.
71. Burrow, T. 1959. The Sanskrit language. London: Faber & Faber.
72. ——. and M. B. Emeneau. 1960. A Dravidian etymological dictionary. Oxford: Clarendon Press.
73. Bykova, E. M. 1966. Bengal'skii i͡azyk. Moscow: Nauka.
74. Caldwell, Robert. (1856). A Comparative grammar of the Dravidian or South-Indian family of languages. 3d rev. ed. Reprinted Madras: Madras University, 1961.
75. Cardona, George. 1965. A Gujarati reference grammar. Philadelphia: University of Pennsylvania Press.
76. ——. 1971. Cause and causal agent: the Paninian view. JOIB 21: 22-40.
77. Carlut, Charles, and Walter Meiden. 1968. French for oral and written review. New York: Holt, Rinehart and Winston.
78. Cartianu, Ana, Leon Levitchi, and Virgil Ştefănescu-Drăgăneşti. 1958. An advanced course in modern Rumanian. Bucharest: Publishing House for Scientific Books.
79. Cecchi, Antonio. 1886. Da Zeila alle frontiere del Caffa. Vol. 1. Rome: Ermanno Loescher.
80. Chandra Sekhar, Anantaramayyar. 1953. Evolution of Malayalam. Poona: Deccan College.
81. Chang, Hei Lee. 1955. Practical Korean grammar. Seattle: University of Washington Press.
82. Chang Kun and Betty Shefts. 1964. A manual of spoken Tibetan. Seattle: University of Washington Press.
83. Chang, Betty Shefts. 1971. The Tibetan causative: phonology. Bulletin of the Institute of History and Philology, Academica Sinica 42.4: 623-766.
84. Chao, Yuen Ren. 1968. A grammar of spoken Chinese. Berkeley: University of California Press.
85. Chatterji, Suniti Kumar. 1926. The origin and development of the Bengali language. Calcutta: University of Calcutta Press.
86. ——. 1927. Bengali self-taught by the natural method. London: Marlborough.
87. Chevalier, Jean-Claude, *et al.* 1964. Grammaire Larousse du français contemporain. Paris: Librairie Larousse.
88. Churchward, C. Malwell. 1953. Tongan grammar. London: Oxford University Press.

89. Cioffari, Vincenzo. 1937. Italian review grammar and composition. Boston: D. C. Heath.
90. Cole, Desmont T. 1955. An introduction to Tswana grammar. London: Longmans, Green.
91. Constantino, Ernesto. 1965. The sentence patterns in twenty-six Philippine languages. Lingua 15:71-124.
92. Cornyn, William. 1944. Outline of Burmese grammar. Lg 20.4 (supplement).
93. ——— and D. Haigh Roop. 1968. Beginning Burmese. New Haven: Yale University Press.
94. Cowan, H. K. J. 1965. Review of H. L. Shorto, ed., Linguistic comparison in Southeast Asia and the Pacific. Lingua 13:305-11.
95. Crazzolara, J. P. 1933. Outlines of a Nuer grammar. Vienna: Anthropos.
96. Christaller, J. G. 1875. A grammar of the Asante and Fante language called Tshi. Basel.
97. Cristo-Loveanu, Elie. 1962. The Romanian language. New York: by the author.
98. Curme, G.O. 1952. A grammar of the German language. 2d rev. ed. New York: G. Ungar.
99. Dambriūnas, Leonardas, Antanas Klimas and William R. Schmalstieg. 1966. Introduction to Modern Lithuanian. Brooklyn: Franciscan Fathers Press.
100. de Bray, R. G. A. 1951. Guide to the Slavonic languages. London: J. M. Dent & Sons.
101. DeFrancis, John. 1963. Beginning Chinese. New Haven: Yale University Press.
102. Delgado de Carvalho, C. M. 1962. Geography of languages. Readings in cultural geography, Philip L. Wagner and Marvin W. Mikesell, eds. Chicago: University of Chicago Press. Pp. 75-93.
103. Dev, Ashu Tosh. N.d. Student's favourite dictionary, Bengali to English. 18th rev. ed. Calcutta: S. C. Mazunder, Dev Sahitya Kutir, Ltd.
104. De Vreese, K. 1965. Review of Siegfried Lienhard, Tempusgebrauch und Aktionsartenbildung in der modernen Hindi. Lingua 13: 198-216.
105. Dezső, L. 1968. Einige typologische Besonderheiten der ungarischen Wortfolge. Acta linguistica 18: 125-59.
106. ———. 1970. A word order typology of three-member sentences. Actes du Xe Congrès (1967) International des Linguistes, 3. Bucharest: Éditions de l'Académie de la République Socialiste de Roumanie. Pp. 55-555.
107. Dhruva, N. M. N.d. Gujarati self-taught. 2d ed. rev. by T. N. Dave. London: Marlborough.
108. Dimock, Edward C., Jr., S. Bhattacharji, and S. Chatterjee. 1964. An introduction to spoken Bengali. Honolulu: East-West Center Press.

109. Dimshits, J. M. 1966. Hindii-vyaakaraṇ kii ruup-rekhaa. Delhi: Rajkamal Prakashan.
110. Driver, G. R. 1925. A grammar of the colloquial Arabic of Syria and Palestine. London: Probsthain & Co.
111. Duka, Theodore. 1887. An essay on the Brahui grammar. Journal of the Royal Asiatic Society 19.1:1-77.
112. Dunn, C. J., and S. Yanada. 1958. Teach yourself Japanese. London: English Universities Press.
113. Dvoriankov, N. A. 1960. I͡Azyk pushtu. Moscow: Vostochnoi Literatury.
114. Dwarikesh, D. P. S. 1971. The historical syntax of the conjunctive participle phrase in the New Indo-Aryan dialects of the Madhyadeśa ('Midland') of Northern India. Unpub. dissertation, University of Chicago.
115. Dzenit, S. I͡A., and N. V. Gurov. 1972. Kratkii grammaticheskii ocherk i͡azyka telugu. Appendix to Lakshmana Rao 1972, pp. 691-744. Moscow: Soviet Encyclopaedia Press.
116. Eliot, C. N. E. 1890. A Finnish grammar. Oxford: Clarendon Press.
117. Elizarenkova, T. I͡A. 1962. Ob asimmetrii v sisteme kauzativnykh glagolov v i͡azyke khindi. Voprosy grammatiki i͡azyka khindi, I. S. Rabinovich and E. P. Chelyshev, eds. Moscow: Vostochnoi Literatury. Pp. 76-86.
118. Elwell-Sutton, L. P. 1941. Colloquial Persian. London: Kegan Paul.
119. Emeneau, M. B. 1944-46. Kota Texts (University of California Publications in Linguistics, 2 and 3). Berkeley: University of California Press.
120. ———. 1956. India as a linguistic area. Lg. 32.1:3-16.
121. ———. 1957. Toda, a Dravidian language. Transactions of the Philological Society (London). Pp. 15-66.
122. ———. 1961. Kolami: a Dravidian language. 2d ed. Annamalainagar: Annamalai University.
123. ———. 1969. Onomatopoetics in the Indian linguistic area. Lg. 45.2: 274-99.
124. ———. 1971. Dravidian and Indo-Aryan: the Indian linguistic area. Symposium on Dravidian Civilization, Andree F. Sjoberg, ed. (Publication No. 1 in the Asian Series of the Center for Asian Studies of the University of Texas at Austin). Austin and New York: Jenkins Publishing Co., Pemberton Press. Pp. 33-68. Discussion by William Bright on pp. 69-71.
125. ———. (1973?) Studies in Dravidian verb stem formation. (Prepub. mss.)
126. ———. (1974). The Indian linguistic area revisited. IJDL 3.1:92-134.
127. Fairbanks, Gordon H. 1958. Spoken West Armenian. New York: ACLS.

128. ——— and Earl W. Stevick. 1958. Spoken East Armenian. New York: ACLS.
129. ——— and Bal Govind Misra. 1966. Spoken and written Hindi. Ithaca, N. Y.: Cornell University Press.
130. ———, James W. Gair, and M. W. S. de Silva. 1968. Colloquial Sinhalese, Vols. 1 & 2. Ithaca, N. Y.: Cornell University Press.
131. Fenn, Henry C., and M. Gardner Tewksbury. 1967. Speak Mandarin. New Haven: Yale University Press.
132. Forbes, Duncan. 1855. A grammar of the Hindùstání language. London: Crosby Lockwood & Son.
133. Foreign Service Institute. 1954, 1956, 1957, 1959. Spoken Persian. Washington, D. C.: Department of State (mimeographed).
134. Fossum, L. O. 1919. A practical Kurdish grammar. Minneapolis: Inter-Synodal Lutheran Orient Mission Society.
135. Frohnmeyer, L. J. 1913. A progressive grammar of the Malayalam language for Europeans. Mangalore: Basel Mission.
136. Gaeffke, Peter. 1967. Untersuchungen zur Syntax des Hindi. The Hague: Mouton.
137. Gair, James W. 1970. Colloquial Sinhalese clause structures. The Hague: Mouton.
138. Gankin, E. B. 1965. Osnovnye russko-amkharskie grammaticheskie sootvetstvii͡a. Appendix to Russko-amkharskii slovar'. Moscow: Soviet Encyclopaedia Press.
139. Ganshina, M., and N. Vasilevskaya. 1945. English grammar. 5th rev. ed. Moscow: Foreign Languages Publishing House.
140. Garusinghe, Dayaratne. 1962. Sinhalese: the spoken idiom. Munich: Max Huebner Verlag.
141. Garvey, Catherine J. 1964. Malagasy introductory course. Washington, D. C.: Center for Applied Linguistics.
142. Geiger, Wilhelm. 1938. A grammar of the Sinhalese language. Colombo: Royal Asiatic Society, Ceylon Branch.
143. Georgiev, V. 1966. Genesis of the Balkan peoples. Slavonic and East European Review 44: 285-97.
144. Gilbertson, George Waters. 1923. The Balochi language, a grammar and manual. Hertford: S. Austin & Sons, for the author.
145. Glover, Warren W. N.d. Three Gurung equivalents of the English *be.* Journal of the Tribhuvan University, Special Linguistic Number: 1-36.
146. Goetchius, Eugene Van Ness. 1965. The language of the New Testament. New York: Scribner's.
147. Gołąb, Zbygniew. 1968. The grammar of Slavic causatives. American contributions to the VIth International Congress of Slavists, Prague 1968, Henry Kucera, ed. Vol. 1, Linguistic contributions. The Hague: Mouton. Pp. 71-94.
148. Goldstein, Melvyn C., and Nawang Nornang. 1970. Modern spoken Tibetan: Lhasa dialect. Seattle: University of Washington Press.

149. ____ and Tsering Dorje Kashi. 1973. Modern Literary Tibetan (Occasional Papers of the Wolfenden Society on Tibeto-Burman Linguistics, ed. F. K. Lehman, vol. 5). Urbana, Illinois: Publications of the Center for Asian Studies, University of Illinois.
150. Gonda, Jan. 1966. A concise elementary grammar of the Sanskrit language. Transl. from the German by Gordon B. Ford, Jr. Leiden: E. J. Brill.
151. Goodwin, William Watson. 1930, 1958. Greek grammar. Rev. by Charles Burton Gulick. Boston: Ginn and Co.
152. Gorgonev, I͡U. A. 1961. Kkhmerskiĭ i͡azyk. Moscow: Vostochnoi Literatury.
153. Grace, G. W. 1961. Austronesian linguistics and culture history. American Anthropologist 63:359-68.
154. Greaves, Edwin. 1933. Hindi grammar. Allahabad: Indian Press, Ltd.
155. Greenberg, J. H. 1959. Current trends in linguistics. Science 130:1165-70.
156. ____. 1963, 1966a. Some universals of grammar with particular reference to the order of meaningful elements. Universals of language (report of a conference held at Dobbs Ferry, New York, 13-15 April, 1961), Joseph H. Greenberg, ed. 2d ed. Cambridge, Mass.: MIT Press.
157. ____ 1966b. Language universals. Current trends in linguistics, vol. 3: theoretical foundations. The Hague: Mouton. Pp. 61-112.
158. Grierson, George A. (ed.). 1903-1928. Linguistic survey of India. Eleven volumes. Reprinted Delhi-Varanasi-Patna: Motilal Banarsidass, 1967-68.
159. Gulian, Kevork H. N.d. Elementary Modern Armenian grammar. Repr. New York: Ungar.
160. Guru, Kamtaprasad. 1962. Grammatika khindi, pts. 1 & 2. Transl. into Russian by P. A. and R. I. Barannikov. Moscow: Vostochnoi Literatury.
161. Hacker, Paul. 1958. Zur Funktion einiger Hilfsverben im modernen Hindi. Mainz: Verlag der Wissenschaften und der Literatur.
162. ____. 1961. On the problem of a method for treating the compound and conjunct verbs in Hindi. BSOAS 24.3: 484-516.
163. Hangin, John G. 1968. Basic course in Mongolian (Uralic and Altaic Series, 73). Bloomington: Indiana University.
164. Hari, Anna Maria (ed.) 1971. Conversational Nepali. Kathmandu: Summer Institute of Linguistics and Institute of Nepal Studies, Tribhuvan University.
165. Harley, A. H. 1944. Colloquial Hindustani. London: Routledge & Kegan Paul
166. Harter, J. Martin, Nanda K. Choudry, and Vijay Budhraj. 1960. Hindi basic course. Washington, D. C.: Foreign Service Institute, Department of State.
167. Haugen, Einar. 1950. Problems of bilingualism. Lingua 2:271-90.

168. Havránek, Bohumil. 1933. Zur phonologischen Geographie: das Vokalsystem des balkanischen Sprachbundes. Archives néerlandaises de phonologiques expérimentales 8-9:119-25.
169. Hebert, Raymond J., and Nicholas Poppe. 1963. Kirghiz manual (Uralic and Altaic Series, 33). Bloomington: Indiana University.
170. Henderson, Eugénie J. A. 1965. The topography of certain phonetic and morphological characteristics of South East Asian languages. Lingua 15: 400-434.
171. Henderson, Harold G. 1945. Handbook of Japanese grammar. London: George Allen & Unwin.
172. Hetzron, Robert. 1969. The verbal system of Southern Agaw. Los Angeles: University of California Press.
173. Hinz, John. 1944. Grammar and vocabulary of the Eskimo language, as spoken by the Kuskokwim and the Southwest Coast Eskimos of Alaska. Bethlehem, Pa.: The Society of the United Brethren for Propagating the Gospel among the Heathen (Moravian Church).
174. Hiremath, R. C. 1961. The structure of Kannada. Dharwar: Karnataka University.
175. Hockett, Charles F., and Chaoying Fang. 1944. Spoken Chinese. New York: Henry Holt & Co.
176. Hodge, Carleton. 1945. Spoken Serbo-Croatian, 1&2. New York: Henry Holt & Co.
177. Hornby, A. S. 1954. A guide to patterns and usage in English. London: Oxford University Press and the English Language Book Society.
178. Horne, Elinor C. 1961. Beginning Javanese. New Haven: Yale University Press.
179. Houghton, Herbert Pierrepont. 1961. An introduction to the Basque language, Labourdin dialect. Leiden: E. J. Brill.
180. Howeidy, A. 1959. Concise Hausa grammar. 2d ed. London: George Ronald.
181. Hrobak, Philip A. 1949. Slovak lessons. Rev. ed. Middletown, Penna.: "Jednota."
182. Hudson, D. F. 1965. Teach yourself Bengali. London: English Universities Press.
183. Innes, G. 1962. A Mende grammar. London: Macmillan.
184. Ishakov, F. G., and A. A. Pal'mbakh. 1961. Grammatika tuvinskogo i͡azyka. Moscow: Vostochnoi Literatury.
185. Jacob, Judith M. 1968. Introduction to Cambodian. London: Oxford University Press.
186. Jacobs, Roderick A., and Peter S. Rosenbaum 1968. English transformational grammar. Waltham, Mass.: Blaisdell Publishing Co.
187. Jakobson, Roman. 1931a. Über die phonologischen Sprachbünde. TCLP 4:234-40.
188. ———. 1931b. K kharakteristike evraziiskogo i͡azykovogo soi͡uza. Paris: Imprimerie de Navarre.
189. ———. 1938. Sur la théorie des affinités phonologiques entre les

langues. Actes du IVe Congrès International de Linguistes (1936). Copenhagen: Munksgaard. Pp. 48-58. Reprinted as Appendix IV to Principes de phonologie, pp. 351-65. See N. S. Trubetzkoy.

190. ——. 1944. Franz Boas' approach to language. IJAL 10.4: 188-95.

191. ——. 1963, 1966. Implications of language universals for linguistics. Universals of language, Joseph H. Greenberg, ed. Cambridge, Mass.: MIT Press. Pp. 263-78.

192. Jamal, Jalal Abdulla, and Ernest N. McCarus. 1967. Kurdish basic course: dialect of Sulaimania, Iraq. Ann Arbor: University of Michigan.

193. Jäschke, H. A. 1954. Tibetan grammar. 2d ed. New York: Ungar (repr.).

194. Jones, Robert B. 1970. Classifier constructions in Southeast Asia. JAOS 90.1:1-12.

195. Jothimuththu, P. 1963. A guide to Tamil by the direct method. Madras; Christian Literature Society.

196. Judson, A. 1888. A grammar of the Burmese language. Rangoon: American Baptist Mission Press.

197. Kachru, Braj B. 1969. A reference grammar of Kashmiri. Unpublished preliminary draft. Urbana: Department of Linguistics, University of Illinois.

198. Kachru, Yamuna. 1966. An introduction to Hindi syntax. Urbana: Department of Linguistics, University of Illinois.

199. ——. 1973. Some aspects of pronominalization and relative clause construction in Hindi-Urdu. Studies in the Linguistic Sciences, 3.2:87-103. Urbana: Department of Linguistics, University of Illinois.

200. Kahane, Henry, Renée Kahane, and Ralph L. Ward. 1945. Spoken Greek. New York: Henry Holt & Co.

201. Kakati, Banikanta. 1962. Assamese, its formation and development. 2d ed. Rev. and ed. by Golock Chandra Goswami. Gauhati (Assam): Lawyer's Book Stall.

202. Karpushkin, B. M. 1964. I͡Azyk Oriya. Moscow: Nauka.

203. Katenina, T. E. 1957. Kratkii ocherk grammatiki i͡azyka khindi. Appendix to Russko-khindi slovar;, A. Beskrovny, ed. Moscow: Gosudarstvennoe Izadatel'stvo Inostrannykh i Natsional'nykh Slovarei. Pp. 1279-376.

204. ——. 1963. I͡Azyk maratkhi. Moscow: Vostochnoi Literatury.

205. Kazazis, Kostas. 1967. On a generative grammar of the Balkan languages. Foundations of language 3.2:117-24.

206. Kellogg, S. H. 1938. A grammar of the Hindi language. 3d ed. London: Kegan Paul.

207. Kholodovich, A. A. (ed.) 1969. Tipologii͡a kauzativnykh konstruktsii: morfologicheskii kauzativ. Leningrad: Nauka.

208. Kiefer, Ferenc. 1967. On emphasis and word order in Hungarian (Uralic and Altaic Series, 76). Bloomington: Indiana University.

209. Kirk, J. W. C. 1903. Notes on the Somali language. London: Henry Frowde.
210. Klimov, G. A. 1969. Die kaukasischen Sprachen. Hamburg: Helmut Buske Verlag.
211. Kochanowski, Jan. 1963. Gypsy studies, Parts 1 & 2 (Sata-Pitaka Series, Indo-Asian Literatures, Vols. 25, 26). Delhi: International Academy of Indian Culture.
212. Kononov, A. N. 1960. Grammatika sovremennogo uzbekskogo literaturnogo i͡azyka. Leningrad: Academy of Sciences of the USSR.
213. Korolev, N. I. 1965. I͡Azyk nepali. Moscow: Nauka.
214. Koski, Augustus A., and Ilona Mihalyfy. 1962. Hungarian basic course. Washington, D. C.: Foreign Service Institute.
215. Koutsoudas, Andreas. 1962. Verb morphology of modern Greek. IJAL 28.4.2. Bloomington: Indiana University.
216. Kraft, Charles H., and Salisu Abubaker. 1965. An introduction to spoken Hausa. East Lansing: African Studies Center, Michigan State University.
217. Krishnamurti, Bh. 1961. Telugu verbal bases (Publications in linguistics, vol. 24). Berkeley: University of California Press.
218. ——— and P. Sivananda Sarma. 1968. A basic course in modern Telugu. Hyderabad, A. P.
219. ———. 1969a. Comparative Dravidian studies. Current trends in linguistics, Thomas A. Sebeok, ed. Vol. 5: Linguistics in South Asia. The Hague; Mouton. Pp. 309-33.
220. ———. 1969b. Koṇḍa or Kūbi – a Dravidian language. Hyderabad: Tribal Cultural Research and Training Institute, Government of Andhra Pradesh.
221. ———. 1970a. Verbs of cognition in Telugu. (Paper prepared for the Seminar on Regional Universals in Indian Grammar, held at University of California, Berkeley, 15-23 August 1970.)
222. ———. 1970b. Stative expressions in Indian languages: some semantic and syntactic aspects. (Paper prepared for Seminar in Regional Universals in Indian Grammar, held at University of California, Berkeley, 15-23 August 1970.)
223. ——— 1971. Causative constructions in Indian languages. IL 32.1:18-35.
224. Krueger, John R. 1962. Yakut manual (Uralic and Altaic Series, Vol. 21). Bloomington: Indiana University.
225. Kruisinga, E. 1924. A grammar of modern Dutch. London: G. Allen & Unwin.
226. Krupa, Viktor. 1967. I͡Azyk maori. Moscow: Nauka.
227. Krušina, Alois. 1963. Say it in Czech. London: Collet's.
228. Kuiper, F. B. J. 1967. The genesis of a linguistic area. Indo-Iranian Journal 10:81-102.
229. Kuroda, S. I. 1965. Causative forms in Japanese. Foundations of language 1.1: 30-50.
230. Kwee, John B. 1965. Teach yourself Indonesian. London: English Universities Press.

231. Lackner, J. A. and J. H. Rowe. 1955. Morphological similarity as a criterion of genetic relationship between languages. American Anthropologist 57: 126-29.
232. Lafitte, Abbé P. N.d. Grammaire basque (navarro-labourdin littéraire). Bayonne (France): Librairie "Le Livre."
233. Lakshmana Rao, Vuppala (ed.) 1972. Telugu-russkii slovar'. Moscow: Soviet Encyclopaedia Press.
234. Lambert, H. M. 1971. Gujarati language course. Cambridge: Cambridge University Press.
235. Lambton, Ann K. S. 1953. Persian grammar. Cambridge: Cambridge University Press.
236. Lanman, Charles Rockwell. 1884-89. A Sanskrit reader, with vocabulary and notes. Boston: Ginn, Heath & Co.
237. Lanyon-Orgill, Peter A. 1955. An introduction to the Thai (Siamese) language for European students. Victoria, B. C.: Curlew Press.
238. Lazard, Gilbert. 1957. Grammaire du persan contemporain. Paris: Librairie C. Klincksieck.
239. Lazdiņa, Terēza Budiņa. 1966. Teach yourself Latvian. London: English Universities Press.
240. Lederer, Herbert. 1969. Reference grammar of the German language. New York: Scribner's.
241. Lee, W. R., and Z. Lee. 1959. Teach yourself Czech. London: English Universities Press.
242. Lehmann, W. P. 1973. A structural principle of language and its implications. Lg. 49.1:47-66.
243. Leslau, Wolf. 1945. The Cushitic influence on the Semitic languages of Ethiopia: a problem of substratum. Word 1: 59-82.
244. ———. 1952. The influence of Sidamo on the Ethiopic languages of Gurage. Lg. 28: 63-81.
245. ———. 1958. Report on Ethiopian linguistics, 1946-56. Journal of Near East Studies 17: 49-55.
246. ———. 1968. Amharic textbook. Berkeley and Los Angeles: University of California Press.
247. Lewis, G. L. 1953. Teach yourself Turkish. London: English Universities Press.
248. ———. 1967. Turkish grammar. London: Oxford University Press.
249. Lewy, Ernst. 1964. Der Bau der europäischen Sprachen. Tübingen: Max Niemeyer Verlag.
250. Li, Ying-chi. 1972. Sentences with *be, exist,* and *have* in Chinese. Lg. 48.3:573-83.
251. Lienhard, S. 1961. Tempusgebrauch und Aktionsartenbildung in der modernen Hindi (Stockholm Oriental Studies, 1). Stockholm. Almqvist & Wiksell.
252. ———. 1962. Dal sanscrito all'hindi. Il nevari (Le civiltà asiatiche, 5). Venice: Istituto per la collaborazione culturale.
253. Liétard, Alfred, 1913. Au Yun-Nan les Lo-lo p'o: une tribu des aborigènes de la chine méridionale. Quatrième partie: la langue des Lo-lo p'o (Anthropos-Bibliothek 1.5). Münster: Anthropos.

254. Lisker, Leigh. 1951. Tamil verb classification. JAOS 71.2:111-14.
255. ——. 1963. Introduction to spoken Telugu. New York: ACLS.
256. ——. 1969. Tamil verb auxiliaries. (Paper delivered at the University of Chicago.)
257. Lorimer, D. L. R. 1915. Syntax of colloquial Pashtu. Oxford: Clarendon Press.
258. ——. 1935-38. The Burushaski language. 2 vols. (Preface by G. Morgenstierne. Instituttet for Sammenlignende Kulturforskning). Oslo: H. Aschehoug & Co.
259. Luckyj, George, and Jaroslav B. Rudnyckyj. 1949. A modern Ukrainian grammar. Minneapolis: University of Minnesota Press.
260. Lukas, Johannes. 1937. A study of the Kanuri language. Oxford: Oxford University Press.
261. Lukoff, Fred. 1945. Spoken Korean, vols. 1 & 2 (USAFI edition).
262. McCawley, James D. 1970. English as a VSO language. Lg. 46. 2(1):286-99.
263. McCormack, William. 1966. Kannada: a cultural introduction to the spoken styles of the language. Madison: University of Wisconsin Press.
264. McGregor, R. S. 1968. The language of Indrajit of Orchā: a study of early Braj Bhāṣā prose. Cambridge: Cambridge University Press.
265. ——. 1972. Outline of Hindi grammar. Oxford: Clarendon Press.
266. Macdonald, R. Ross, and Darjowidjoyo Soenjono. 1967. A student's reference grammar of modern formal Indonesian. Washington, D. C.: Georgetown University Press.
267. Macdonnell, Arthur A. 1927. A Sanskrit grammar for students. 3d ed. London: Oxford University Press.
268. MacLeod, A. G. 1967. Colloquial Bengali grammar: an introduction. 3d ed. Calcutta: Mission Press.
269. Macphail, R. M. (ed.) 1953. Campbell's Santali-English dictionary.
270. Mainwaring, Col. G. B. 1876. A grammar of the Róng (Lepcha) language. Calcutta: Baptist Mission Press. Reprinted 1971 as Vol. 5, Series II, Bibliotheca Himalayica (H. K. Kulöy, ed.) New Delhī: Mañjuśrī Publishing House.
271. Maisale, J. D., S. V. Bhat, and Candulal Dube. 1957. Sacitra kannaḍa-hindii aadarś koś. Dharwar (Mysore): Ramasraya Book Depot.
272. Mann, S. E. 1932. A short Albanian grammar. London: David Nutt, A. G. Berry.
273. Marsack, C. C. 1962. Teach yourself Samoan. London: English Universities Press.
274. Martin, Samuel E. 1954. Korean in a hurry. Tokyo: Tuttle.
275. —— and Young-Sook C. Lee. 1969. Beginning Korean. New Haven: Yale University Press.
276. Masica, Colin. 1972. Relative clauses in South Asia. The Chicago which hunt: papers from the relative clause festival, Paul M. Peranteau, Judith N. Levi, Gloria C. Phares, eds. Chicago: Chicago Linguistics Society. Pp. 198-204.
277. —— 1974. The basic order typology as a definer of an Indian

linguistic area. IJDL 3.1: 154-80. (Contact and convergence in South Asian languages, Franklin C. Southnorth and Mahadev L. Apte, eds.)

278. Master, Alfred. 1947. Introduction to Telugu grammar. London: Luzac & Co.

279. ———. 1964. A grammar of Old Marathi. Oxford: Clarendon Press.

280. Maun Maun Nyun, *et al.* 1963. Birmanskii i͡azyk. Moscow: Vostochnoi Literatury.

281. Mazur, I͡U. N. 1960. Koreiskii i͡azyk. Moscow: Vostochnoi Literatury.

282. Mikula, Bohumil E. 1948. Progressive Czech. Chicago: Czechoslovak National Council of America.

283. Miller, Roy Andrew. 1967. The Japanese language. Chicago: University of Chicago Press.

284. ———. 1971. Japanese and the other Altaic languages. Chicago and London: University of Chicago Press.

285. Mistry, P. J. 1969. A generative syntax of Gujarati. Unpublished dissertation, University of California at Los Angeles.

286. Mitchell, T. F. 1972. Colloquial Arabic: the living language of Egypt. London: English Universities Press.

287. Moag, Rodney, and Rachel Moag. 1967. Peace Corps spoken Malayalam materials. 2d version (offset process).

288. Monier-Williams, Monier. 1899. A Sanskrit-English dictionary, etymologically and philologically arranged, with special reference to cognate Indo-European languages. New edit., revised and enlarged. Oxford: Clarendon Press.

289. Moravcsik, Edith A. (ed.) 1970-72. Working papers on language universals, Nos. 1-8 (Language Universals Project, Committee on Linguistics). Stanford University.

290. Moreno, M. M. 1939. Grammatica della lingua Galla. Milan: Mondadori.

291. Morland-Hughes, W. R. J. 1947. A grammar of the Nepali language in the Roman and Nagri scripts. London: Luzac.

292. Nandriş, Grigore. 1945. Colloquial Rumanian. London: Kegan Paul, Trench, Trübner & Co.

293. Neffgen, H. 1918. Grammar and vocabulary of the Samoan language. Transl. from the German by A. B. Stock. London: Kegan Paul, Trench, Trübner.

294. Nguyen-Dinh-Hoa. 1966. Speak Vietnamese. Rev. ed. Tokyo: Tuttle.

295. Noss, Richard B. 1964. Thai reference grammar. Washington, D. C.: Foreign Service Institute.

296. Okell, John. 1969. A reference grammar of spoken Burmese. Two volumes. London: Oxford University Press.

297. O'Leary, De Lacy. 1958. Colloquial Arabic. London: Routledge & Kegan Paul

298. Olli, John B. 1958. Fundamentals of Finnish grammar. New York: Northland Press.

299. Pakhalina, T. N. 1959. Ishkashimskii i͡azyk. Moscow: Nauka.

300. Palmer, F. R. 1957. The verb in Bilin. BSOAS 19.1:131-59.
301. Panfilov, V. Z. 1962. Grammatika nivkhskogo i͡azyka, 1 & 2. Leningrad: Academy of Sciences of the USSR.
302. Parker, G. W. 1883. A concise grammar of the Malagasy language. London: Trübner.
303. Pattanayak, D. P. 1970. Outline of Oriya grammar. Unpublished mss.
304. Penzl, Herbert. 1955. A grammar of Pashto: a descriptive study of the dialect of Kandahar, Afghanistan. Washington, D. C.: ACLS.
305. Perrott, D. V. 1951. Teach yourself Swahili. London: English Universities Press.
306. Perry, Edward Delavan. 1936. A Sanskrit primer. 4th ed. New York: Columbia University Press.
307. Petrunicheva. Z. N. 1960. I͡Azyk telugu. Moscow: Vostochnoi Literatury.
308. Phillott, D. C. 1918. Hindustani manual. 3d ed. Calcutta: by the author.
309. Pinnow, Heinz-Jürgen. 1960. Über den Ursprung der voneinander abweichenden Strukturen der Munda- und Khmer-Nikobar Sprachen. Indo-Iranian Journal 4.
310. Plam, I͡Urii I͡Akovlevich. 1965. Morfologicheskii kategorii v taiskom i͡azyke (na materiale glagola). Moscow: Nauka.
311. Poetzelberger, Hans Andreas. 1965. Einführung in das Indonesische. Wiesbaden: Otto Harrassowitz.
312. Pop, Sever. 1950. La dialectologie: aperçu et méthodes d'enquête linguistique. (Recueil de travaux d'histoire et de philologie, 3 sér., fasc. 38.) Louvain.
313. Pope, G. U. 1904. A handbook of the ordinary dialect of the Tamil language. 7th ed. Oxford: Clarendon Press.
314. Pořízka, Vincenc. 1963. Hindština: Hindi language course. Prague: State Pedagogical Publishing House.
315. Praetorius, Franz. 1879. Die amharische Sprache. Halle: Verlag der Buchhandlung des Waisenhauses.
316. ———. 1893. Zur Grammatik der Gallasprache. Berlin.
317. Prakasham, V. 1970. The syntactic patterns of Telugu and English: a study in contrastive analysis (Monograph No. 5, ed. S. K. Verma). Hyderabad, India: Central Institute of English.
318. Pray, Bruce. 1970. Topics in Hindi-Urdu grammar (Research Monograph No. 1, Center for South and Southeast Asian Studies). Berkeley: University of California.
319. Punjab, Government of: Language Department. 1961. Panjabi manual and grammar.
320. Puzitskii, E. V. 1968. Kachinskii i͡azyk (ya chzhingpkho). Moscow: Nauka.
321. Rabel, Lili. 1961. Khasi: a language of Assam. Baton Rouge: Louisiana State University Press.
322. Ramamurti, G. V. 1931. A manual of the So:ra: (or Savara) language. Madras: Government Press.
323. Ramanujan, A. K., and Colin Masica. 1969. Toward a phono-

logical typology of the Indian linguistic area. Linguistics in South Asia (Current Trends in Linguistics, 5. Thomas A. Sebeok, ed.). The Hague: Mouton. Pp. 543-77.

324. Ramaswami Aiyar, L. V. 1928. Causal verbs in Dravidian. Madras: Educational Review.

325. Rastorgueva, V. S. 1963. A short sketch of Tajik grammar. Transl. and ed. by Herbert Paper (Indian Research Center for Anthropology, Folklore and Linguistics, Pub. 28). IJAL 29.4.2.

326. ——— and A. A. Kerimova. 1964. Sistema tadzhikskogo glagola. Moscow: Nauka.

327. Raun, Alo. 1969. Basic course in Uzbek (Uralic and Altaic Studies, 59). Bloomington: Indiana University.

328. Ray, Punya Sloka, Muhammad Abdul Hay, and Lila Ray. 1966. Bengali language handbook. Washington, D.C.: Center for Applied Linguistics.

329. Reddy, G. M., and Dan M. Matson. 1964. Graded readings in modern literary Telugu. Madison: University of Wisconsin (dittoed).

330. Rerikh, I͡U. N. (= G. N. Roerich). 1961. Tibetskii i͡azyk. Moscow: Vostochnoi Literatury.

331. Rice, Frank A., and Majed F. Sa'id. 1960. Eastern Arabic: an introduction to the spoken Arabic of Palestine, Syria, and Lebanon. Beirut: Khayat's.

332. Riggs, Stephen Return. 1893. Dakota grammar, texts, and ethnography (U. S. Geographical and Geological Survey of the Rocky Mountain Region). Washington, D. C.: Department of the Interior.

333. Robbins, R. H. 1959. Nominal and verbal derivation in Sundanese. Lingua 8.4: 337-69.

334. Robinson, C. H. 1905. The Hausa language: Hausa grammar. London: Kegan Paul.

335. Ross, J. R. 1970. Gapping and the order of constituents. Actes du Xe Congrès International des Linguistes (Bucharest, 1967), 2. Bucharest: Éditions de l'Académie de la République Socialiste de Roumanie. Pp. 841-54.

336. Saihgal, M. C. 1958. Saihgal's modern Hindi grammar. P. O. Subathu, Simla Hills, Punjab: by the author.

337. Sandfeld, Kristian. 1930. Linguistique balkanique: problèmes et résultats. Paris: E. Champion.

338. Sankaranarayana, P. 1964. An [*sic*] Telugu-English dictionary. Rev. ed. Madras: V. Ramaswamy Sastrulu & Sons.

339. Sarma, Nirmaleswar. 1963. A guide to Assamese. Gauhati, Assam: Lawyer's Book Stall.

340. Sarma, Paresh Chandra Deva. 1962. Assamese Tutor. Gauhati, Assam: Lawyer's Book Stall.

341. Schmidt. Wilhelm. 1926. Die Sprachfamilien und Sprachenkreise der Erde. Mit Atlas von 14 Karten. Heidelberg: C. Winter.

342. Scholberg, H. C. 1940. A concise grammar of the Hindi language. 3d ed. Bombay: Oxford University Press.

343. Schrijnen, Josepf. 1933. Essai de bibliographie de géographie linguistique générale. Nijmegen: N. V. Dekker.
344. Schwarz, J. 1945. Colloquial Czech. 2d ed. London: Routledge & Kegan Paul.
345. Scotton, Carol Myers, and John Okeju. 1973. Neighbors and lexical borrowings. Lg. 49.4: 871-89.
346. Sebeok, Thomas A. 1945. Finno-Ugric and the languages of India. JAOS 65: 59-62.
347. ——. 1950. The meaning of 'Ural-Altaic'. Lingua 2.2: 124-39.
348. —— *et al.* (ed) 1969. Linguistics in South Asia (Current trends in linguistics, 5). The Hague: Mouton.
349. Seidel, E. 1958. Probleme und Methoden der Balkanlinguistik. Omagiu lui Iorgu Iordan. Bucharest: Editura Academiei Republicii Populare Romîne. Pp. 775-88.
350. Semeonoff, Anna K. 1962. A new Russian grammar. Part 3: Russian syntax. New York: E. P. Dutton.
351. Sevortian, E. V. 1962. Affiksy glagolo-obrazovanii͡a v azerbaidzhanskom i͡azyke. Moscow: Nauka.
352. Shackle, C. 1972. Punjabi. London: English Universities Press.
353. Shafeev, D. A. 1964. A short grammatical outline of Pashto. Transl. and edited by Herbert H. Paper (Indiana Research Center in Anthropology, Folklore, and Linguistics, Pub. 33.3.3). Bloomington: Indiana University.
354. Sharma, Aryendra. 1958. A basic grammar of modern Hindi. Delhi: Government of India.
355. Sharma, M. V. Shivram. 1967. Hindii-telugu vyaakaraṇõ kaa ek tulanaatmak adhyayan. Hyderabad: Andhra Pradesh Sahitya Akademi.
356. Sharma, S. N. 1956. Hindi grammar and translation. 2d ed. Bombay: Lakhani Book Depot.
357. Shenai, K. Vittal. 1962. English-English-Kannada dictionary. Bombay: Orient Longmans.
358. Shorto, H. L. 1962. A dictionary of modern spoken Mon. London: Oxford University Press.
359. —— (ed) 1963. Linguistic comparison in South East Asia and the Pacific (Collected papers in Oriental and African Studies). London: SOAS.
360. Sjoberg, Andrée F. 1963. Uzbek structural grammar (Uralic and Altaic Series, 18). Bloomington: Indiana University.
361. Skalička, V. 1933. Zur Charakteristik des eurasischen Sprachbundes. AO 6: 272-74.
362. Skorik, P. I͡A. 1961. Grammatika chukotskogo i͡azyka.1. Leningrad: Academy of Sciences of the USSR.
363. —— (ed.) 1968. Mongol'skie, tunguso-man'chzhurskie i paleoaziatskie i͡azyki. (I͡Azyki narodov SSSR, vol. 5. Gen. ed. V. V. Vinogradov.) Leningrad: Nauka.
364. Sofroniou, S. A. 1962. Teach yourself Modern Greek. London: English Universities Press.

365. Southworth, Franklin C., and Naresh B. Kavadi. 1965. Spoken Marathi: first year intensive course. Philadelphia: University of Pennsylvania Press.

366. Southworth, Franklin C. 1971a. Detecting prior creolization: an analysis of the historical origin of Marathi (Pidginization and creolization of languages: proceedings of a conference held at the University of the West Indies, Mona, Jamaica, April 1968). Dell Hymes, ed. Cambridge University Press. Pp. 255-73.

367. ———. 1971b. The student's Hindi-Urdu reference manual. Tucson: University of Arizona Press.

368. ———. 1974. Linguistic stratigraphy of North India. IJDL 3.1: 201-23.

369. Spencer, Harold. 1914. A Kanarese grammar. Mysore; Wesleyan Mission Press.

370. Spies, Otto. 1968. Türkische Chrestomathie aus moderner Literatur. Wiesbaden: Otto Harrassowitz.

371. Starosta, Stanley. 1967. Sora syntax: a generative approach to a Munda language. Unpubl. dissertation, University of Wisconsin.

372. Stebnickii, S. N. 1934. Itel'minskii i͡azyk. Moscow: Nauka.

373. Stevens, Alan M. 1968. Madurese phonology and morphology (American Oriental Series, 42). New Haven: American Oriental Society.

374. Stevenson, C. H. 1970. The Spanish language today. (Hutchinson University Library: Modern Languages.) London: Hutchinson & Co.

375. Stewart, J. A. 1955. Manual of colloquial Burmese. London: Luzac.

376. Stilo, Donald L. 1970. Language communities in contact: the Sprachbund in Northwest Iran and the South Caucasus. (Paper delivered at the Oriental Institute, Chicago, 18 March 1970.)

377. St. John, R. F. St. A. N.d. Burmese self-taught. London: Marlborough.

378. Stockwell, Robert P., J. Donald Bowen, and John W. Martin. 1965. The grammatical structures of English and Spanish (Contrastive Structure Series). Chicago: University of Chicago Press.

379. Sturtevant, E. H. 1947. Hittite and areal linguistics. Lg.23:376-82.

380. Subrahmanyam, P. S. 1968. A descriptive grammar of Gondi (Annamalai University, Department of Linguistic Publication No. 16.)

381. ———. 1971. Dravidian verb morphology: a comparative study (Annamalai University, Department of Linguistic Publication No. 24).

382. Summer Institute of Linguistics. 1973. Clause, sentence and discourse patterns in selected languages of Nepal. 4 vols. Norman, Oklahoma: Summer Institute of Linguistics.

383. Sutton-Page, W. 1934. An introduction to colloquial Bengali (James G. Furlong Fund, 13). Cambridge: W. Heffer & Sons.

384. Swadesh, M. 1959. Linguistics as an instrument of prehistory. Southwestern Journal of Anthropology 15:20-35.
385. ———. 1961. The culture-historic implications of Sapir's linguistic classification. To William Cameron Townsend on the 25th Anniversary of the Summer Institute of Linguistics. Cuernavaca, Mexico: Tipográfica Indígena. Pp. 663-71. Reprinted in Swadesh 1971, pp. 313-23.
386. ———. 1962. Linguistic relations across Bering Strait. American Anthropologist 64: 262-91.
387. ———. 1971. The origin and diversification of language. Joel Sherzer, ed. Foreword by Dell Hymes. Chicago: Aldine-Atherton.
388. Swanson, Donald C. 1959. Vocabulary of Modern Spoken Greek. Minneapolis: University of Minnesota Press.
389. Temple, Richard C. 1907. A plan for a uniform scientific record of the languages of savages (applied to the languages of the Andamanese and Nicobarese). Indian Antiquary, July-Dec. 1907: 181-364.
390. Teslar, Joseph Andrew. 1947. A new Polish grammar. 5th ed. Edinburgh: Oliver and Boyd.
391. Thomas, Lewis V. 1967. Elementary Turkish. Rev. ed. by Norman Itzkowitz. Cambridge, Mass.: Harvard University Press.
392. Thompson, Laurence C. 1965. A Vietnamese grammar. Seattle: University of Washington Press.
393. Thompson, Sandra Annear. 1973. Resultative verb compounds in Mandarin Chinese: a case for lexical rules. Lg.49.2:361-79.
394. Thumb, Albert. 1964. A handbook of the Modern Greek language. Transl. from the 2d improved and enlarged German edition by S. Angus. Chicago: Argonaut Publishing Co.
395. Trubetzkoy, N. S. 1931. Phonologie et géographie linguistique. TCLP 4:228-34 (repr. in Trubetzkoy, Principes de phonologie, J. Cantineau, tr. Paris: Librairie C. Klincksieck, 1957, as App. III, pp. 343-50).
396. ———. 1939. Gedanken über das Indogermanenproblem. Acta linguistica 1:81-89.
397. Tschenkéli, Kita. 1958. Einführung in die georgische Sprache. 2 vols. Zurich: Amirani Verlag.
398. Turner, Nigel. 1963. A grammar of New Testament Greek, 3: syntax. Edinburgh: T. & T. Clark.
399. Turner, R. L. 1966. A comparative dictionary of the Indo-Aryan languages. London: Oxford University Press.
400. Tyler, Stephen A. 1968. Dravidian and Uralian: the lexical evidence. Lg. 44.4:798-812.
401. Ullrich, Helen Elizabeth. 1968. Clause structure of Northern Havyaka Kannada (Dravidian): a tagmemic analysis. Unpub. dissertation, University of Michigan.
402. Unbegaun. B. O. 1957. Russian grammar. Oxford: Oxford University Press.

403. Vaccari, Oreste, and Elisa Enko Vaccari. 1954. Complete course of Japanese conversation-grammar. 11th rev. ed. Tokyo: Tuttle.
404. Van Wagoner, Merrill Y. 1949. Spoken Iraqi Arabic. New York: Henry Holt & Co.
405. Voegelin, C. F. 1945. Influence of area in American Indian linguistics. Word 1:54-58.
406. ——. 1955. On developing new typologies, and revising old ones. Southwestern Journal of Anthropology 11:355-60.
407. Vogt, Hans. 1971. Grammaire de la langue géorgienne (Instituttet for Sammenlignende Kulturforskning). Oslo: Universitetsforlaget.
408. Wagner, P. L. 1958. Remarks on the geography of language. Geographical review 48: 86-97.
409. Waley, A., and C. Armbruster. 1934. The verb *to say* as an auxiliary in Africa and China. BSOS 7:573-76.
410. War Department. 1945. Dictionary of spoken Russian (Technical manual 30-944). Washington, D. C.: U. S. Government Printing Office.
411. Warsama, Solomon, and Maj. R. C. Abraham. 1951. The principles of Somali. (By the authors: mimeographed.)
412. Weigand, Gustav Ludwig. 1971. Bulgarische Grammatik. 2d ed. Leipzig: J. A. Barth.
413. Weinreich, Uriel. 1954. Is a structural dialectology possible? Word 10: 388-400.
414. ——. 1965. College Yiddish. 4th ed. New York: Yivo.
415. Wessén, Elias. 1968. Vårt svenska språk. Stockholm: Almqvist & Wiksell.
416. Whitney, Arthur H. 1950. Colloquial Hungarian. 2d rev. ed. London: Routledge & Kegan Paul.
417. ——. 1963. Teach yourself Finnish. London: English Universities Press.
418. Whitney, William Dwight. 1889. Sanskrit grammar, including both the Classical language, and the older Dialects, of Veda and Brahmana. 2d ed. Tenth issue, 1964. Cambridge, Mass.: Harvard University Press.
419. Whymant, A. Neville J. 1926. A Mongolian grammar. London: Kegan Paul, Trench, Trübner & Co.
420. Wickremasinghe, Don M. de Zilva. 1916. Sinhalese self-taught. London: Marlborough.
421. —— and T. N. Menon. 1927. Malayalam self-taught. London: Marlborough.
422. Winfield, W. W. 1928. A grammar of the Kui language (Bibliotheca Indica, 245). Calcutta: Asiatic Society of Bengal.
423. Worth, Dean Stoddard. 1961. Kamchadal texts collected by W. Jochelson. The Hague: Mouton.
424. I͡Akovleva, V. K. 1963. I͡Azyk ioruba. Moscow: Vostochnoi Literatury.
425. Yale University: Institute of Far Eastern Languages. 1966. Dictionary of Spoken Chinese. New Haven: Yale University Press.

426. Zandvoort, R. W. 1966. A handbook of English grammar. 3d ed. Englewood Cliffs, N. J.: Longmans/Prentice-Hall.
427. Ziadeh, Farhat J., and R. Bayly Winder. 1957. An introduction to modern Arabic. Princeton: Princeton University Press.
428. Zide, Arlene, R. K. 1972. Transitive and causative in Gorum. JL8:201-15.
429. Ziegler, F. 1953. A practical key to the Kanarese language. Mangalore: Basel Mission.
430. Zograf, G. A. 1960. I͡Azyki Indii, Pakistana, Tseilona i Nepala. Moscow: Vostochnoi Literatury.

INDEX

(Numbers in italics refer to items in the Bibliography.)